D1613211

Why do Research in Psychotherapy?
Introduction to a Revolution

Why do Research in Psychotherapy?

Introduction to a Revolution

ALVIN R. MAHRER PhD

University of Ottawa, Canada

W

WHURR PUBLISHERS
LONDON AND PHILADELPHIA

© 2004 Whurr Publishers Ltd
First published 2004
by Whurr Publishers Ltd
19b Compton Terrace
London N1 2UN England and
325 Chestnut Street, Philadelphia PA 19106 USA

British Library Cataloguing in Publication Data

A catalogue record for this book
is available from the British Library.

ISBN 1 86156 441 4

Typeset by Adrian McLaughlin, a@microguides.net
Printed and bound in the UK by Athenæum Press Ltd, Gateshead,
Tyne & Wear.

Contents

Acknowledgements

I gratefully appreciate those philosophers of science whose writings introduced me to an exciting, stimulating, challenging new world.

I gratefully appreciate those psychotherapists and researchers whose passionate curiosity inspires further and deeper inquiry into the secrets of psychotherapy.

I gratefully appreciated the School of Psychology of the University of Ottawa, for providing such a welcoming atmosphere; Sarah Prud'homme, for her ready and responsible expertise in transforming cut-and-paste notes into a publishable manuscript; and Colin Whurr for his precious readiness to take a risk.

Introduction and overview

I want to tell you about some serious problems that I believe underlie the field of psychotherapy research, are ingrained into and characterize much of psychotherapy research, constrain and limit most psychotherapy research, and can have a profound effect on the future of psychotherapy research. I want to tell you about these serious problems partly because I believe that they are not commonly talked about, but ought to be. They ought to be talked about for at least two reasons.

One is that I believe these serious problems can be serious road blocks in doing research on psychotherapy. They are so serious that they can very well constrain, derail and prevent the researcher from achieving what might be achieved if these road blocks were removed. There can be some directly practical consequences from solving these serious problems.

A second reason for identifying and openly talking about these serious problems is that, if these serious problems can be solved, I believe that the larger field of psychotherapy can move in the direction of a revolutionary shift forward.

I also want to tell you about a reason for doing psychotherapy research, an approach to research, that is relatively uncommon, but one that I believe can have exciting promise for the field. My hope is that some psychotherapy researchers can welcome and allow a little room for what may be called a discovery-oriented approach to research on psychotherapy.

I keep saying 'I believe' because I am not all that sure. My intent is to try to build a suitable case for at least some interested researchers to be willing to talk about these serious problems, to discuss them openly, to try to solve them, and even to leave a little room for the discovery-oriented approach to psychotherapy research.

For you to make your own sense of my involvement with these issues, it may be helpful to describe something about the relationship I have had with the field of psychotherapy research.

Four kinds of relationships with psychotherapy research

I have had four kinds of relationships with psychotherapy research. My first relationship consisted of a rather naïve and unsystematic study of psychotherapy audiotapes to try to learn first hand what this thing called psychotherapy is and how to do it. Picture a small group of newly graduated psychotherapists huddled in an office, listening to audiotapes of seasoned practitioners so that we could actually learn what these practitioners did in their sessions. We were supposed to have learned how to do psychotherapy when we were in school or on internship or in residency, but here we were in actual jobs, and we were all scared because this was for real, and none of us had studied what seasoned practitioners actually did in their actual sessions.

My first two jobs were in large medical training hospitals where physicians and nurses learned their trades in large part by studying seasoned and experienced practitioners on the job, in actual work with patients. They worked side by side with their teachers, both as trainees and as graduated professionals on the job. In my own doctoral training, I had few if any opportunities to learn from, to observe and study with, seasoned and experienced psychotherapists in actual psychotherapeutic work with actual patients. I had read a great deal about psychotherapy, about the theories and various therapies, and talked over my work with my supervisors. But I had not seen psychotherapists first hand, or studied what psychotherapists actually did in their sessions.

For about 13 years, in those first two jobs, I tried to beg and borrow audiotapes of professional psychotherapists in order to learn how to do my craft. In those early days, it was virtually impossible to get audiotapes, so the small number that I was able to get were precious. Over the years, a small group of us studied the audiotapes as carefully as we could in order to learn what psychotherapy was truly like and how to do it.

This was not genuine research in most of the traditional meanings of that term. On the other hand, we were serious about trying to find answers to questions such as the following:

> What do you think she is going to do now? . . . Let's play that part again to see how he got that change . . . I think that was a great change; do you think it was a great change? . . . I never started a session like that; did you ever start a session that way? . . . What do you think she was trying to accomplish by doing that? . . . Do you think she'll get what she seems to be trying to get? . . . That patient seems so different; let's play the tape again from the beginning to try and see what happened. . . . We have two consecutive sessions, so what do you think is going to happen in the next session? . . .

I never heard that method done like that; have you? . . . Right here, I have no idea what I would do; what do you think he is going to do? . . . What she did is altogether new to me; how would you describe what she did? . . . What do you think he is going to do with the dream the patient just mentioned?

My first relationship with psychotherapy research did not seem to be with genuine research, but it was in the general neighborhood. I was more of an on-the-job student, with a few other students, trying to learn the rudiments of what we were supposed to do in our jobs. We studied those audiotapes carefully and in depth, but we never thought of this as psychotherapy research.

My second and third relationships occurred when I moved from hospitals to universities. The luggage included a cache of audiotapes which gradually grew to almost 500 tapes from over 80 practitioners, over the course of four decades or so in universities.

The university setting meant doing research, and doing research meant trying to use my library of audiotapes. Doing research also meant becoming familiar with the rich literature on the study of psychotherapy, if only to help students produce acceptable theses. The psychotherapy research team was rather large, including a few professors, partly because none of us was especially familiar with what psychotherapy research was or how to do it, so we spread the work around.

The second relationship with psychotherapy research consisted of doing it. We studied audiotapes from my growing library. We had weekly meetings, read research articles, managed to have things to study, learned about design and methodology, gathered data, published the studies and had parties for the graduates. After a decade or so, we became fairly good at doing psychotherapy research, although we were not especially fascinated with why we were doing it or what we were after. We were mainly just doing psychotherapy research, and that seemed sufficient to continue.

I had moved from many years of being in a hospital office, with a few colleagues, trying to learn from listening to audiotapes of seasoned practitioners. Now I was spending many years, in a university research room, with a few colleagues and a fair number of students, trying to 'do research' by listening to the same audiotapes. Our way of listening became much more careful and systematic. What we were listening for became much more concrete and specific. What we got from listening to the tapes became much more organized. The procedures we used became much more identifiable and careful. And we published what we believed we were finding. However, in essence, we were still a group of people, interested in psychotherapy, listening carefully to audiotapes of seasoned practitioners, except that we were doing psychotherapy research.

My third relationship with psychotherapy research took place in my office at the university, not in the research room. In the research room, I met each week with my research team. We studied audiotapes and did research. My university office is down the hall from the research room. In my office, either by myself or with a colleague or two, I studied some of the tapes that I studied with the research team. I also studied audiotapes of my own sessions, none of which was studied by the psychotherapy research team.

In my office, I studied, I dissected, I explored in detail audiotapes of gifted therapists in sessions that inspired me. Even though the research team may have studied these precious audiotapes, I studied them in infinite detail so that I could uncover their secrets, learn how to help achieve their magnificent changes. By carefully learning from these inspirational tapes, and by comparing these audiotapes with audiotapes of my own sessions, my aim was to learn how to do psychotherapy better and better and still better.

Over the decades, these parallel meetings gradually led to my own way of doing psychotherapy and I do believe that my own way of doing psychotherapy was mainly inspired by, was the outcome of, careful examination of these audiotapes. Of course these two parallel tracks of meetings, over the decades, affected one another. However, over all that time one track was aimed at doing and publishing psychotherapy research studies, and the other was fueled by my fascination with developing a way of doing psychotherapy that seemed fitting for me, and somehow evolved into an applied therapeutic approach that was, in many ways, somewhat distinctive from many other therapeutic approaches.

My fourth relationship with psychotherapy research started, innocently enough, with reading philosophy of science. By 'innocently enough', I mean that I do not know how or why I returned to this body of writings. However, after arriving at my own way of making sense of and carrying out psychotherapy and deep-seated personal transformation, and after doing a number of studies on psychotherapy, I turned to philosophy of science in a big way. Somehow, it just seemed like the next thing to do.

Here are some of the philosophers of science, and their friends, whom I studied, and whose work was such an inspiring wellspring for me to try to draw applications and implications for the field of psychotherapy and research on psychotherapy: Achenbach, Avey, Bartley, Bergmann, Bergson, Bernstein, Bertalannfy, Block, Braten, Bridgman, Brodbeck, Brown, Bunge, Campbell, Carnap, Chalmers, Churchland, Cohen, Derrida, Dewey, Duhem, Einstein, Erwin, Feibleman, Feigl, Feyerabend, Fodor, Frank, Fuller, Gadamer, Goldman, Gorman, Grunbaum, Habermas, Hammerschmidt, Hegel, Heidegger, Heisenberg, Hempel, Husserl, James, Kant, Kantor, Keynes, Kneale, Koch, Kuhn, Lakatos, Leibniz, Mach, Mays, Medawar, Meehl, Mitcham, Nagel, Newton-Smith, Oppenheim, Oppenheimer, Pap,

Peirce, Planck, Poincaré, Polanyi, Popper, Quine, Radnitsky, Reichenbach, Rorty, Rychlak, Ryle, Russell, Sartre, Schlick, Schroedinger, Simon, Slife, van Fraassen, Weimer, Whitehead, Wittgenstein.

This body of writings rarely talked about the field of psychotherapy and psychotherapy research. It talked about sciences that I knew essentially nothing about. My first challenge was to try to grasp what these people were talking about, were studying, were saying. Much of what they were saying I did not understand. However, I did understand some of the issues, the problems, the matters they were discussing.

When I was able to grasp what they were saying, the challenge was to see if there might be some ways that it applied to the field of psychotherapy and psychotherapy research. The answer seemed to be yes. This point seemed to apply to our field. This issue seemed to be here for our field. This problem is one that our field also faces. So much of what I could understand had relevance to and implications for the field of psychotherapy and psychotherapy research.

Philosophers of science talked about the history of physics, and how a particular issue was dealt with before the Middle Ages and after the Middle Ages. Not only does the issue apply to our field, but it almost seems that we might be dealing with that issue in much the same way physics did before the Middle Ages. Philosophers of science discussed particular problems and how sciences solved these problems over the course of centuries. It seemed that our field still faces these problems. Philosophers of science are eminently familiar with the advantages and disadvantages, the strengths and weaknesses, of different conceptual and research mind-sets. It seemed that the field of psychotherapy research was not especially aware of the various mind-sets, and seemed preponderantly wedded to a given common mind-set that may not be the strongest and most useful for our field. Philosophers of science were exceedingly familiar with an exciting range of issues, problems and options in doing research in many sciences, whereas our researchers seemed generally limited to a few common ways of thinking about and doing their research.

It seemed to me that the field of philosophy of science had a great deal to offer to the field of psychotherapy and psychotherapy research. The more I read, the more I seemed to have wave after wave of reactions to what I was reading, what I was learning and what I believe philosophy of science could offer to our field.

One reaction was like coming home. During my graduate school years I had secretly wallowed in underground philosophy of science readings. For decades thereafter, my way of thinking was at the level of sophomore philosophy of science without knowing I was so close to philosophy of science. When I finally studied these writings as a 'mature student', it was indeed like coming home to a field that was truly my home.

Another reaction was made up of almost equal parts embarrassment and suspicion. I was embarrassed that I was only now coming to truly appreciate philosophy of science. I had spent a whole career without fully appreciating this neighboring field, and it seemed to me that I missed a great deal in my education, my training and my knowledge. The sense of suspicion was punctuated when I came across some philosophy of science writings by psychotherapy researchers who were knowledgeable in and contributing to this field. My suspicion was that most of my psychotherapy research colleagues knew philosophy of science while I had hobbled along in comparative ignorance.

Still another strong reaction was curiosity about programs of education and training in psychotherapy and psychotherapy research. Did many of these programs provide a relatively sound base of knowledge in philosophy of science? I knew that some psychotherapy researchers were also scholars in philosophy of science, but how much of this knowledge was an integral part of most doctoral programs in psychology, psychiatry and the other psychotherapy-related disciplines?

A final reaction was sheer excitement. The more I read, the greater was my fascination with the implications of philosophy of science for the field of psychotherapy research. Here seemed to be a rich field of study that had serious, powerful, almost astounding implications for psychotherapy research. The implications dealt directly with the fundamental ways of thinking about and doing psychotherapy research, with deep-seated issues and problems in psychotherapy research, with the very reasons why psychotherapy research was done and the feasibility of being successful in doing research for these reasons. The implications also seemed to open up challenging and exciting new possibilities for what psychotherapy research can do, can accomplish, can become, and to offer promising avenues and ways for the field to become what it could become. My excitement lay in the revolutionary possibilities that philosophy of science opened up for the field of psychotherapy and psychotherapy research.

It was the respect and appreciation of the field of philosophy of science, of what this field might have to say to the field of psychotherapy and psychotherapy research, that inspired and led to this book.

What are the purposes of the volume?

When I entered the library of philosophy of science, my aim was to read, to try to understand what I could, and to try to see how these writings might have something helpful to say to the field of psychotherapy research. It was only later that the purposes of this volume took some form and shape. In this section, I hope to be clear about what the purposes are. In a subsequent section I hope to be clear about what the purposes are not.

Invitation to psychotherapy researchers to appreciate what philosophy of science can offer

There was a time when education in psychology and related disciplines included little or no knowledge and training in either psychotherapy or psychotherapy research.

At the present time, some psychotherapy researchers are quite familiar with philosophy of science. However, it seems safe to say that most psychotherapy researchers have only a limited appreciation of philosophy of science and a limited base of foundational knowledge in this neighboring field. Few programs in psychology, psychiatry and related fields include courses that provide a foundational knowledge in philosophy of science.

The purpose of this book is to invite psychotherapy researchers to gain a broader and deeper appreciation of this body of knowledge, to respect what this field may have to offer to the advancement of the field of psychotherapy research. To whatever extent psychotherapy researchers have such an appreciation, the purpose is to enhance, increase, broaden and deepen this sense of appreciation. The purpose is also to help provide a groundwork for future education and training of future psychotherapy researchers to include a foundational knowledge of philosophy of science. If this is already a part of some education and training programs, so much the better. Again, the purpose is to extend and broaden this part of the education and training of future psychotherapy researchers.

Identification of some of the reasons for doing research on psychotherapy

What are some of the reasons for doing research on psychotherapy? Why is such research done? What are these researchers seeking to learn, to know, to find, to accomplish? Philosophers of science seemed to study why researchers in other sciences did their research, what they were after, their aims and goals. What about the field of research on psychotherapy?

One way of answering this question is to start with somewhat formal analyses, category systems of reasons for doing research on psychotherapy. It seemed relatively clear that careful development of such category systems was not much of a priority in this research field. There was little if any emphasis on arriving at a somewhat comprehensive set of reasons for doing psychotherapy research.

The way that seemed sensible was to ask a research team to sample a broad range of journals with studies of psychotherapy. The team collected a sample of approximately 400 studies from these journals, going back to the 1940s, and including randomly selected studies from representative issues of each journal, regardless of the nature of the study.

Arriving at a category system meant starting with each study, and trying to get a simple answer to what the study was after and why it was done, and to make an effort to arrive at an answer by emphasizing simple description over technical, research-sophisticated terms and phrases. Once we became familiar with emphasizing simplicity and non-technical vocabulary, we gradually evolved a provisional set of reasons which we were quite ready to revise a little bit or a great deal. The category system seemed somewhat evolved after trying to use the simple descriptions from about 80 of the 400 studies.

At that point, we stopped and asked another team of researchers to arrive at their own category system from the simple descriptions of the balance of the studies. Comparing the two category systems indicated remarkable, and unexpected, similarities. The differences were more in regard of exact wording than of substantive content. When we discussed the final wording, the two teams were quite satisfied with the general idea of each reason for doing research on psychotherapy, the number of reasons and the actual wording for each category.

We had arrived at a category system of reasons for doing research on psychotherapy. There were 10 reasons, described in words that were admittedly simple and non-technical. Although we had few if any formal category systems to compare ours against, and although we knew our category system was arrived at in a way that was relatively amateurish, not especially rigorous or stringent, we were generally satisfied that our 10 reasons covered most of the 400 studies, and would seem to do until a better one came along.

In other words, the purpose was to identify some of the reasons for doing research on psychotherapy, to provide a category system of reasons. The purpose was not to identify 'the' reasons for doing this research, or to provide 'the' category system of reasons. The other side of this purpose is to invite others to modify and improve this set of 10 reasons, or even to replace the proposed reasons with a better set.

Offer researchers a choice of available reasons for doing research on psychotherapy

It seems relatively easy to rise to a sufficiently high level of abstraction so that most of the reasons for doing this research blend into one or a few large categories such as gaining psychotherapeutic knowledge or helping to advance the field of psychotherapy. On the other hand, the purpose was more to try to identify what may be considered the working reasons, the on-the-job reasons, the reasons that may be contrasted with other workable reasons.

Accordingly, the purpose was to provide researchers with a set of options, a menu of available choices of reasons – picture researchers who are in training, or who have a track record of doing research on psychotherapy, or who are perhaps at a place where they are ready to consider varying their reasons for doing this research. The aim is to invite these researchers to pause for a while, to take some time to consider the available reasons, and to arrive at their own personal choice of what reason to select for the next project or line of research. The aim is to offer these researchers a chance to decide whether or not to continue their reason for doing research or to consider some alternative reasons.

Does this particular reason for doing research have a substantial likelihood of finding how to do psychotherapy better and better?

For each reason for doing research on psychotherapy, the question may be phrased along the following lines: How likely is it that this reason will produce the kinds of findings that can show practitioners how to do their in-session work better and better? How likely is it that doing research for this reason can tell us much about how to do psychotherapy? Even before the researcher begins the actual study, it can be rather clear that some reasons would have a rather low likelihood and some may well have a rather high likelihood that the findings could tell how to do in-session work better and better.

Some reasons may have little if anything to do with finding ways to do in-session work better and better. These reasons have other things in mind. They may concentrate on seeing whether a given therapy is better than a rival therapy, or checking out the applicability of a given therapy for a particular kind of problem or disorder.

Some reasons may involve testing of new and better ways that practitioners actually carry out in their in-session work. However, a careful distinction can be made between research that sheds interesting new light on how to do psychotherapy better and better and, on the other hand, research that aims at checking out, testing, what practitioners already use to help in-session work become better and better. Finding how to do psychotherapy better and better is a separate issue from testing ways that practitioners already use in their in-session work.

For psychotherapists who are interested in doing in-session work better and better, the hope is that most reasons for doing research would have something useful to say. On the other hand, it might well be disappointing if most reasons for doing research were characterized by a low likelihood of finding how to do psychotherapy better and better.

Introduce a 'discovery-oriented' reason for doing research on psychotherapy

Perhaps the word 'introduce' is somewhat inappropriate because the spirit of this reason has been around for a while. However, there seem to be very few studies that expressly exemplify this reason.

The 'discovery-oriented' reason borrows bits and pieces of an underlying spirit that is not entirely alien to some of the other reasons for doing research, and combines these bits and pieces into an integral reason that emphasizes discovery of the secrets of psychotherapy. The discovery-oriented reason highlights exploration of what psychotherapy can be and can become, opening up more and more of what is essentially not yet known in the field of psychotherapy, pushing the envelope of what psychotherapy can achieve, and doing research expressly dedicated to discovering more and more of how to do psychotherapy better and better.

The purpose is to put a flag on what may be termed a 'discovery-oriented' reason for doing research on psychotherapy, to describe some of its philosophical and conceptual foundations, what it is and how it works, how it can contribute to the field of psychotherapy, and ways in which this reason may be distinguished from most other reasons for doing research on psychotherapy. This purpose may be achieved if the field granted some acceptance of this reason for doing research, if there were even a little room set aside for this reason, and if some researchers adopted and used this reason for doing research.

Are there some serious problems associated with the various reasons for doing research on psychotherapy?

For many philosophers of science, a large part of their subject matter consists of some of the serious problems associated with doing research. This is also clear in their examination of the historical development of many sciences as the story of encountering and eventually solving some of these serious problems.

The problems may be serious in various ways. They may be serious in that they effectively block progress in the science. Particular avenues of research can be handicapped or derailed because of serious problems and these can also be serious because they arise out of deeper issues, so that the right solution can virtually revolutionize the particular field of research.

A few philosophers of science were also psychotherapy researchers, but most were not. Indeed, most of their subject matter seemed to involve fields other than that of psychotherapy research. Accordingly, one purpose of this volume is to try to see whether the serious problems that philosophers of science talked about seemed to apply to the field of psychotherapy research. Given these serious problems, to what extent do they seem to apply to the various reasons for doing research on psychotherapy? Trying to provide a fair answer to that question was a major purpose for this volume.

I started out with no predetermined intent to answer yes or no for any of the reasons for doing research on psychotherapy, i.e. I was mainly curious to see if these serious problems did or did not apply to psychotherapy research, to see the extent to which the serious problems might apply, and to see which of the reasons for doing this research might be vulnerable to which serious problems, if any.

On the other hand, when I began, I tried to be clear on how serious these problems might be for each of the reasons for doing research on psychotherapy. Were they mainly minor interferences so that increasing sophistication and progress in design and methodology could overcome them? Or did they seem to be serious enough that they may well effectively hamper, handicap, block or derail doing research for the various reasons? Did these serious problems seriously reduce the likelihood of successfully pursuing each avenue of psychotherapy research? Might these serious problems seriously weaken the case for doing research for some or many or all of the reasons for doing it?

The purpose was to examine each of the reasons for doing research on psychotherapy, and to see whether or not each was especially associated with any of the serious problems. I was open to the possibility that each reason might be associated with its own relatively unique set of serious problems, that a pool of serious problems may cut across most of the reasons for doing this research, or that most of the reasons had both their own unique serious problems while sharing some common ones.

Invite interested researchers and others to discuss and solve the serious problems

If philosophers of science found serious problems in many other fields of research, and if a case can be made that many of these serious problems can also be found in the various reasons for doing research on psychotherapy, then one purpose is to invite interested psychotherapy researchers and others to discuss and solve these serious problems. To a large extent, these are separate but related matters: one is serious discussion of the serious problems and the other is searching for serious solutions.

My purpose is to provide a case on behalf of serious, open, fair, careful discussion of the serious problems. If the net result of these discussions is that the case is weak, that such discussions are already ongoing, that there are no such serious problems or that there are substantial efforts to solve the serious problems, then that is that. I am wrong; there is little or no solid basis for such discussions. On the other hand, if the net result of these discussions is that the field of psychotherapy research can be readily seen as accompanied by these kinds of serious problems, a next step seems to be that of searching for serious solutions to these serious problems.

My purpose is not to provide solutions to the serious problems. I am satisfied to flag them and to encourage others to take up the task of solution. In each of the following chapters, I make some friendly suggestions in the direction of solutions, but these are offered more in a spirit of amateur first attempts, helpful gestures, first approximations. I leave the serious solution to those better equipped and better able to solve the serious problems.

It is important to keep in mind that there are at least two solid reasons why it seems important to solve the serious problems. One is that solving the problems would probably help to remove the road blocks that effectively hamper and derail efforts to do research for each reason. If this is one way that the serious problems are indeed serious, their solution might well be an important gift to researchers dedicated to doing research for that particular reason.

A second reason why solving these serious problems can be important is that the solutions may very well help nudge the field in the direction of a revolutionary shift. If the problems are serious because their roots lie in deep-seated, foundational, fundamental issues in the field of psychotherapy, their solution may very well have revolutionary implications even beyond the area of psychotherapy research.

Special qualities of those interested in discussing the issue of serious problems

The purpose is to offer a friendly invitation to those who could be interested in discussing the issue of serious problems underlying research on psychotherapy. The key is a genuine interest in simply discussing the issue of the serious problems, in simply believing that the issue may be important enough to warrant talking about.

Not everyone has such an interest. Indeed, I believe that having such an interest is rather special, especially for those who are actively involved in psychotherapy research. The purpose is to talk with these interested people, to promote discussion of the issue of serious problems. It is also to find those who already have at least a glow of interest, rather than (1) to try to convince those who are not especially interested, who have little or no interest, or (2) to argue with those who are actively disinterested, resistant or opposed to discussing the issue of the serious problems.

Those who can be interested may be described as having at least five special qualities:

1. They have a special quality of being able to accept differences in ways of thinking, perspectives, approaches, mind-sets, without one way having to be dominant, superior, right, better, or having to cope with and defeat its rivals (Mahrer, 2000a, 2002, 2003, 2004). I can confidently confirm that the object is ceramic, rather than paper or metal or plastic, but I can also accept your description of the object as white, rather than blue or red or green, and I can also accept that the object is a cup, rather than a screwdriver or a brush or a pencil. We can share an interest in discussing the issue of the serious problems, even though we differ in our basic beliefs, our fundamental principles, our dictums, canons, foundational beliefs, mind-sets.

   However, it can be hard to have a genuine interest in discussing the serious issues if my way of thinking sees your way of thinking as a rival, a threat, a competitor who must not defeat me, a rival whom I must defeat, overcome, dominate, compete against. I cannot have an honest interest in open discussion when my power has to oppose your power, when your attack is to be met by my counter-attack, when I must get you to bend to my will, to accept my truth, to see things and do the way I see things and do.

2. There can be an interest in discussing the serious problems provided there is even a sliver of readiness and willingness to change one's way of thinking, outlook, at the more basic level rather than just superficially. This special quality means that one's basic ideas are at least slightly open to questioning, to challenge, to modification and improvement, to change, perhaps even to replacement (Mahrer, 2000a).

   On the other hand, it can be hard to have a genuine interest in honest discussion of the serious problems if one's basic ideas are set, rigid, inflexible, especially if one does not know or is inclined to deny that one's basic ideas are essentially immune from change. These conditions essentially defeat an interest in genuine discussion of the serious problems.

   For example, under these conditions the side that lacks a genuine interest can take a position in which the interested side is challenged to provide increasingly higher piles of evidence in a game in which the uninterested side takes a position of the one who judges the adequacy of the presented evidence. The outcome of the game is predetermined because the interested side is caught in the unwinnable game of the 'eternally insufficient evidence'. No matter what kind or how much evidence is presented, the uninterested judge can pronounce it as insufficient.

3. Those who have a genuine interest in discussion of the serious problems can accept that they are caught in a catch-22 dilemma of insufficient support by recognized authorities and by a supporting body of research. There are two sides to the catch-22 dilemma:

   (a) Those with a genuine interest in open discussion know that the presence of serious problems is more a conclusion drawn from careful thinking and reasoning than from research findings. It is virtually inevitable that such a conclusion cannot be drawn from a body of research findings, and therefore the search for supporting research findings is a catch-22 dilemma.

   (b) The other side of the catch-22 dilemma can be equally exasperating. If there were plenty of available support from psychotherapy researchers and recognized authorities, saying that the serious problems are indeed serious problems, there would be little or no need to discuss the importance of the serious problems. It would be a case where psychotherapy researchers and recognized authorities were busy studying and discussing the serious problems, and they were asked if they were interested in studying and discussing the serious problems that they were already studying and discussing!

4. The quality of being ready, willing and interested in discussing the issue of the serious problems means only that the person is ready, willing and interested in discussing the issue. Nothing more. It does not mean that the person regards, or will regard, the issue of serious problems as important, as strong. After due discussion, the person may well regard discussion of the issue as trivial, unimportant, weak. It also does not mean that the person regards, or will regard, the case as strong for a particular serious problem. The person may well conclude that the case for a particular serious problem is trivial, unimportant, weak. The special quality is limited to a readiness, a willingness and an interest in entering into discussion of the serious problems.

5. A special quality is a realistic appreciation that reason and logic can be the properties of those who can be interested in discussing the issue of the serious problems, and the properties of those who are not especially interested, and also the properties of those who are actively opposed to discussing this issue. In other words, each side can have confidence that it must be right because reason and logic are on its side. In still other words, the special quality is knowing that the interest in discussing the issue of serious problems is not especially bolstered by the use of reason and logic.

Copernicus relied on reason and logic to plead for open discussion of his ideas that the earth is not really the center of the universe, and that the sun is the center around which the earth rotates. The scholars, authorities and scientists who vehemently opposed his ideas were not raging monsters, threatened by the power of his reason and logic. They raised the reason and logic stakes by judging his plea on the twin pillars of reason and logic: would a studious analysis indicate that his ideas conform to what was known to be basically true and the cumulative body of scientific knowledge?

On the basis of the twin pillars of reason and logic, here was the erudite, studious, careful, reasonable and logical conclusion in the words of Clarius: 'Copernicus's position contains many absurd or erroneous assertions: it accepts that the earth is not at the center of the world . . . . All these things are in conflict with the doctrine commonly received by philosophers and astronomers. Moreover . . . these assertions seem to contradict what Holy Scriptures teach us' (Duhem, 1996, p. 146). In other words, Clarius concludes, 'The two censured propositions did not present either of the two characteristics that marked an admissible astronomical hypothesis, therefore, both must be totally rejected' (Duhem, 1996, p. 146). Copernicus was defeated by his own twin pillars of reason and logic.

The special quality is knowing full well that reason and logic can be used to bolster the interest in open discussion of the issue of the serious problems or in defeating such discussion by using the scales of reason and logic to see if such discussion fits in with or violates (a) what the field of psychotherapy knows are the foundational canons and axioms of psychotherapeutic truth, and (b) what is contained in the hallowed cumulative body of psychotherapeutic knowledge. In other words, reason and logic can be in full supply on all sides of the issue, and the special quality is knowing this full well.

I sincerely hope that some psychotherapy researchers and others have these special qualities, and can be interested in open discussion of the issue of serious problems in the field of research on psychotherapy.

Some advantages of specificity over generality in identifying serious problems

Serious problems may be identified in their more or less specific forms with regard to given reasons for doing research. On the other hand, serious problems may be identified as falling in such large topics or issues or categories as research methodology, logic and reasoning, or researcher objectivity. Although both can make sense, there are some advantages in

leaning toward a preference for specificity rather than generality in identifying the serious problems.

Serious problems can lose their identity, diffuse out of existence, if the
level of generality rises sufficiently high. Indeed, one effective way to deny
serious problems their concrete nature is by rising to a sufficiently high
level of generality. Where there had existed a number of concretely different serious problems, at the level of relative specificity, there can be
merely a few general topics such as experimenter objectivity, research
design, quantitative–qualitative data analysis or stability of measurement.
At the level of specificity accepted in this book, there are 42 concretely different serious problems spread over 10 reasons for doing research on
psychotherapy. At a sufficiently high level of generality, the 42 serious
problems vanish and are replaced by perhaps five general topics or issues
or problems.

Serious problems can be discussed and solved when the level of specificity is sufficient to enable discussion and solution of the serious
problems. Concretely serious problems have a hard time being
discussed and solved when the level of generality is high enough so that
the serious problems no longer exist. The serious problem of the sudden
high rise in fatalities at the intersection of King and High Streets may be
discussed and solved when the level of discussion is specific enough to
allow for discussion of the sudden high rise in fatalities at the intersection
of King and High Streets. That concrete problem is not likely to be discussed and solved when the level of discussion is limited to 'traffic issues
in general'. In much the same way, many concretely specific serious problems are inclined to be lost, diffused away, unlikely to be discussed and
solved, when discussion is limited to the high level of researcher objectivity, measurement stability and design power.

For example, it seems that discussion of the general problem of
'researcher objectivity' would not be likely to include serious discussion of
many specific serious problems that can fall under 'researcher objectivity'.
Some of these overlooked or excluded serious problems may include: (1)
a comparison of researchers' single-truth perspective with researchers'
multiple-truth perspective; (2) researcher preference for hypothesis confirmation versus hypothesis falsification; (3) evidence-based grounds for
abandoning a theory or a psychotherapy; and (4) the presence or absence
of independent, theory-free criteria of the nature and content of a presumed real world of psychotherapeutic events. For purposes of enabling
serious discussion of the serious problems, the case is that specificity can
be superior to generality in identifying serious problems.

It can be more conducive to searching for and finding solutions when
the serious problems are identified in their relatively specific form rather
than in their relatively general form. Although the aim is not to describe a

serious problem in excruciatingly fine detail, there is probably a level of specificity that is useful and helpful in enabling solutions to be found, and this level is typically not that of high-level generality.

To take one example from above, searching for and finding solutions to the serious problem of comparing single-truth and multiple-truth perspectives are more likely to occur when the serious problem is identified at a reasonable level of specificity, rather than if the problem is identified as a problem of 'researcher objectivity' (Mahrer, 2004). Identified at such a high level of generality, the specific problem is unlikely to be identified and, therefore, even more unlikely to be solved.

It is possible to identify a smaller number of relatively general problems. However, for purposes of constructive discussion and finding solutions, the case is in favor of identifying serious problems in their relatively specific form.

The roles of consultants with regard to the serious problems

I was fortunate to have two sets of colleagues who served as consultants, especially with regard to the important matter of identifying the serious problems in doing research on psychotherapy. These colleagues did more than provide reader-friendly comments on the drafts of the manuscript. They served as consultants in answering some explicit questions with regard to the serious problems.

One set consisted of colleagues in the field of philosophy of science. They served in the role of consultants with regard to two explicit questions:

1. As few philosophers of science concentrated directly on the field of psychotherapy research, I did what I could to try to draw the connections, to carry out the applications from their writings to my trying to identify the serious problems in psychotherapy research. Did I do the job adequately or inadequately? How could I do the job better?
2. There were occasions when I put on the robes of a philosopher of science, and tried to see some of the truly serious problems that a genuine philosopher of science might see. Did I do a job that was grossly inadequate, or perhaps merely frail and feeble, or possibly might I earn a passing grade in their estimation?

A second set of substantive consultants included colleagues in the field of psychotherapy research. I turned to these consultants for answers to three explicit questions:

1. Who has written about the serious problems in psychotherapy research? What are the important references?

2. What are the fatal flaws in my attempts to identify the serious problems? How and where did I fail, go wrong, do an inadequate job?
3. In my own way of setting forth what I believe are some serious problems, what do they find bothersome, offensive, objectionable, insulting, excessively provocative, excessively aggressive, excessively critical?

Dilemma of finding like-minded psychotherapy researchers

A large part of my case is that there seem to be very few psychotherapy researchers who emphasize and acknowledge the importance of these serious problems, or who are engaged in searching for solutions. If there were, then much of the case for this book happily disappears. This is not the dilemma.

On the other hand, I am caught in an almost impossible-to-solve dilemma if I am challenged to cite an impressive number of psychotherapy researchers who agree with my case that precious few psychotherapy researchers see these serious problems as serious problems, or are engaged in finding solutions, i.e. the case itself disappears if I could cite a fair number of like-minded psychotherapy researchers. This is a catch-22 dilemma.

Nudging the field in the direction of a revolutionary shift

The overall, long-range purpose is to nudge the field in the direction of a revolutionary, radical, qualitative shift. This includes a revolutionary solution to each of the serious problems, a revolutionary shift in the underlying foundations of the field of psychotherapy, in the positions and answers to basic issues and questions, in what psychotherapy is and can achieve, in the reasons for doing psychotherapy research, and in the ways and means of doing this research.

However, the style and spirit of this purpose are more in keeping with gradual and incremental changes, more a matter of friendly nudging than wrenching explosions or implosions. The changes are thought of more in little baby steps rather than in giant leaps, and the emphasis is on an appreciation of the field's own readiness and pace, with plenty of room for open consideration and discussion along the way.

Nevertheless, the purpose is to move in the direction of a revolutionary shift in what the field of psychotherapy is and can become, and in what psychotherapy research is and can become.

These were the main purposes. Were they achieved? Before turning to a consideration of what fell outside the intended purposes, of what were not the purposes, it seems appropriate to provide a glimpse of the final conclusions and invitations.

A glimpse of the final conclusions and invitations

Each chapter concentrates on one reason for doing research on psychotherapy, and ends with its own set of conclusions and invitations. However, the present purpose is to provide an abbreviated preview of the final conclusions and invitations. These are spelled out more fully in the final chapter.

1. A case can be made that there are different reasons, aims, goals for doing research on psychotherapy. The invitation is to keep improving the list of reasons for doing research on psychotherapy.
2. It is probably helpful to take your time, and to make a careful choice of your particular reason for doing research on psychotherapy.
3. A case can be made that there are different packages of serious problems associated with the different reasons for doing research on psychotherapy. The problems can be serious obstacles and road blocks, sufficiently serious to effectively block, derail and defeat doing research for these reasons.
4. Researchers and interested others are invited to discuss and solve the serious problems associated with most of the reasons for doing research on psychotherapy. Solving these serious problems: seems to call more for careful thinking than for further research; can help remove some serious road blocks in doing research on psychotherapy; can perhaps seriously weaken the case for many of the reasons for doing research on psychotherapy; and can help nudge the field of psychotherapy in the direction of a revolutionary shift.
5. Doing research for nine of the 10 reasons is not designed to, nor can it tell us much about, how to discover more and more of what psychotherapy can accomplish, and better and better ways of accomplishing these things.
6. Discovery-oriented research is an effective way of doing research to discover more and more of what psychotherapy can accomplish, and better and better ways of accomplishing what psychotherapy can accomplish. Researchers are invited to provide some room for the discovery-oriented approach to psychotherapy research, and interested researchers are invited to adopt and improve the discovery-oriented approach to psychotherapy research.
7. The field of psychotherapy and psychotherapy research is invited to become friends with the field of philosophy of science.

What are not the purposes of the volume?

It is easy to be unclear about the limits of the purposes that were mentioned, and about what the purposes are and are not. It is easy to attribute or read in other purposes. Accordingly, the aim of this section is to take a clarifying look at what are not especially the purposes of this volume.

Not proposing some grand new way of looking at the field of psychotherapy research

The purpose is to propose some serious problems, the solution of which may well have revolutionary implications for what the field of psychotherapy is, is like, and is for. However, if there is some grand way of looking at the field of psychotherapy, the purpose is not to propose a new one – and not to propose some grand new epistemology, general framework or metatheory. Although much of the material for this book is drawn from philosophers of science, the purpose is not to propose some grand new philosophy of science for the field of psychotherapy.

The purpose is also not to propose a way of looking at the field of psychotherapy research in regard to such debates as: (1) whether the field is or ought to become more of a science, more of an art or more of some combination of the two; (2) the comparative value of basic and applied research; (3) how research may interface with practitioners; or (4) the advantages and disadvantages of using psychotherapy research for upholding professional standards, for professional lobbying and politics, and for public relations.

Not comparing the 'world views' of each reason for doing research on psychotherapy

Each reason for doing research on psychotherapy is entitled to be embedded in its own world view, to have its own general outlook on whether the world is orderly or chaotic, whether the world is ultimately knowable or can only be somewhat approximated, on what science is and is not, on the relationship between science and the world of ordinary events. Each reason may well have its own world view of: what research is and could be, the guiding principles of research, the appropriate methodologies and designs, the general framework for research and what research is for.

The purpose is not to compare these underlying 'world views' – not to judge them, not to see where they agree or disagree, not to look for common principles, not to see which comes closer to some so-called 'scientific world view'.

Not providing a formal category system of 'the reasons' for doing research on psychotherapy

The purpose is not to provide an authoritative, finalized, research-confirmed category system of 'the reasons' for doing research on psychotherapy. The 10 reasons suggested in this book came from trying to take a careful look at about 400 studies from a representative sampling of most of the journals publishing psychotherapy research, trying to frame the guiding reason for doing each study, and gradually evolving a set of reasons that seemed sensible and useful.

However, the way of arriving at these 10 reasons is admittedly amateurish and unsophisticated. It may very well be that the set of 10 reasons falls short of ringing the bell on the hard criteria for developing a category system, and it is acknowledged that there may be better ways of categorizing the reasons. This is a provisional category system; the 10 reasons are a good beginning, rather than being dressed in the robes of 'the reasons' for doing research on psychotherapy. The 10 reasons are neither fixed nor formal. The invitation is to improve or replace the 10 reasons with a better category system.

Not suggesting that some reasons are superior to others

It is not the purpose to suggest that some reasons are more worthy than others, have more value, deserve more support or are superior to others. By extension, the purpose is not to suggest that some reasons ought to be abandoned. Perhaps they can be put 'on hold' for a while, but not abandoned.

An appreciation that there are different reasons seems to be more important and useful to the field than trying to elevate some reasons as more superior. An appreciation that there are some serious problems in each of the reasons is done in the spirit of flagging the importance of solving the serious problems, rather than either turning to some other reason or abandoning that reason because of its serious problems.

One purpose is to introduce a 'discovery-oriented' reason for doing research, to implore researchers to allow a little room for this additional reason, and to invite interested researchers to adopt and follow this reason. However, the underlying spirit is not to elevate this above other reasons, and certainly not to proclaim that researchers ought to abandon their reasons and adopt the discovery-oriented reason.

Not providing a summary review of familiar problems in the field of psychotherapy research

The purpose is to suggest, perhaps even to introduce or to present in a new light, some problems that seem to emerge from an examination of the writings of philosophers of science, problems that may well bear substantially important relevance to the field of psychotherapy research. It is acknowledged that some of these problems, perhaps many of these problems, may already be more or less familiar to some or many psychotherapy researchers. It is also acknowledged that there may very well be problems, already familiar to psychotherapy researchers, that fall outside the scope of this book.

The purpose is not to offer a comprehensive summary review of the problems of psychotherapy research, to bring together in a single volume the many problems already noted and discussed in the psychotherapy research literature. This literature is rich in its own examination and inquiry into many problems and limitations of the field of psychotherapy research, and the purpose is therefore not to deal with this territory.

Not assessing the current status of solutions to the serious problems

The purpose is to flag some of the serious problems in each reason for doing research on psychotherapy, to highlight the importance of resolving these problems and to open the door to some suggested avenues toward solution. However, the purpose is not to make cases for any particular avenues toward solution, and expressly not to assess the status of current attempts to resolve these problems.

Accordingly, the purpose is not to provide a comprehensive review of the various attempts to solve these problems by means of such recent developments as the use of manuals, checks on treatment adherence, the development of increasingly sophisticated designs, methodologies and statistics, or the use of both quantitative and qualitative methods. If they are successful at resolving the problems, so much the better.

Not arguing on behalf of any particular solutions

For some of the serious problems, the door will be opened to some possible directions of solution. Some of these will come from solutions that may be somewhat familiar, some from relatively unfamiliar possible solutions and some from my own attempts to frame possible avenues of solving these serious problems.

However, the aim is mainly to open the way toward solution, and to beat the drum for more and better efforts to solve these problems. The importance lies in addressing these problems, gearing up to solve them and coming up with possible solutions. The purpose is not to try to make a case on behalf of any particular solution.

The real work of solving these serious problems lies, I believe, in the hands of those who are genuinely interested in seeing these problems as serious problems, and in searching for better and better solutions. These people include some psychotherapy researchers, researchers in related fields, philosophers of science, psychotherapy theoreticians, psychotherapy practitioners, and anyone else drawn toward helping to find better and better solutions for these serious problems.

Not replacing the current reasons for doing psychotherapy research with the discovery-oriented reason

The intent is to identify some of the serious problems in each of the current reasons for doing research on psychotherapy. Why? For what purpose? The purpose is to encourage efforts to solve these serious problems so that (1) researchers interested in these reasons can more fruitfully, constructively and successfully pursue these reasons when the serious road blocks are solved and removed, and (2) solutions to these serious problems can help nudge the field of psychotherapy in the direction of a revolutionary shift forward.

The intent is also to provide an introduction to the discovery-oriented reason and approach to psychotherapy research. Again, why and for what purpose? The purpose is to encourage the field of psychotherapy research to allow some room for the discovery-oriented reason and approach. The intent, aim and purpose are not to replace the current reasons and approaches with the discovery-oriented reason and approach.

Who is this book 'in conversation' with?

It is relatively common to think of the reader as part of an audience to whom the book is addressed. The relatively common question is: 'Who are the audiences for this book?' However, this picture did not especially fit what I had in mind as I was writing. Instead of an audience, I pictured being in conversation with the reader, a talking with each other, a dialogue.

When I was writing and rewriting the first drafts, I pictured being with philosophers of science, and talking with them about whether I was reasonably accurate in trying to understand the main points of their work. When I was writing the final drafts, the picture included at least three groups of readers in a genuine talking together, an honest dialogue. I hope to hear from these three groups. I hope we can talk with one another.

One group includes those who are doing psychotherapy research, whether they are just beginning or have a seasoned track record, and who have at least a spark of interest, and the essential open-mindedness, to discuss the issues and problems raised in this book. These people can be in a special position to appreciate the value of what philosophers of science may have to say, to engage in serious and constructive discussion of these matters, and to take steps toward enabling the field to become what it can become.

A second group includes those who may become the future psychotherapy researchers. Some of these people may be in, or not yet in, undergraduate programs of psychotherapy-related fields and disciplines. Some of these may not be students in psychotherapy training programs. Some may be in the field of psychotherapy but not involved with psychotherapy research. Some may be in related or neighboring fields of inquiry and study. What this group shares is a glow of interest in the study of psychotherapy, in exploring what psychotherapy is and can become, and perhaps in becoming the future psychotherapy researchers.

A third group includes those who are not involved with psychotherapy research, who will probably not become future psychotherapy researchers, but who share a genuine interest in the serious problems and their resolution, in the possibilities and potentialities of the developing field of psychotherapy and psychotherapy research. This group includes some practitioners and their clients, some psychotherapy teachers and their students, some supervisors and their trainees, some psychotherapy administrators and bureaucrats, lobbyists and mental health groups, some researchers in neighboring fields, some philosophers of science, and those who simply want to know more about the field of psychotherapy and psychotherapy research.

A few comments about 'vocabulary'

My intent was to try to use a vocabulary that highlighted simplicity, clarity and concreteness, rather than a vocabulary that was more abstract, high level or filled with technical terms, a vocabulary of in-group jargon, a vocabulary that was perhaps more familiar to research sophisticates than to the uninitiated. The emphasis on simple, clear, concrete, non-technical vocabulary can be seen in the titles, headings and subheadings in each of the chapters. There are at least three reasons for this preference in regard to vocabulary.

One reason is that I found it easier to talk about what this book tries to talk about when the vocabulary emphasized simplicity, concreteness and non-technicality. It is almost as if the issues, in examining the serious problems of why researchers do research on psychotherapy, could be illuminated and described when the vocabulary was simple, clear and non-technical, and seemed to become fuzzy and diffuse when this vocabulary was replaced by the more traditional, professional, technical vocabulary. In other words, the simpler vocabulary seemed much more useful in getting at the subject matter of this book.

A second reason is that this vocabulary seemed much more helpful in talking to readers who are not necessarily psychotherapy researchers. These people may not be especially familiar with fashionable technical terms and phrases dealing with psychotherapy research, design, methodology, statistics, and other terms and phrases such as contingency responding, conceptual schemata, fractures in the helping alliance, empathic attunements, rigid supraordinate constructs, assimilation phases, vicarious learning expectancies, and hundreds of other technical terms and phrases that we researchers are thoroughly familiar with, of course, and can define with accuracy and precision! Most psychotherapy researchers can adopt a technical vocabulary that is generally found in our books, and especially in our research journals. This is recognizable as a professional or academic style of writing. Students tend to become familiar with this vocabulary and style, and most researchers adopt them in their publications. Although a case can be made for the virtues and advantages of such a vocabulary and style for most psychotherapy researchers, for the purposes of this book that vocabulary and style would probably alienate and lose many of the readers with whom this book hopes to talk. Accordingly, although something may be sacrificed by opting for a more simple, concrete, clear, non-technical, non-jargon vocabulary, this is the vocabulary of choice.

A third reason is that the more technical terms and phrases, the more professional and academic vocabularies, generally seem to contain their own, somewhat implicit, built-in mind-sets, ways of thinking or conceptual frameworks (Mahrer, 2000a). The problem is that these implicit conceptual frameworks and ways of thinking can easily mask, hide or block many of the issues and problems discussed in this book. In other words, many of the reasons for doing psychotherapy research, many of the problems and possibilities in each of the reasons, tend to be concealed or defeated when the vocabulary is the more fashionable and traditional professional vocabulary.

For example, it is common for psychotherapy researchers to talk about 'process-outcome' research. The idea of 'process outcome' may well be common, sensible and appealing. It has a respectable history and a sound track record of many studies. However, the words 'process' and 'outcome' come with a great deal of accompanying conceptual baggage that is presumed when one accepts the innocent-appearing phrase 'process-outcome' research. If one accepts the idea of 'process' and 'outcome', one is thereby virtually adopting a more or less particular mind-set, way of thinking, conceptual system or way of making sense of what psychotherapy is, is for, and how it works. The 'process-outcome' way of thinking insinuates itself into the user, imposes itself on the user, elevates itself above and crowds out other ways of making sense of psychotherapy.

The 'process-outcome' mind-set typically comes with a conceptual system that virtually forces the user to accept propositions such as:

1. Most of what occurs in a psychotherapy session is a means to a subsequent end, a 'process', the relevance and importance of which lie mainly in its culminating in or leading toward the more relevant and important subsequent aim or goal.
2. Psychotherapy aims toward successful achievement of an 'outcome' of the in-session 'process'; generally, this 'outcome' is the culminating product of the sessions and occurs at the end of the series of sessions.
3. Psychotherapy ordinarily consists of a longer or shorter program or series of sessions.
4. Initial sessions are typically aimed at identifying the general contours of what is to be taken as the post-treatment 'outcome.'
5. Most psychotherapy sessions with the client are characterized by a relatively stable and continuing conception of the post-treatment aim, goal or 'outcome', although this conception may be subject to modification over the course of the sessions.

Quite aside from whether this particular 'process-outcome' mind-set, this particular way of thinking about what psychotherapy sessions are and are for, is common, good or useful, it nevertheless is only one mind-set or way of thinking about psychotherapy and psychotherapy sessions. Therefore, in order to get at and discuss the issues that this book seeks to talk about, the preference is to try to use a vocabulary that emphasizes simple, clear, non-technical words, terms and phrases rather than a more professional technical vocabulary with its built-in, intrinsic, implicit mind-set, ways of thinking and conceptual frameworks, whatever these may be.

How is the book organized?

There are 10 chapters in the main body of the book, each dealing with one reason for doing research on psychotherapy. Chapters 1–9 deal with some relatively common reasons. Chapter 10 introduces the discovery-oriented approach to doing research on psychotherapy.

Chapter 1 focuses on research simply aimed at showing that this psychotherapy thing is connected to and goes with that psychotherapy thing.

Chapters 2–4 deal with research showing that some aspect of psychotherapy is good, worthwhile and effective. Chapter 2 deals with psychotherapy in general, Chapter 3 with any selected psychotherapy and Chapter 4 with comparing psychotherapies with regard to a particular problem or disorder. Each reason is relatively distinctive and each is associated with its own set of serious problems.

Chapter 5 focuses on research showing that this particular thing is connected with successful post-treatment outcome, the traditional process-outcome research, and Chapter 6 highlights research showing commonalities across successful psychotherapies. Although both deal with successful therapies, the two reasons differ, and so do the serious problems associated with each.

Chapters 7 and 8 deal with psychotherapeutic theory, with Chapter 7 concentrating on research aimed at showing that a particular theory is good and Chapter 8 concentrating on research comparing several theories. The explicit reasons differ, and there are differences in the serious problems associated with each.

Chapter 9 focuses on research aimed at contributing to the cumulative body of psychotherapeutic knowledge.

Chapter 10 provides an introduction to the discovery-oriented approach to psychotherapy research. As this reason is comparatively uncommon, Chapter 10 is longer and fuller, and covers more territory than the preceding nine chapters.

The final chapter offers the volume's final conclusions and invitations.

CHAPTER 1

Does this kind of psychotherapy thing go with that kind of psychotherapy thing?

It can be appealingly sensible to look for connections between psychotherapeutic things. Doing research for this reason can be thought of as helping to establish a factual, empirical base for the field, a way of checking out theoretically predicted connections, or getting closer to the content and structure of particular psychotherapeutic phenomena.

In any case, the purpose of this chapter is to explore this kind of research to see whether it can reveal some serious problems.

Relatively easy to appreciate this kind of research

I have had first-hand, personal appreciation of this kind of research, and have not looked for or encountered any deeper serious problems. In introducing this reason for doing research, perhaps a little bit of personal storytelling might be excusable.

When I graduated, I worked in two large hospitals for about 13 years. In the course of my work, I interviewed almost 1000 patients who were admitted to the psychiatric ward. For some reason, which seemed sensible during that time, I interviewed each one about their problems, complaints, symptoms and personal life histories. This led to a problem checklist of 300 items and a life history questionnaire of 300 items. I used this information to help write intake reports about each patient.

Then, I went to a university. As the faculty and the masters and doctoral students had to do theses, my students and some of my colleagues were very pleased that I had brought along a large and useful data pool. They could do research on this data pool. They showed me how to select an item from one checklist and see what items from the other checklist were statistically related. If I took patients who were 'only children', I could see what problems they tended to have. If I started with patients with headaches, I could see what life histories went with headaches. The students and my colleagues impressed me with the

1

sophisticated statistics and designs that could be called on. This research could be quite scientific. We could go on and on. We should apply for research grants.

When I began doing research on psychotherapy, I remember sitting with some doctoral students at other universities and in other countries. These students liked doing research on psychotherapy. When I asked how they arrived at whatever connections they were studying, many of the students simply said they were honestly curious. One doctoral student told me that she had a hunch that clients who talk a lot or easily tended to have good working relationships with therapists. I remember a fellow from another university who was interested in the relationship between the number and specificity of the presenting complaints and the severity of the illness. Where did their hunches come from? Again, in honesty and openness, they said the hunches came from something they noticed in working with their clients, something that struck them in their readings or something their thesis supervisors were interested in studying.

The students explained to me that, to meet the standards of a doctoral thesis, they were to go to the library to study the theory and review the research on the things they wanted to see related to each another. Sure enough. When I read published research on both topics, and the publications from their theses, none of the studies started by simply saying that the researchers wanted to see if this thing and that thing went together. Instead, almost without exception, all of the studies started with grand, careful, scientific reviews of the theory and the body of related research. The studies gave the impression that the studies were inspired by a scientific urge to examine and test hypotheses drawn from the theory, and also to add to the body of studies on the topic. Yet, when I had opportunities to talk with the researchers, they admitted that they simply were interested in the relationships between this thing and that thing.

The journals are filled with studies that are inspired by a simple interest, curiosity or hunch that this thing and that thing go together. The relationships between these things are often the underlying reason for doing this kind of research. The researcher wonders or guesses whether these things go together.

Connections between psychotherapeutic things can open up worlds of possibilities

Do they correlate, go with one another? What kinds of 'psychotherapy things' are we talking about? The answer is: almost any kinds of psychotherapy things. Picture hundreds of ways of describing clients, scores of mental disorders, hundreds of kinds of problems, hundreds of personality dimensions and qualities, hundreds of ways of describing therapists, thousands of things that happen in sessions, scores of things about the way that therapists and clients are with one another, hundreds of therapies and methods, hundreds of outcomes and goals. Mix these thousands of things in a big pot, and reach in. Your reason for doing research is to see if this kind of psychotherapy thing and that kind of psychotherapy thing somehow go together.

Here is just one example that might spawn hundreds of studies for a number of psychotherapy research teams. The research question is: 'What kinds of patient characteristics go with what kinds of personal problems and mental disorders?' The hypothesis would be that certain kinds of patient characteristics occur regularly with certain kinds of personal problems and mental disorders. The big category on the left contains personal problems and mental disorders such as attention deficit disorders, depression, post-traumatic stress syndromes, schizophrenias, borderline disorders, bulimia, conduct disorders, paranoid personalities, problems of overachievement and underachievement, obesity, spouse abuse, eyebrow-pulling, insomnia, too many or too few orgasms, feeling anxious or gloomy or mad, and about 500 more personal problems and mental disorders. The big category on the right includes thousands of client characteristics such as autonomy, stress sensitivity, affiliation, mental imagery, expectations about psychotherapy, achievement, concrete thinking, regressive tendencies, altruism, receptivity to interpretations, internal control, extraversion and perhaps a few thousand other client characteristics measured on hundreds of scales, inventories, checklists, measures or questionnaires.

Just by using these two big categories, researchers can answer thousands of research questions and test thousands of research hypotheses. Researchers can see what client characteristics go with clients who have attention deficit disorders, insomnia, conduct disorders or some kind of schizophrenia. Reversing the question, researchers can see what kinds of personal problems and mental disorders go with clients who are sensitive to stress, altruistic, internally controlled or left-handed, Lutheran, like playing hockey.

If we expand way beyond these two categories, inventive researchers, with clever computers, can tease out the way just about any psychotherapy thing relates or correlates with just about any other psychotherapy thing. Here is just a sample of some other categories with connections that can warrant study: the whole potful of therapist methods and techniques, the whole system of therapy orientations and approaches, lots of kinds of outcomes, all sorts of therapist intentions and aims, the range of client pre-therapy expectations, the package of ways that therapists and clients relate to and get along with one another, the range of helpful in-session process events, pertinent case history data, and on and on.

The net result is that the researcher does research to see if this kind of psychotherapy thing goes with that kind of psychotherapy thing, or to see what kinds of psychotherapy things go with this kind of psychotherapy thing, or just to see what kinds of psychotherapy things go together. And there is almost no foreseeable end to the possible kinds of psychotherapy things that can go with one another.

Should the researcher believe in the things that are studied?

The things that are found to go together usually depend on the kinds of things in which the researcher has some faith. It is relatively rare for the researcher to toss into the pot, and come up with relationships between, things like conditions of being a warlock or a witch, the therapist–client magnetic field, the client's astrological signs, eye color of the client's great grandparents, the patterning of bumps on the client's head or the phlogiston content of the client's nostril hair. Maybe researchers in the future may well be amused that researchers of today study connections between believed-in things such as catharsis, mediating cognitions, intermittent conditional reinforcement, affiliation needs, unconscious impulses, internal control or schizophrenia. If the researcher does not truly believe in things such as 'unconscious pathogenic beliefs' or 'self-efficacy', the findings will probably not include connections between these things and other things:

> If the unconscious pathogenic beliefs postulated by Weiss, Sampson, et al. (1986) are a myth, or play no important causal role in the development of psychopathology, then the research program of these investigators is likely to prove sterile. If self-efficacy expectations either do not exist or make little difference to human behavior, then social learning theory research programs are also likely to prove fruitless.
>
> Erwin (1992, p. 165).

Doing this kind of research usually means having faith in the things that are to be studied. Faith in what goes into the pot goes a long way in determining what the findings can yield.

Should the psychotherapist truly believe in the things that are studied?

A study that says these things go with those things speaks to psychotherapists who place some value and importance in these things and those things. If none of the things is of interest to the psychotherapist, then the findings, whatever they are, would probably have little or no meaning or value.

For example, consider three questions that may be put to a group of psychotherapists:

1. Do you treat 'test anxiety'?
2. If you do, are you inclined to use a treatment method that the client selects from a number of methods you offer the client?
3. Are these among the methods you would invite the client to select from, including giving a little information on each – cognitive coping skills, systematic desensitization, biofeedback, rational–emotive therapy, study skills training, test-wiseness training, empty chair technique, double technique?

A study examining the relationship between providing some information on these methods and participants' preferences for the methods (e.g. Ertl and McNamara, 2000) may well be of interest to practitioners who are ready and willing to do these things if the findings are friendly. The study itself, regardless of the findings, would not especially be of interest to psychotherapists who are not especially inclined to provide information on a menu of methods to see which method is preferred by the client and likely used by the therapist.

Consider another study of whether this thing and that thing go together. One thing is called the patient's core conflictual relationship themes. It consists of themes in regard to what the patient wanted from other people, how the other people reacted and how the patient reacted to that reaction, with the pattern giving the patient's basic transference template (Luborsky and Crits-Christoph, 1998). One study looked for the core conflictual relationship themes in patients with major depression (Eckert et al., 1990). Another study looked for the core conflictual relationship themes in patients with combat-related post-traumatic stress disorder.

It is easy to see how a whole program of studies may be launched, starting from a search for the relationship between the core conflictual relationship themes in each pathological diagnosis. The findings would probably be of interest to practitioners who truly believe in and use what is meant by patients' core conflictual relationship themes, and who accept and truly believe in and use the patients' pathological diagnosis. However, I would find little or no relevance in whatever the findings are from these studies. Nor would other practitioners whose ways of thinking and working do not especially use the meaning of 'core conflictual relationship themes' or the patients' determined pathological diagnosis.

It seems that both the researcher who does the study, and the psychotherapist to whom the study is addressed, should truly believe in the things that are studied, and should be truly interested in what the findings find.

Are the things studied connected parts of a single belief system?

To a rather large extent, the researcher usually studies things that the researcher thinks belong to some particular belief system or conceptualization. It is relatively rare that a researcher will look for connections between intermittent reinforcement schedules and Jungian archetypes, or between ego lacunae and the degree of permeability of cognitive structures. As a result of the way the researcher thinks, the things that are studied tend to be parts of a single belief system. In other words, because they are already a part of a single belief system there is already a reasonable basis for believing that they go together.

Should you check each day, or presume that if present yesterday it will be the same today?

If you are looking at the relationship between diagnosis and gender, you would probably figure that if the patient were diagnosed as schizophrenic and female today she would probably be diagnosed as schizophrenic and female tomorrow. If she was described as left-handed and brown-eyed yesterday, you probably presume that she would be left-handed and brown-eyed today. Some things and some qualities are presumed to remain pretty much the same from day to day.

It is common to do what is called an intake evaluation or pre-therapy assessment. If the client is said to have a post-traumatic stress disorder, it is generally presumed that the client will still have a post-traumatic stress disorder during the first therapy session, and also the second. Diagnoses are rarely done for each session. The same holds for things like the case history, problem and expected length of treatment.

Many of the things that are studied, to see if they go together, are presumed to be relatively stable. Assess them once, usually at the beginning of treatment, and they are supposed to remain generally the same when treatment is begun. This is a common mind-set in doing research to show that this kind of psychotherapy thing goes with that kind of psychotherapy thing.

It is hard to do research for this reason if you presume that the thing you are studying is not so stable, or can change significantly from day to day, e.g. if the person's concerns, worries, troubles and problems are seen as being one way in the initial session, a different mind-set can hold that the practitioner or the researcher really ought to check again in the next session and perhaps in each subsequent session because these things can change substantially. According to this alternative mind-set, the case history that the therapist elicits in or before the initial session can be quite different from the case history obtained in the second or fifth or tenth session.

The researcher may ask the client, before treatment 'How many visits do you think you'll attend?' (Mueller and Pekavik, 2000). A traditional mind-set is that the answer is supposed to hold for the next session, and probably most of the subsequent sessions. Then the researcher can study the relationship between expected length of treatment and some other thing(s). The alternative mind-set is that how many sessions the person expects to have is easily modified by what happens in the next session(s). If one set of things happen, the person may, if asked, expect to have many more or far fewer sessions. Doing or not doing this kind of research depends a lot on whether you presume the thing you are studying might well be checked almost each session, or whether you presume that you have to check it only once because if it was present yesterday it will of course be present today.

Hoped-for payoffs of showing that these things go together

Suppose that studies proclaim that depression goes with perceptual rigidity and low scores on internal control, that extraversion goes with higher levels of experiencing and affiliation, and that client manner of expressiveness goes with involvement and productivity in treatment. These psychotherapy things go with those psychotherapy things. So what? What are the hoped-for payoffs of showing that these things go together?

There may be at least three nice payoffs. One is that we might learn more about and have greater understanding of things such as depression or extraversion or whatever we study that is found to go with other things. Second, we may come face to face with puzzling things that call for a solution, real problems with a solution that would move us ahead. Just how do we explain that depression goes with being an only child or that extraversion goes with being near-sighted? Third, maybe we can find out a little about what helps to bring about, to cause, one thing by seeing what things seem to go with it. In this hoped-for payoff, correlation just might shed some light on causality. These are some attractive payoffs. But there are problems.

Much ado about nothing: the big connections

In the title of the study, and in the conclusions, what usually appears are high-level concepts and constructs. The title trumpets that the study found new and improved connections between big and important things such as self-esteem and ego identity, meta-cognitions and tears in the helping alliance, perceptual rigidity and manner of expressiveness, internal control and a depressogenic family patterning.

However, a little closer inspection usually reveals that the actual connections are not between these high-level concepts and constructs, but rather between measures and tests, scales and questionnaires, which are heralded as measuring these high-level concepts and constructs. If we let our curiosity go even further, the differences are between three particular items of this 12-item scale and those four items that comprise the subscale of this other measure.

The close examination shows that the actual connections were between items such as the following:

1. I rely on a personal agenda organizer.
2. For most things, I usually prefer working by myself rather than as part of a group.
3. I worry about my mood swings.
4. My parents would generally talk things over with one another.

These interesting little items would then be expanded until they were labeled as connections between self-esteem and ego identity, meta-cognitions and tears in the helping alliance, perceptual rigidity and manner of expressiveness, or internal control and a depressogenic family patterning. The problem is making much ado about questionably little.

Grand connection: more of an illusion hiding a shared common element?

On the surface, to all appearances, it looks as if the study examines the connection between two different psychotherapy things. Almost always, these psychotherapy things are abstract, highly conceptual. However, if you take a closer look into each of the two psychotherapy things, there is usually a reason for a bit of skepticism. Strip away the abstract jargon, the high-level concept, and look for what each consists of, what each is. At base, they consist of the same thing. Each rests on a common element.

The study is offered as a study of the connection between this high-level thing and that high-level thing. But this is an illusion. The study is really a study of this simple common element. It is truly a study that this element is here and also there. It is really a study of a single element, elevated into an illusory study between two high-level psychotherapy things.

Consider a study of the relationship between two high-level notions. One is called a 'stages of change model' and the other a 'helping alliance'.

The understandable aim of the study was to see whether the person's state, before starting therapy, relates to, is connected with or can predict the nature of the person's relationship with the therapist (Derisley and Reynolds, 2000). However, a closer examination indicates that 'the client's readiness to actively engage in the change process' was perhaps the core feature of the stages of both the stages of change model and the helping alliance, and the study becomes a study of whether a person with a certain degree of readiness to engage actively in the change process is a person with a certain degree of readiness to engage actively in the change process. Unfortunately, what appears to be a study of the connection between two grand psychotherapy things turns out to be a study of their important shared common element.

Can it be too easy to make sense of how and why these things go together?

Most of our ways of understanding things such as depression, extraversion, psychopathology or anxiety are so vague, soft, expansive or flexible that it is usually too easy to make sense of how and why things go together. It would be nice if the ways of making sense of these things were sophisticated enough to be able to declare it hard to explain why particular things seem to go together. But that is rare. It is more common that our ways of making sense of things would be almost unfazed if we said 'Oops, I was wrong. Depression does not go with low scores on internal control; it goes with high scores'.

As it is usually so easy to make sense of things that go together, it is hard to be faced with a genuine puzzle, some phenomenon or pattern of things that almost defies explanation, some exciting challenge. Easy explanations replace challenging puzzles.

Wandering in the seductive world of groundless abstraction

The field of psychotherapy can be thought of as having created an entire world of high abstractions, ungrounded jargon, cloudy conceptualization and generalized notions that are essentially its own world, cut off from the ground of concrete events (Mahrer, 2004). It is a world of vague abstractions such as superegos, identity diffusions, archetypes, anhedonia, anomie, actualization forces, cognitive boundaries, proactive inhibitions, and an entire dictionary of ethereal terms and phrases, all part of an aerie faerie world of high abstraction.

If you start looking for which things go with which other things, watch out. You may well wander around endlessly, seeing connections at higher and lower levels of abstraction, connections within and between packages of loosely ethereal notions. You can spend a career following up seductively appealing possibilities. As long as you wander around in this world of high abstraction, your possibilities can be virtually endless.

Suppose that you start with the idea of 'transference'. The first task is to decide if you want to distinguish 'transference' from overlapping terms and phrases such as the therapist–client relationship, the helping relationship, the alliance, the real relationship, and other intertwining and connected terms and phrases. The important next task is to look for things that you believe might bear some connection with transference. You wonder what other things might help account for transference, be related to transference, go with transference.

Once you start wandering around, you may never be heard from again. Starting from transference, you can find yourself in a never-ending world of beliefs that transference relates to the client's and the therapist's degree of identity diffusion, kind of repressed affect, amount of unconditionality of positive regard, level of disidentification, nature of their respective core cognitions, shared cultural background, history of early family relationships, content of their mutual role relationships, strength of ego boundaries, reinforcement histories, level of dependency, role of transitional objects, nature and kind of defense mechanisms, strength of affiliation needs, patterns of contingency respondings, power of parental surrogates, degree of effectance motivations, and on and on.

You may begin by being drawn toward the generalized notion that transference is likely to be related to a number of interconnected ethereal concepts such as self-esteem, ego identity development, and the clients' perception of the degree of similarity between their parents and therapist on other vague things such as empathic attunement, positive regard and unconditionality of positive regard (e.g. Arachtingi and Lichtenberg, 1999). From there, you may wander around, almost forever, drawn toward all sorts of other high-abstraction notions and ideas that might be connected to transference or to the dozens of things that you believe might be related to the dozens of things that are thought to be related to transference.

Once you are up in the world of ethereal psychological abstraction, looking for what might be connected with what could leave you wandering around in an endless search for seductive possibilities.

Is yet another psychotherapy thing connected to it?

Suppose that you are drawn toward seeing what is connected with, may help to account for and predict, a psychotherapy thing called drop-out, premature termination, early drop-out. Your idea is that clients who are high on 'effectance motivation' will be more inclined to stay only a few sessions and those who are low on effectance motivation will be more inclined to remain for the full treatment.

You check the research literature to see if your study has been done, and what other psychotherapy things have been found to relate to early drop-out. Your review shows that dozens of psychotherapy things have been found to connect with drop-out, including gender of client and therapist, religious affiliation of client and therapist, diagnosis, pathological problem, length of stay in therapy of friends and acquaintances, cultural background variables, lots of demographic variables, length of previous relationships with friends, clients' expectations of length of treatment, precursors of the helping alliance and the therapeutic relationship, readiness for change, therapist orientation and approach, therapist experience and expertise, socioeconomic variables, cost of treatment, client psychological mindedness, and many kinds of client psychological dimensions including effectance motivation.

What do you make of your review of the relevant literature? There are at least four options, each pointing toward the likely fruitlessness of your going ahead with your intended study:

1. If so many things are connected to early drop-out, what does the practitioner actually do if any of these things is present with this practitioner and this client? Does the practitioner expect an early drop-out if his or her brand of therapy is one of these things, if the cultural background of the client is one of these things, or if the client's social class is one of these things? One option is to ignore the research findings in general, unless perhaps the practitioner is strongly impressed that this client will drop out, regardless of the research findings.

2. The researcher can shift the aim of the study to see which particular combination or cluster of the many psychotherapy things proves to be a more powerful predictor of client drop-out.

3. The researcher can believe that the larger the sheer number and kinds of psychotherapy things that are connected to early drop-out the less likely is any one psychotherapy thing to be strongly connected to early drop-out.

4. The researcher can gain appreciation and respect that clever researchers and clever designs can show that an almost unlimited number and kinds of psychological things can be shown to be connected with drop-out.

As a consequence, the researcher can be excused for wondering if it is sensible or fruitless to do yet another study to see if yet another psychotherapy thing is connected to drop-out. In other words, it is under-standable that some researchers will drop out of doing this kind of research.

Problems in trying to make causal sense of things that go together

If a number of studies show that manner of expressiveness and client pro-ductivity or involvement in treatment go together, it can be attractive to conclude 'that manner of expressiveness is a key factor in determining client productivity or involvement in treatment' (Hill, 1990, p. 290). But there can be some problems in trying to make causal sense of things that are found to go together.

One problem is that the case is rather weak if an almost plausible causal connection can be said to go either way. One way is that client man-ner of expressiveness is an important causal determinant of client productivity or involvement in treatment. But the equal and opposite direction also makes some sense: client productivity or involvement in treatment is an important causal determinant of client manner of expres-siveness; the more productive and the more involved in treatment the better is the client's manner of expressiveness.

A second problem is when the two things are not really separate. They may overlap, or one is included in the definition or meaning of the other. If one part of the definition of 'client productivity' has to do with the client's manner of expressiveness, then 'client productivity' and 'manner of expressiveness' go together, not in some causal way, but rather because one is a part of the definition of the other.

Consider a study of the connection between 'therapeutic alliance' and 'drop-out' (e.g. Piper et al., 1999). The idea was that, if therapeutic alliance was poor, the clients would be inclined to drop out of therapy. At a distance, it may appear that 'therapeutic alliance' and 'drop-out' were separate things, but the boundaries become much too fuzzy when 'thera-peutic alliance' is found to include things that virtually indicate that the client is headed for the door, e.g. things such as having a negative reac-tion to the therapist and what the therapist says, virtually direct indications of intending to end therapy, the therapist and the client argu-ing with each other, the client's showing frustration with the therapist and the sessions, and the client's general dissatisfaction with continuing ther-apy. It is like studying the relationship between the start of the client leaving therapy and actually leaving therapy, between starting to drop out and actually dropping out.

This second problem is quite common, i.e. it is common that the things that are supposed to go together are components of each other, overlap and help define each other. Consider a study of the relationship between the therapist's judgment of the client's active, steadfast, confident engagement and investment in treatment and (1) the therapist's judgment of client progress or (2) the therapist–client alliance (Hatcher, 1999). Although the researcher stretched and strained to show that the three things could be measured independently, it nevertheless seems embarrassingly clear that the therapist's judgment of the client's active, steadfast, confident engagement and investment in treatment also shows itself in (1) the meaning of the therapist's judgment of the client's progress and in (2) the meaning of the therapist–client alliance. In so many studies, the researcher is studying the relationship between one thing and itself, but dressed in different costumes.

Or suppose that you are looking into the causal or predictive relationship between homophobia and empathy, i.e. whether homophobia in the therapist makes it difficult for the therapist to be empathic with the gay client (e.g. Hayes and Erkis, 2000). On the surface, it looks as if homophobia and empathy are separate things that do not overlap with one another. The difficulty comes when elements of one are similar to elements of the other, when what is used to assess one also may be used to assess the other, when the same measure may be used to assess both. Consider this item: 'I don't think it's possible for a gay man to be really psychologically healthy.' Does this indicate or assess homophobia? Does it indicate or assess a low degree of empathy? Or does it perhaps indicate or assess both? Unfortunately, a careful examination of two things that may be causally or predictively related can reveal that you are often looking at two sides of virtually the same thing.

A third problem is believing that simple correlation equals causality. Although it is common to heed this warning, it is far more common to churn out hundreds of studies on the notion that if these two things are correlated then one causes the other, e.g. the researcher can start with a belief that the therapist–client relationship is causally related to desired outcome, and specifically that there is a 'predictive relationship' between 'therapeutic bond' and 'cognitive change'. You then study the relationship between, for example, 'pre-treatment depressogenic beliefs' and 'patients' perception of the therapist–patient alliance' (Rector, Zuroff and Segal, 1999). Underlying this and so many related studies is the familiar erroneous principle that simple correlation does indeed equal causality.

Finding a few laws or causes underlying most instances versus opening up worlds of possibilities to account for multiple instances

Researchers like to look for what things go together, correlate with one another, especially if researchers have a belief that with enough good studies they can uncover the small number of laws or causes or factors that account for or explain whatever phenomenon they are studying, e.g. researchers can have a belief that after 10 or 200 well-done studies, the findings would tend to identify two or four main factors that seem to predict or correlate with length or duration of treatment. This belief can make such a program of studies sensible.

On the other hand, it seems to be much more likely that the more studies that are done, the more researchers think of factors that might be related to length of duration of treatment, it is likely that there can be ever-unfolding worlds of possibilities. Rather than two to four or so main factors, there may be 200–400, and the quest is just opening up more and more worlds. If this is the future of such research, is the researcher still likely to wade into a never-ending search for whatever seems to predict or relate to or correlate with length of duration of treatment?

For example, just a few minutes of speculation might well come up with those kinds of factors that perhaps bear a relationship to length or duration of treatment, and there are studies on each: therapist skill and expertise, client perceptions of the therapist, client socioeconomic status, client diagnosis, degree of psychopathology, defensiveness, motivation, psychological mindedness, degree and level of therapist experience, cost of treatment (e.g. Berrigan and Garfield, 1981; Hattie, Sharpley and Rogers, 1984; Dubrin and Zastowny, 1988; Garfield, 1994; Sue, McKinney and Allen, 1996; Renk, Dinger and Bjugstad, 2000). If a week of serious speculating produces about 400–1000 or more possibilities, would the researcher still be enthusiastic about opening the door to this line of research? I wouldn't. Maybe some would.

Almost from the time research on psychotherapy began, a stream of researchers has been concerned with what they termed 'drop-out', meaning, usually, that the therapist believed the client stopped treatment before the therapist believed treatment was finished. Typically these clients leave after just a few sessions, and their therapists believe therapy has barely begun, much less finished.

Most of these researchers look for things that are connected with, correlated with, go with what they term 'drop-out'. They study dozens and dozens of different things on the belief that with enough studies they can uncover a small number of laws, causes or factors that can account for clients leaving treatment before they should. Researchers can identify these few things because they have what the researchers call 'significant effect sizes'.

The trouble is that the researchers typically have trouble coming up with the small number of underlying laws, causes or factors that the researchers believe underlie most instances of drop-outs. Unhappy about what they did not find, after examining lots of things that ought to have predicted drop-outs, Piper and his colleagues (1999, p. 116) lamented: 'A number of demographic, personality, and initial disturbance outcome variables, as well as interactions between certain personality variables and the form of therapy, failed to differentiate all drop-outs from all completers . . . .' Reviewing virtually the whole history of studies looking for the one or two things that hopefully would predict drop-outs, Brogan, Prochaska and Prochaska (1999, p. 106) are equally dismal: 'After 125 studies and 30 years of research, all too little data are available for understanding why so many clients terminate therapy prematurely.' It is easy to see researchers resolutely marching through the next 30 years, using increasingly clever and more sophisticated statistical procedures, searching for the holy grail of one or two underlying laws, causes and factors.

There is another mind-set that believes we can keep on thinking of worlds of possible things that can be found to go with, correlate with drop-outs. Furthermore, each instance of a client leaving before the therapist believes therapy is done may well have its own explanation or mode of understanding. There is no law that there must be a small set of underlying laws, causes or factors. There may be worlds of possibilities.

Even a cursory examination of the many drop-out studies can show how clever researchers have been at thinking of dozens and dozens of different things that can go with drop-out, from cost of service to therapeutic approach, from treatment setting to client diagnosis, from developmental status to client demographics, and on and on. The next 125 studies are limited only by the cleverness of the researchers in thinking of what might go with drop-out, e.g. from the experiential perspective, clients use being with a therapist to undergo important personal feelings and experiencings (Mahrer, 1996/2004; 2002). Similarly, therapists are with clients in order to be able to gain the personal feelings and experiences that are important for the therapist. If there is low goodness of fit between the important feelings and experiences of the two, they will be inclined to part company, e.g. if the client is here to feel protected and safe, to find someone to be on his or her side, and if the therapist is here to rescue the client from serious psychopathology and mental illness, then their agendas differ and they will probably part company after a session or two. Calculate the number of conceivable studies if the researcher finds 30–50 important personal feelings for clients and 30–50 important personal feelings for the therapist!

All in all, there are lots of hoped-for payoffs from showing that these things go together. The problem is that there seem to be some serious problems in the hoped-for payoffs of doing research to show that these things and those things seem to go together.

Concentrate on studying the exceptional cases rather than trying to find laws and principles of truth

It seems that most researchers are searching for the true laws of the psyche, of human behavior, the basic canons of what human beings are like, the principles of truth about psychotherapy (Mahrer, 2004).

In this grand search, it is common to have studies that examine large numbers of cases, hundreds or thousands of instances, and to sort out the connections between these things and those things. When these connections include large numbers of cases and instances, the researcher can frame a law, a principle of truth. These things go with those things. This is the way nature is, or human nature, or at least something about psychotherapy.

This is one way of looking at what research is for. In its quest for truth, for laws and principles of truth, it is understandable that there is little or no careful attention to the few cases or instances of what may be exceptional, remarkable, impressive. These are typically overlooked, lost in the grand search.

There are many examples of such research, and of the understandable brushing aside of the exceptional exceptions. Here is one: the aim of the study was 'to specify further how interpretations influence the therapy process' (Caspar et al., 2000, p. 310), 'to sharpen our understanding of how therapist interpretations take effect – or fail to take effect – in the context of a particular dyad' (p. 318). More specifically, the study wanted to establish the differential contributions of 'content' and 'process' to 'plan compatibility' and to patient progress. 'Plan compatibility' referred to the goodness of fit between the therapist's interpretations and the patient's goals of therapy. 'Content' referred to the fit between the therapist's interpretations and the patient's plan. 'Process' referred to how an interpretation took its effect as an act in the context of the interpersonal relationship.

By emphasizing an approach that highlights interpretation, and by examining each instance of interpretation in a number of cases, the study generated plenty of instances to study what goes with what in the grand search for general principles of truth about the differential contributions of content and the process of interpretations in therapy.

However, as with most studies of this kind, there was little or no intent to examine the exceptional exceptions, i.e. another researcher, intent on learning from these special instances, might have concentrated on outstanding and impressive instances of interpretations having profound effects on in-session therapeutic change or progress. The missions are different. One mission is to search for laws and principles of truth. A different mission is to learn what can be learned by examining exceptional instances. The general search for showing that this thing goes with that thing almost certainly loses the opportunity to learn from the exceptional exceptions.

Conclusions, serious problems and suggestions

A case is raised that there can be some serous problems in doing research to show that this kind of psychotherapy thing goes with that kind of psychotherapy thing. The case holds that these problems can be serious enough to interfere with this reason, to reduce the chances of success, and to make it exceedingly difficult to do research for this reason.

Some researchers may accept that there can be some serious problems; other researchers may be much less inclined, and instead more inclined to argue against these serious problems. The suggestion is that some of the interested and concerned researchers at least consider taking some time out, and for them to put their attention to solving these serious problems.

The suggestion is that solving these problems can perhaps clear the way for researchers interested in doing research for this reason. Even further, the larger suggestion is that solving these serious problems can help nudge the field in the direction of a revolutionary shift forward.

Here is an attempt to summarize some of the serious problems that await solution by and for researchers interested in doing research for this reason:

1. Some connections warrant relatively stronger consideration as 'causal connections', whereas other connections warrant relatively weaker consideration. The problem is: How can principles of causality be used, adapted, modified and refined, to enable researchers to identify and to differentiate connections that may and may not qualify as 'causal connections'?

2. Some connections seem to be between things that are relatively grounded and real. This psychotherapy thing and that psychotherapy thing go together, and both can be taken as essentially real. On the other hand, some connections can be between things that appear to be more illusory, groundless, unreal. The problem is how the researcher can identify and distinguish between the two, and what value, if any, can be found in connections between psychotherapy things that are essentially illusory, groundless and unreal.

3. One kind of beguiling connection is with almost anything and everything that can be shown to be connected with psychotherapy outcome. Although this is discussed more fully in Chapter 5, the mushrooming problem seems to occur in the form of a widely expanding and seemingly inexhaustible supply of conceivable things that can connect with

psychotherapy outcome. The problem is how researchers can determine whether an apparently inexhaustible supply of connecting psychotherapeutic things is relatively useful or useless, if researchers are better advised to withdraw from the morass or to remain and try to find connections that may be worthwhile.

4. There can be at least two rather different research mind-sets in looking for connections between psychological things. One mind-set holds that there is a small number of identifiable laws and general principles linking psychological things, and it can be the task of researchers to find them. An alternative mind-set holds that psychotherapeutic events are open to multiple modes of description and understanding. One side of the problem is which mind-set the researcher is to hold, because the former mind-set is conducive to this reason for doing research, whereas the latter mind-set has little or no place for this line of research. The other side of this problem is whether researchers who do research for this reason are ready and willing to acknowledge that this research can stand or fall on the particular mind-set that the researcher holds.

5. The study of large group distributions and aggregate normative analyses can submerge, dissolve or bypass the importance and significance of exceptional instances. The problem is how research on the connections between psychotherapeutic things can learn and benefit from close scrutiny of exceptional instances.

6. Some researchers may be interested in learning more and more of what psychotherapy can help to achieve, and how to achieve these changes in better and better ways. The problem is that this is not an especially likely consequence of doing research to show that this kind of psychotherapeutic thing goes with that kind of psychotherapeutic thing.

Except for the final problem, each of these serious problems seems to be especially tied to this particular reason for doing research on psychotherapy. The suggestion is that these serious problems deserve solution in order to help remove some serious roadblocks in doing research for this reason, and also in order that the field of psychotherapy move in the direction of a revolutionary advance. The suggestion is also that solving these serious problems is much more likely to occur by means of careful thinking than by further research.

CHAPTER 2

Is psychotherapy good, worthwhile, helpful and effective?

Almost from the beginning of professional psychotherapy, the field was entitled to show that it had a legitimate place, that it could provide something of value, that psychotherapy was good, worthwhile, helpful, effective. There were, and still are, a number of reasons why it can be useful for researchers to do such research.

One reason is that there are several other fields that have ample histories of helping: to reduce mental anguish and pain, turmoil and trouble, unhappiness and suffering; to reduce mental problems and difficulties, troubles and conditions; to deal with lost souls, with people who have drifted away from what is normal, who act in ways that seem bizarre and unusual. There are faith-healers and counselors, herbs and essences, alienists and helpers of lost souls, mind-healers and witch-doctors. There are fields such as medicine, sociology, pharmacology. From the perspective of many fields, professional psychotherapy is relatively new, and there can be reasons for professional psychotherapy to show that it is legitimate and respectable, perhaps even superior to these other fields that have a history of squatters' rights to what professional psychotherapy also wants to provide.

A second reason is economic. Professional psychotherapists want money for their services. Training psychotherapists can cost a great deal of money. Clinics and agencies that house psychotherapists cost a great deal of money. Mental health lobbyists know how hard it can be to justify their piece of the financial pie. Insurance companies and others who pay the bills can demand worth for their dollar. All in all, professional psychotherapy can be big business, and this can be sufficient reason for researchers to do research to show that psychotherapy is worthwhile and effective.

A third reason is that there can be skeptics both outside and inside the field. These skeptics may represent rival professions, the so-called 'hard sciences', intellectuals, rival movements, cultures that place little value on professional psychotherapists, influential members of the community.

19

The skeptics can also include colleagues who are doubtful about the substantial worth of professional psychotherapy (e.g. Eysenck, 1952, 1961,
1966).

All in all, it seems that there has been and continues to be a basis for
researchers doing research to show that psychotherapy is indeed good,
worthwhile, helpful and effective.

One of the main purposes of this chapter is to suggest that there can
be some serious problems underlying research for this reason, and to suggest that this package of serious problems can be relatively unique to this
reason for doing research. In other words, doing research for this reason
is accompanied by a package of serious problems that substantially differ
from doing research, e.g. to show that a given psychotherapy is good,
worthwhile, helpful, effective (see Chapter 3), or to show that a given psychotherapy is more helpful and effective than other psychotherapies for a
particular problem or disorder (see Chapter 4).

If researchers are to be unbiased and objective, who will do the research to show that psychotherapy is good?

Doing research for this reason can put researchers in a catch-22 bind. To
have trustworthy findings, the researcher ought to be eminently unbiased,
uninvolved, and objective on the issue of whether or not psychotherapy
is good, worthwhile, helpful, effective. But the problem is that, to do
research for this reason, the researcher is almost certainly already convinced that psychotherapy is or is not good, worthwhile, helpful, effective.

This is like trying to convince ourselves that researchers' findings are
rigorously trustworthy when researchers study the effects of smoking on
health and they work for a tobacco company. It is hard to picture
researchers doing research to show that psychotherapy is good, worthwhile, helpful, effective, and to picture the researcher as eminently
unbiased, objective and essentially neutral (compare Siegel, 1996). It is
easier to picture very few researchers left when we discount researchers
who are essentially biased and dedicatedly unobjective.

There seem to be at least three large rivals in treating personal problems, emotional problems and bad feelings: the fields of medicine,
pharmacology and psychotherapy, each of which is powerful, with a great
deal of money involved (Newman and Tejeda, 1996; Strupp, 1996). If
each of these three competitors held a conference in the same hotel, there
would be researchers working for, sponsored by and affiliated with medicine or pharmacology or psychotherapy. What would be essentially

missing at these conferences are researchers who are not in the pocket of medicine or pharmacology or psychotherapy, researchers who may be distinctively unbiased and objective. Indeed, a conference for these researchers may not occur for at least two reasons: one is that there is probably no big organization to pay the bills for the conference; the other is that the number would be so small, they could meet in the home of one of the relatively unbiased and objective researchers.

Valued payoffs from the desired findings, and how they help you get the desired findings

Even before you actually do the research, try being exceedingly honest with yourself. What are the valued payoffs from getting the kinds of findings that you want? How would you, or your boss or agency, benefit from the right findings? Once you can spell out these valued payoffs, take a careful look at your research design to spot the ways in which your valued payoffs help to determine the way the research is to be carried out.

The payoffs depend on your own personal intentions or those of your employer or the agency that gave you the money to do the research. Your findings may show that psychotherapy works, and that is fine because you are employed by the Academy of Psychotherapy, not a group of pharmaceutical firms, or your findings will be used to lobby a government committee to fund training programs for psychotherapists. Pay attention to the payoff reasons why the researcher is doing research aimed at showing that psychotherapy is a fine treatment, or that medicine works, or that pharmaceuticals are truly effective. Proponents can have an investment in getting friendly findings (Brooks, 1971; Newman and Tejeda, 1996; Peebles, 2000).

It is invitingly wicked to picture journals as publishing research studies in sets, with each study on much the same problem. Here is a study, the findings of which can be used to get practical payoffs for psychotherapists, grouped with a study with findings that will be used by the field of medicine, followed by a third study, the findings of which will be used by the pharmaceutical industry. Each study is on much the same problem, but done by researchers with quite different intentions for getting the right findings. The idea comes from the established practice in law, where experts testify for either the prosecution or the defense.

Suppose that you are going to do a piece of research. The neutral way of describing the study is that it is to evaluate the effectiveness of short-term treatment in reducing 'psychosocial symptomatology' (e.g. Vonk and Thyer, 1999). Suppose that is true. But suppose it is also true that, if you get the right findings, your university counseling center can help fend off pressure from the university administration to close the center, or to reduce the budget by 15 per cent, or to change the mission of the center to one that emphasizes working with students with learning and educational problems. These stand as rather practical payoffs from doing the research and getting the right kind of findings.

The public reasons for doing the research are typically high-minded and conceptually pure. In addition, what ought to be acknowledged are the other, more practical, payoffs from doing the research in the first place, and for getting the right kinds of findings.

Imagine that a research study flagged the ways in which the actual research design was geared to help obtain the right kinds of findings. Usually these are diplomatically omitted. Here are a few that seemed to have been included in the report by Vonk and Thyer (1999). As, perhaps, a way of nudging the design to help guarantee the right findings, the pretest was explained as a way of giving both the client and the counselor the right information that might be helpful both to the client her- or himself and to the counselor in understanding the client's needs. Such an invitation is much more likely to get the client to provide the right information, rather than interrogating clients for their pathological symptoms. After therapy, the client was told that the assessment was to evaluate the effectiveness of the center. Although it was not directly stated, it is easy to understand that only a mean and cold-hearted client would want to stick a dagger in the bowels of the innocent university center. Furthermore, clients agreed to participate in a planned termination program. What a good idea. Just based on these three pieces of the research design, it might well be expected that short-term psychotherapy was indeed shown by research to be effective.

If research is to show that psychotherapy is effective, the research will probably show that psychotherapy is effective, especially if there are valued payoffs from getting the right findings, and if the research design includes effective ways of almost ensuring that the research comes up with the right findings.

Generally accepted, universal meaning of success effectiveness versus that belief is a myth

Doing research to show that psychotherapy is good almost requires a firm conviction that there is a generally accepted meaning of success effectiveness, that all or most orientations and approaches salute the meaning, and that the meaning is virtually free of the particular value system of some particular orientation or approach. Here are some candidates (Hollon and Flick, 1988; Jacobson, Follette and Revenstorf, 1984; Jacobson and Revenstorf, 1988):

1. Success and effectiveness mean the reduction of presenting complaints such as low back pain, lack of sexual desire or feeling tense when being criticized.
2. Success and effectiveness mean the reduction of mental disorders and psychopathology.
3. Success and effectiveness mean movement from a dysfunctional range to a normal range.

There are some considerations for a case that belief in such a criterion of success effectiveness is a myth, and therefore this reason for doing research can be in serious trouble. One consideration is that we are quite far from general agreement on the meaning of success effectiveness (e.g. Strupp, 1986b). The sheer existence of a fair number of candidates, such as the three above, is some evidence that we have not yet reached general acceptance of any one meaning. More proof is that the single, generally accepted criterion has yet to appear, together with evidence that it is indeed generally accepted.

A second consideration is that just about every family of psychotherapies has its own criterion or meaning of psychotherapeutic success effectiveness. Looked at the other way, I know of no single meaning of success effectiveness that has won the unqualified support of all or even most psychotherapeutic orientations and approaches.

A third consideration is that most of what is taken as criteria of success and effectiveness can be seen as representing some kind of choice of morals and values (e.g. Heaton, 1976). As Heaton argues, there are distinctive differences in the value systems of orientations such as existential, behavioral, psychoanalytic, client centered and others, including the various integrative/eclectic orientations.

If a fair enough case can be made that it is a myth to believe in a generally accepted, universal meaning of success effectiveness, it is indeed questionable to do research aimed at showing that psychotherapy is good.

Single monolithic thing called psychotherapy versus that belief is a myth

In doing research for this reason, should the researcher be careful to select a particular kind of psychotherapy or use a balance of representative therapies? Not really. Psychotherapy is psychotherapy. Doing research for this reason quietly assumes that there is a single monolithic thing called psychotherapy.

The idea that there is a single monolithic thing called psychotherapy was there when Eysenck (1952, 1961, 1966) issued his famous challenge that psychotherapy may not be any good. It was there in the hundreds of studies trying to show that psychotherapy really is good, and in the reviews of those studies (e.g. Meltzoff and Kornreich, 1970; Bergin, 1971; Smith and Glass, 1977; Bergin and Lambert, 1978).

There may be a single monolithic psychotherapy if the day ever comes when one approach, perhaps cognitive–behavioral therapy or some other, takes over the field. Or if the integrative movement gradually integrates the whole field. Or if there are such broad and deep commonalities that they eventually coalesce into some single grand psychotherapy.

But, for now, a stronger case can be made that the very idea of a single monolithic psychotherapy is more of a collectively believed myth. There are simply too many differences between too many psychotherapies in everything from their notions of how patients got to be the way they are to their notions of what patients can become, from their notions of why patients feel bad to their notions of how to make things better. If doing research for this reason means believing in a single monolithic thing called psychotherapy, and if a stronger case can be made that this belief is more of a collectively held myth, then it seems the grounds for doing research for this reason may be more non-existent than real.

Is psychotherapy good: comparison with a plausible alternative?

When Eysenck (1952, 1961, 1966) first challenged the field to show that psychotherapy is any good, he looked at the studies. Virtually none of those studies compared psychotherapy with a reasonably plausible alternative. Since that time there have been so many studies purporting to show that psychotherapy is good and effective that reviewers sing a collective chorus that psychotherapy has indeed been proven to be good, worthwhile, helpful, effective, e.g. Maling and Howard (1994) cheerfully announced: 'Indeed, psychotherapy is the best-documented medical intervention in history! . . . there no longer exists a reason to investigate the general question of treatment efficacy' (p. 247).

It looks as if psychotherapy has been compared with truly plausible alternatives, but looks can be deceiving. Although some studies have compared psychotherapy against such alternative treatments as drugs or social-community programs, many of the studies compared psychotherapy with control groups, consisting of either doing nothing and leaving patients alone, or having the control patients on a waiting list. The problem is that a body of studies has yet to be done in which psychotherapy has been compared with control groups that constitute reasonably plausible alternatives.

If psychotherapy were a chemical ingredient in a pill, the control groups ought to be given a pill that looks like psychotherapy, tastes like psychotherapy, is administered in the same context as psychotherapy, but does not contain psychotherapy. Perhaps the control group should have sessions with people who are not professionally trained psychotherapists. A plausible alternative should offer something close to what the patient expects, should aim at being a plausible means of accomplishing what psychotherapy aims at accomplishing, should come in the general trappings of psychotherapy.

Until researchers figure out and use control groups that genuinely meet the standards of a plausible alternative, it is hard to be able to conclude that psychotherapy has been shown to be good, worthwhile, helpful, effective, no matter how many studies have been done.

Is the researcher's belief system about psychotherapy friendly and fitting?

To be inclined to do research for this reason, and to do this kind of research well, it probably helps if the researcher has a particular kind of belief system about psychotherapy, e.g. the researcher should probably believe that (1) there is a single monolithic thing called psychotherapy and (2) there is a generally accepted meaning, and way of measuring, something called success and effectiveness of psychotherapy.

In addition, the researcher's belief system should also include notions such as:

3. Patients come to therapy for treatment of their personal problems.
4. A main purpose of initial sessions is diagnosis and identification of the patient's problems and mental disorder.
5. Psychotherapy is treatment of personal problems and mental disorders.
6. The problem or mental disorder that was there in the beginning of treatment is the one that persists over treatment, and is the one to be assessed and evaluated when treatment is done.

If the researcher does not believe in these ideas, or does not have beliefs that are reasonably similar, it would be rather difficult for the researcher to do research for this reason.

For good and effective psychotherapy, wrap research in vocabulary that sounds scientific to outsiders

Even outsiders can be impressed that the broken typewriter now works, or that the crack in the glass is gone, or that the bald spot is now filled with hair. But outsiders might have a harder time telling that psychotherapy was good, worthwhile, helpful, effective. Researchers can have a better chance of impressing other researchers and especially outsiders if the whole research enterprise is wrapped in vocabulary that makes sense mainly to other psychotherapy researchers, and impresses outsiders as very scientific, specialized, technical.

Proclaim that the research findings have shown that psychotherapy is effective in treating things like ego diffusion, subclinical depression, emotional instability, an expressive learning disorder, a punitive superego. Describe the research design and findings in impressive language that mainly other psychotherapy researchers would probably understand. If the research is wrapped in vocabulary that sounds scientific, very few outsiders would be inclined to argue. They would hardly know what the researcher is talking about.

Conclusions, serious problems and suggestions

A case is offered in this chapter that there can be some serious problems in doing research to show that psychotherapy is good, worthwhile, helpful, effective. According to this case, the problems can be serious enough to block the chances of success, and to cast some doubt on a respected body of research generally accepted as showing that psychotherapy is, indeed, good, effective, worthwhile.

Especially for those researchers, and others, who can accept that there can be some serious problems, the suggestion is to (1) take some time out from doing this kind of research, (2) solve these serious problems and (3) use these solutions to re-evaluate the body of research that has generally been accepted as indicating that psychotherapy has been shown to be good, worthwhile and effective.

If these serious problems can be solved, it would seem that not only would this help to open the way for those interested in doing research for this reason but, on a grander scale, solving these problems may well help to nudge the field toward a wholesale revolutionary leap forward. Here is a summary of some of these serious problems in doing research for this reason:

1. Some researchers do the actual research, and some do the reviews of bodies of studies. In either case, designs and methodologies can be careful, rigorous and sophisticated, with double and triple masking to ensure experimenter objectivity. Nevertheless, standing behind the research paraphernalia are real-life researchers with built-in notions about whether psychotherapy is truly worthwhile. Here is the problem: 'How can research on the worth and effectiveness of psychotherapy include and benefit from researchers representing a range of built-in affinities, from a conviction that psychotherapy is good and effective, to researchers with substantial doubts, and to researchers who believe psychotherapy is rarely worthwhile and effective?'

2. Doing research to show that psychotherapy is good and worthwhile almost requires a belief in a single, identifiable entity called psychotherapy. Perhaps not, but, if it does, this belief practically puts itself nose to nose with a contrary position that there is little or no basis for a single grand entity called psychotherapy, that there are simply too many different therapies, with too many different philosophical foundations, with too many different programs and methods, and for too many different purposes and uses.

   The problem is what researchers can do to answer the challenge posed by the contrary position: 'How can researchers defend their position on grounds that are philosophical, rely on logic and reasoning, or emphasize evidence-based data?'

3. Doing research for this reason virtually requires that psychotherapy be compared with something, and researchers have called on a variety of increasingly sophisticated alternatives. Nevertheless, the challenging problem remains what alternative to psychotherapy qualifies as a rigorously stringent alternative, one that looks like psychotherapy, acts like psychotherapy in going through the motions of psychotherapy, and yet lacks the defining ingredients of psychotherapy.

4. Doing research to show that psychotherapy is good and worthwhile can invite researchers to be complicit with one another in backing into a vocabulary that looks impressive to outsiders, i.e. scientific sounding, filled with jargonesque technical terms and vulnerable to being labeled 'psychobabble'. Especially in communicating with the consumers of this line of research, including those in related professions, the problem may be stated as follows: How much of the vocabulary, in this kind of research, can and should be replaced by vocabulary that is more understandable, grounded and meaningful, both to researchers in related fields and to interested consumers?

5. Doing research to show that psychotherapy is good, worthwhile, helpful, effective is not especially designed to bring the field closer to discovering more and more of what psychotherapy can help accomplish, or to

discovering better and better ways of helping to accomplish what psychotherapy is found to accomplish. This may well have been a problem in the first reason for doing research on psychotherapy (see Chapter 1). It continues as a problem in this second reason for doing research on psychotherapy.

Interested researchers, and others, are invited to take some time out from doing research for this reason, and to address and solve these serious problems. It is hoped that solving these serious problems would help to remove some serious road blocks in doing research for this reason. In addition, solving these serious problems may well help nudge the field of psychotherapy in the direction of a giant revolutionary leap forward.

CHAPTER 3

Is this particular psychotherapy good, worthwhile, helpful, effective?

In Chapter 2, the reason for doing research was to show that psychotherapy in general is good, worthwhile, helpful, effective. In this chapter, the reason is to show that a particular psychotherapy, some given psychotherapy, is good, worthwhile, helpful, effective, either in general or in doing something about a given ailment, problem, difficulty or mental disorder.

The purpose of this chapter is to look at the serious problems that seem to go with, to underlie, this reason for doing research. Interestingly, perhaps surprisingly, it seems that the serious problems in doing research for this reason are relatively unique and distinctive. It might seem that the serious problems associated with this reason would be those associated with doing research to show that psychotherapy in general is good, worthwhile, helpful, effective. It turns out that a case can be made for a relatively distinctive package of serious problems in doing research to support a given psychotherapy.

Interested researchers and others are invited to address these problems, and to do what they can to solve these problems. The continuing theme is that solving these serious problems not only would remove some serious roadblocks in doing research for this reason, but, perhaps more importantly, would also help to nudge the field toward a revolutionary shift forward.

Is the psychotherapy associated with a body of friendly studies?

Picture a group of consultants to a particular psychotherapy. Suppose that the psychotherapy is Daseinsanalysis or primal integration therapy or Jungian analysis. The consultants advise the proponents of the therapy to do research on the therapy, to get a body of reasonably friendly studies.

'But suppose the findings are negative?' The consultant answers: 'Look, the important thing is that you have to be able to say that your therapy is associated with research. Just have a fair number of studies. No, they should not be grossly negative. But nor do they have to be authoritatively positive. Just get a fair number of reasonably friendly studies. Trust me. It works.'

An important purpose of many studies is to contribute to a body of studies so that the therapy can announce that it is supported by a body of studies. What is important is the existence of this body of associated studies, and the more studies the better for public relations purposes. Daseinsanalysis and primal integration therapy might be better off if they heeded the advice of the consultant. The steering committee for Jungian analysis may well have a serious discussion about the advantages and disadvantages of entering the research market.

Looked at in this way, the purpose of this research is not merely to get at the truth, to see if the therapy is good, worthwhile, helpful, effective. The reasons for associating a therapy with an impressive body of studies are also for purposes of public relations, marketing, sales, enhancing the reputation of the therapy, politics, business, power, money, e.g. a review of the research on eye movement desensitization and reprocessing therapy (Herbert et al., 2000) can be read as demonstrating how these kinds of high-powered considerations seem to be important in the research both in favor of and critical of that therapy. These considerations seem to play an important role in much of the research on many therapies, i.e. research can be big business, with implications that make doing research for the simple pursuit of truth both naïve and unimportant. Bigger issues are often at stake.

Those who come up with a new therapy are easily caught in a catch-22 situation in which their new therapies have serious trouble being published because there is little or no supporting research, and yet it can be hard to foster supporting research unless the new therapies are published. There are usually two ways to try to solve this problem. One is to publish the new therapy by citing other research studies and to do one's best to dress the new therapy as a 'theoretical' contribution in the hope that 'theory' is an acceptable way of dressing up a proposal for a new therapy. A second solution is to try to do a few studies on one's own new therapy, and thereby to get one's new therapy inserted into the literature inside research articles.

No matter how it is done, the important thing is to outfit the new therapy with a body of friendly studies.

Therapeutic effectiveness versus specification of nature and degree of change

Researchers generally try to evaluate a therapy's effectiveness in treating something relatively specific, rather than just whether or not a therapy is effective in general. The focus is on a person's temper or stuttering or feeling anxious and scared in airplanes. Most researchers can and do see if a therapy is good for some particular problem. But suppose we go somewhat further.

One way of going further is to see what degree of change this therapy is able to help bring about in that specific problem (Kazdin and Wilson, 1978; Barlow, 1980; Garfield, 1980, 1981). Does this therapy reduce the stuttering a little bit or a great deal? Are the person's feelings of anxiety and being scared in airplanes reduced somewhat or is the person virtually free of the bad feelings in airplanes? Is the cancer reduced a tiny bit or has it gone completely?

Rather than pronouncing a therapy as effective or ineffective, it can be more useful to say that this therapy can reduce the stuttering a little bit or moderately. I would not like to call a therapy ineffective if it is only able to bring about a 50 per cent reduction in the cancer in the left lung. Perhaps it is better to replace the words 'successful' and 'effective' with the degree of change this therapy is able to bring about in this specific thing.

Failure to identify the impressive changes that occurred

Suppose that a therapy is tried out with 100 patients. The therapy would probably be called unsuccessful if the desired outcome were achieved in only five of the patients. The study is over and that is that.

But suppose that the therapy had been carried out with people who had been dead for three days, and the five people were brought back to life, alive and well, free of whatever was thought of as having killed them. Or suppose that the desired outcome was growing in height, and there were increases in only five of the 100 patients, with four growing about one inch, and one growing four inches.

If the study is to show that a given psychotherapy is effective for this problem or kind of patient, the findings will probably conclude that the psychotherapy was or was not effective. A clearly different question is: 'What seems to account for the impressive changes that did occur?' If the therapy is pronounced ineffective, perhaps there were some instances of impressive changes, or impressive outcomes. If the therapy is pronounced effective, what accounts for the impressive changes in the big changers, in those with conspicuously impressive outcomes?

The pity is that doing research for this reason tends to fail to study the impressive changes that did occur, whether or not the therapy was found to be effective.

Relatively immediate, conspicuous and impressive in-session consequences

Almost always, whether or not a therapy works means that a researcher waits for weeks, months or years until treatment is over, and then tries to see if there is a change in some mental illness or pathological problem. The researcher starts when the client is diagnosed as having this or that mental illness, or this or that pathological problem. Therapy is applied, and the researcher tries to see if the treatment has been successful or effective. It is understandable that a researcher is needed to make this determination.

On the other hand, there are thousands of ordinary circumstances when a person does not necessarily turn to a researcher to see if a change has occurred. Most people can tell if the refrigerator light works or not, if the cigar is lit or not, if the traffic light has turned from green to red, if water does or does not come when the tap is turned, if the trembling hand is no longer trembling, if the person is no longer stuttering on almost every word, if the person can or cannot hold and stroke the snake. You don't need a researcher to tell if the change has happened when the change is relatively immediate and conspicuous.

You do not especially need a researcher to tell if the person is or isn't carrying out this task: 'Right now, in the session, look directly at your wife, see her, put all your attention on her. Now go ahead and be tearful, cry, have a strong sense of loving her and caring for her, show this genuinely and convincingly, as you say, with real meaning, "I love you! You mean more to me than anything in this world. I love you!" Ready? Is this all right to do? Yes? Then go ahead, and do it with real feeling!'

Here is a big change, an important change. You do not necessarily need a researcher to tell if the person did this or not, or even if the person continued being this whole new way for the next 10 or 20 minutes. Most people can tell if the person was being this way or not, especially if the change occurs right here in the session, if the change is a rather stark contrast with the way the person has been up to that point and if the change is rather conspicuous and blatant.

If the person seems to have been mainly quiet throughout the session, spoke occasionally and with obvious glumness and depression in saying that he is ready to die, has nothing to live for and feels an absolute failure in every way, most people could tell if he is that way now, as he is saying:

'I know I never told you how much I care about you! Well, that's over now. I love you. I really love you. See these tears? Go ahead, touch them! They are real. They are proof. Have I ever cried? Never. Diana, I love you. I love you. God, this feels good! Can we get married again? I mean for the first time, really!'

Most people could tell if the person is so withdrawn, pulled in, depressed, ready to die, when the therapist says, 'Now go ahead and be depressed. Talk about dying, giving up, killing yourself. Be you again.' And the person giggles, 'That is not easy! . . . Diana, Diana, I am really depressed . . . [He laughs.] Oh shit! I can't do it! I want to have a joint with you and walk in the woods and see if I can race you to the pond, and start having great sex like we used to! That's more fun cause I really love you! I feel too good!'

You don't really need a researcher to tell that a change has occurred when the changes are immediate and conspicuous right here in the session.

Weak and strong controls: a reasonably plausible alternative

It is common for researchers to be pleased that their studies used a control group, and that this is superior to studies that lack a control group. But if we take a closer look at control groups, it seems that a case can be made that some are relatively strong, whereas so many others are relatively weak. What is a relatively strong control group? It may well have at least two characteristics:

1. The patient should think of it as a reasonably plausible means of accomplishing what the psychotherapy is supposed to accomplish.
2. It should be essentially equal to the psychotherapy except for the ingredients that the psychotherapy regards as responsible for bringing about psychotherapeutic change.

Both of these characteristics are somewhat indicated in Erwin's (1997, p. 152) description of a placebo control:

> Ideally, a placebo control should control for a number of factors that might plausibly explain improvement, such as therapist attention, demand for improvement, and therapeutic rationale. At a minimum, it must be at least as credible to the patient as the therapy to which it is being compared.

Using these two characteristics of a reasonably plausible alternative, most control groups utterly fail to qualify as strong or even moderately strong. Picture a patient who is concerned with whether or not to leave her husband, or who is so fretful about being so fat he cannot fit into an air-plane wash room, or who is just tired of being generally miserable and gloomy. Being put on a waiting list does not even come slightly close to either characteristic of a strong control group. If most of our control groups are relatively weak, research that uses such control groups stands little chance of being able to show that a particular psychotherapy is good, worthwhile, helpful, effective.

A reasonably plausible alternative: placebo therapist

If we follow the lead of a placebo, the placebo pill at least has the trap-pings of the experimental pill. One way to do this is for the placebo therapist to look like a real therapist and to play the role of a therapist, but to lack the key ingredients of the real therapist. All the placebo therap-ist offers is the raw role, nothing more. The placebo therapist lacks the key ingredients of the particular psychotherapy that is being tested.

Suppose, for example, that our placebo therapist is an actor who has had no training as a psychotherapist. All the actor is going to provide is the mere role of therapist. The real therapist contains all the key ingre-dients of the therapy.

If the real pill looks pink and circular, the placebo should likewise look pink and circular. How can we find out what role or roles the placebo therapists should offer so that they can look like the real therapist but without the active ingredients? One way is to look at the actual pill and make the placebo look sort of similar. Picture the researcher looking at the real therapists, just to see what roles they offer. Picture the researcher as observing that half the real therapists seem to play the role of the patient's good friend, liking the patient, a confidante of the patient, and the other half seemed to play the role of the one who has both feet on the ground, is anchored in reality, is solid and reality based. When half of the actors are schooled to offer one role and the other half are rehearsed to play the second role, the placebo therapists are ready to carry out the session with the patients.

Researchers have placebo therapists providing control patients with placebo therapist roles that are reasonably comparable with those of the real therapists. The real and placebo therapists should look somewhat alike, dress somewhat alike, use somewhat similar offices and offer some-what similar therapist roles – except that the placebo therapists have no training in administering psychotherapy and they do not even contain or offer the active therapeutic ingredients. The placebo therapists don't even know what the real therapists are providing as the active ingredients!

To look like the real therapists, the actors play the role of, for example, the one who is fascinated with just about everything about the patient, the patient's thoughts, hopes, worries, early childhood, hobbies, everything, or the one who is wise, sage, knowledgeable, seasoned and experienced. All the placebo therapist offers is a placebo therapist's role. This is a reasonably plausible alternative, a fine control group. In this careful use of a control group, the odds may be on the control group!

What do experimental therapists provide that control placebo therapists do not?

If the placebo control testing is done with pills, the experimental pill contains the experimental ingredient and the placebo pill does not. What precisely does the experimental therapist provide that the placebo therapist does not?

Is one of these active ingredients training? After all, our actors have been selected because they had no training in psychoanalytic methods, in cognitive–behavioral or Gestalt or client-centered methods, or even in how to obtain and use the kind of patient–therapist relationship in any of those or any other therapies. Without training, the actors ought to lack the effective ingredients. An actor may play the role of a professional boxer, pilot or surgeon, but would not do so well boxing with a trained professional boxer, or piloting a real airplane, and no patient would be pleased to have surgery performed by an actor with no training in surgery.

If the researcher is testing psychoanalytic therapy or cognitive–behavioral, gestalt or client-centered therapy, what precise ingredients will characterize the real therapists – ingredients that should not be there in the placebo control therapists? What should the psychoanalytic therapist do that the placebo therapist does not? What is the placebo control therapist not to do because it is what helps make cognitive–behavioral therapy what it is? Clearly, each therapy should spell out what the experimental therapists are to do, and these things must be missing in the placebo control therapists. In general, this task has still to be done by researchers. Only a sliver of a proportion of studies, if there are any at all, have listed what the psychoanalytic or cognitive–behavioral experimental therapists must do and the placebo control therapists must not do.

When, some day, it is relatively common to have such a list for researchers to use, what is left for the placebo control therapists to do? What is our version of the little white pill that looks like the real thing and is like the real thing except for the active ingredients? After all, the placebo pill should not provide some rival active ingredient so that it stops being a placebo control and becomes a rival active ingredient. Therefore, the placebo control therapists should not do experiential therapy or solution-focused therapy. So what do they do?

One solution to start with is for the placebo control therapists to carry out a placebo therapist's role that the researcher judges is free of the active ingredients in the experimental therapists, and yet the researcher deems reasonably fitting for this patient, e.g. while the psychoanalytic therapist does psychoanalytic therapy, the placebo control therapist may be (1) an actor with no training in psychoanalytic therapy, (2) an actor who, with this patient or these patients, carries out a placebo therapist's role of careful and interested tracking and clarification of what the patient says and does, and (3) instructed by the researcher, and regularly screened, to ensure that the placebo therapist is essentially free of doing the things on the active ingredient list.

All of this is perhaps sensible and meets what is meant by a placebo control therapist. But it would be surprising to find two-thirds or one-third or even 5 per cent of studies using such controls.

In general, it seems safe to conclude that almost all control groups are exceedingly weak, almost none is impressively strong; on this score at least, it can be quite difficult to do research that can convincingly show that this particular psychotherapy is good, worthwhile, helpful, effective.

Comparison with plausible rivals versus comparison with a friendly control

It is relatively common for therapies to demonstrate their effectiveness against their own friendly control groups, and then to proclaim themselves as effective. But this proclamation can be accused of deceptive marketing because it can give the impression that the therapy is to be preferred over its rivals because it is effective. Either directly, or indirectly by implication, proclaiming the effectiveness of a therapy is comparing with plausible rivals (compare Erwin and Siegel, 1989). This almost amounts to clever and deceptive advertising.

The field of psychotherapy seems to lack a criterion of effectiveness that all contestants agree on. If there were one, it probably would mean that no control group is needed at all, e.g. if a special track contest were held for all runners who run the mile in four minutes or less, each candidate may qualify for the big race without competing against a control runner. But there is very little to compare with a 4-minute mile in the field of psychotherapy.

In our field, one common way to justify proclaiming a therapy as effective is to compare it with its own selected friendly control. Four therapies can therefore each proclaim themselves as effective, with the impression that they are all effective, and the therapist or patient can make a selection from the four. But this can be deceptive for at least two reasons: first each tested itself against its own friendly control and second such a pronouncement may well disguise the more careful conclusion that some of the four therapies are far more effective than others, even though each pronounces itself as effective.

One plausible conclusion is that proclaiming a therapy as effective is far stronger if the therapy is indeed compared with its plausible rivals. Otherwise, proclaiming effectiveness by comparison with a friendly control is, or can be, very deceptive – good public relations, but very deceptive.

Does effectiveness presume a continuing problem or condition as the treatment target?

Effectiveness almost always presumes that some problem or condition is identified before treatment, or early in treatment, and this problem or condition remains the target over the course of treatment. The researcher can have a fairly good idea of what to assess to see whether or not the psychotherapy is effective. If the problem or condition is identified as a fear of high places or a bipolar disorder, effectiveness means that the researcher sees whether therapy was effective in reducing the fear of high places or the bipolar disorder. Whether treatment took 10 sessions or 50 sessions, the researcher reasons that, if the problem was a fear of high places, the thing to look for is to see if the patient, after treatment, still has the fear of high places.

Sometimes the researcher can have a reason for believing that the initial problem might have been a fear of high places, but subsequent sessions indicate a bipolar disorder, so the researcher sees if treatment was effective by looking at both the fear of high places and the perhaps more important bipolar condition. In any case, the researcher typically presumes that, once the target is a fear of high places or a bipolar condition, then (1) it almost certainly means that in subsequent sessions the target remains essentially the fear of high places or the bipolar condition, and (2) effectiveness means that treatment was successful in reducing the fear of high places or the bipolar condition.

Some psychotherapies, however, simply do not fit. In experiential psychotherapy, for example, the start of each session gives the person plenty of room to find the scene of strong feeling that is front and center for the person right now, and to discover the inner deeper potential for experiencing that is found by probing down into the scene of strong feeling. The aim of each session is to enable the person to become a qualitatively new person, based on the deeper potential for experiencing that was discovered in this session, and for the person to be free of the scene of strong bad feeling that was front and center for the person in the session. In other words, each session can give rise to, and can be judged as successful or unsuccessful with regard to, its own distinctive changes (Schon, 1982; Mahrer, 1996/2004, 2002). There simply is no continuing problem or condition.

The traditional way of seeing whether a psychotherapy is effective is based on a presumption that the initial target of a fear of high places or the bipolar condition remains in the second and middle sessions, and throughout the course of treatment. The researcher then knows what to look for when treatment is over to see whether or not it was effective. In other psychotherapies, this presumption would be wholly ineffective. Instead, the researcher would have to figure out some way of seeing whether or not the aims and goals of each session were accomplished effectively. Whether or not the initial problem or condition is presumed to remain, the continuing target over the course of treatment can make a big difference to both what and how some change is seen as making the therapy effective or ineffective.

Who decides if the therapy accomplished its job?

Catherine had six sessions with a psychotherapist. It was a festival of fractiously different perspectives to listen to so many stakeholders argue about what changes had occurred and whether they were good ones or bad ones. The stakeholders included many more than just the client and the therapist (Strupp and Hadley, 1977; Patton, 1986; Howard et al., 1996; Newman and Tejeda, 1996; Strupp, 1996). The stakeholders included the researcher, the reviewers on the editorial board of the journal to which the reviewer submitted the study, Catherine's husband, her parents and older sister, Catherine's lover who referred Catherine to the psychotherapist, advocates of the feminist therapy the therapist followed, advocates of other therapies, Catherine's co-workers and work supervisor, and the company that paid the bill for the treatment.

The researcher, a colleague of Catherine's therapist, wrote up the study with conspicuous self-assurance that Catherine leaving her husband and family and becoming 'empowered' was an indication of successful treatment. Very few of the other stakeholders agreed. Most of them had their own justified notions of what would qualify as the desirable changes that treatment was supposed to accomplish.

There are ways of resolving or compromising this apparent party of different perspectives, but the dilemma remains. In many instances, there are different stakeholders who feel that they have a justified role in determining what changes should occur and whether or not they did occur.

The dilemma is made somewhat harsher because each stakeholder would probably be able to justify what changes should have occurred, whether or not they occurred, and the degree to which they occurred. Each stakeholder had relatively strong opinions about the desirable direction of change and how to justify that change as welcome and desirable.

The researcher provided a fine justification of the kinds of changes that were to be considered desirable, even though many of the other stakeholders seriously disagreed in favor of their own changes. In studying tapes of each session, it seemed relatively clear where the therapist was trying to go and what changes the therapist regarded as valued and important as indicators of success and effectiveness. If the other stakeholders had listened to each session as it moved along, many of the stakeholders would have objected to what the therapist was trying to accomplish.

There are often several people with stakes in what would constitute a successful and effective treatment. The dilemma is acknowledging the presence of these different stakeholders, and answering the question of who gets to decide if the therapy accomplished its job.

Is there room for greater openness, fairness and ingenuousness when testing for effectiveness?

Most testing for the effectiveness of a therapy may be seen as relatively careful, rigorous and objective. However, there can be ways in which much of this testing can be seen as rather disingenuous, artful, indirect, or less straightforward, frank, candid, open or fair than it could be. Here are some ways in which there may be some room for greater openness, fairness and ingenuousness in testing for effectiveness:

1. The testing is generally done by a therapy-friendly researcher. How to test to see whether this therapy is effective, and what tests to use, are typically decided by the therapy's own researchers, and often by the owners, developers and proponents of the very therapy that is being tested for effectiveness. Indeed, these are usually the very people who carry out the research. This can perhaps be somewhat deceptive and unfair. All of this can be done by researchers who are invested in testing a therapy's effectiveness, but not invested in showing that the therapy is effective.

2. A carefully selected control group is used that is weak, and chosen to make the therapy look as effective as possible. Some studies seem to use a weak and inert control group to show that the therapy does better than the control group. Proclaiming that the therapy's effectiveness has been shown by 'controlled studies' gives the impression that the

therapy accomplishes the goals that the consumers believe the therapy sets out to accomplish. But this is not always true. It means only that the therapy does better than a weak and inert control group. A fair test uses a robust control group, and the therapy is shown to be effective in attaining the particular goals that it seeks to attain.

3. Something that defines the therapy in the first place is used as an indication that the therapy is effective. If the therapy is defined as Adlerian partly because it emphasizes social interest, it can be somewhat deceptive and unfair to say that the therapy is effective when the patient talks about herself in terms of social interest. If a therapy is defined as being used because there is a good patient–therapist relationship, it is hardly a fair test of the therapy's effectiveness if the patient, after therapy, says she previously had a good relationship with the therapist. Many tests of a therapy's effectiveness are little more than indications that the therapy being used was cognitive therapy or psychoanalytic therapy. Perhaps a more open and fair-minded test may identify some other goal that the therapy seeks to attain with this patient, such as being free of the pounding headache, rather than the presence of what defines the therapy in the first place, such as talking about the pain and shock of birth, or keeping careful records of the circumstances surrounding the occurrence of the headache, or having a heightening of scores on a scale of voice quality.

4. This concerns the circumstances in which the testing takes place. It is inviting to picture the circumstances as somehow neutral, unbiased, objective. That might be nice, but the problem arises when the circumstances push or pull for the right kinds of findings (compare Kazdin and Wilson, 1978). Imagine the final therapy session, friendly talk about the patient's future, about having more sessions at some future time, warm and friendly conversation, and then the therapist asks the patient if he wouldn't mind filling out this questionnaire, giving some friendly reason to explain why it would be helpful to have the patient's feedback. Or, some time after the friendly last session, the patient is called by a friendly secretary or by a friendly researcher to help with a therapy-friendly check-up, and the ex-patient is greeted by a friendly, appealing, attractive secretary or research associate in a friendly office, and asked therapy-friendly questions. Under each set of conditions, the pull can well be for a therapy-friendly assessment.

5. A somewhat artful and clever, rather than open and trustworthy, way is when the emphasis is on the buyer rather than on the product bought. If marketing professionals want to get reactions to a new store, they may be more likely to ask shoppers in the store rather than homeowners in the community. They are more likely to get yes answers from sweet kindly people than from gruff tough codgers.

If the researcher asks the right questions, the yes answer is more likely to come from the consumer of a program of therapy sessions. Otherwise, the researcher is almost entitled to ask: 'If you didn't like the therapy, then what kind of an idiot are you to keep coming week after week for so long?'

If the researcher asks the right question, the yes answer is more likely to come from people who are inclined to give yes answers. Clever researchers know that there are all sorts of personality characteristics of consumers who are likely to indicate satisfaction with treatment (Lebow, 1982). Practitioners whose clients are asked whether they were satisfied with treatment are entitled to wince about some patients. 'Not Hilda! She bad-mouths everything. Besides, she always takes shots at me. I don't think she liked me much.' Saying yes often means that the clients were nice people, more inclined to be yes-sayers than no-sayers, rather than that the treatment was effective. It almost means that treatment is getting the clients to say yes when the program ends.

6. Finally, testing for effectiveness can be more artful than innocent inquiry when the researcher gathers so much data and is so clever at scrutinizing the data from so many angles that surely something good can be found. Give five or 10 different measures made up of hundreds and hundreds of items, with each item scaled from very little to very much. Then study the data to look for broad patterns and concrete units of change, look for global scores and all sorts of subscales. Go down to a level of concreteness and specificity, and rise up to higher levels of abstraction. Be creative and inventive. Keep searching, organizing and reorganizing, until you come up with something that you can show to indicate that the therapy was effective. If you are clever enough, you will find something.

Most testing for effectiveness is not quite an exemplar of open, innocent inquiry. It is often quite artful and disingenuous, especially in elements that are not usually reported in the publication. Testing for effectiveness ought to be open, fair and ingenuous. It seldom is.

Research designs providing friendly findings: a solution to the problem

Most researchers are good at coming up with research designs that are rigorous, scientific, sophisticated and equipped with the latest fashion in statistics. When researchers want to show that their therapy is good, their research designs can be impressively careful and rigorous.

The problem is that clever researchers come up with research designs that are heavily inclined to provide the kind of findings that the researchers want. Picture proponents of a given therapy, or even the actual developers of the therapy, as either doing the research or hiring the graduate students who are to do the research. The research design is stringent, rigorous and so heavily inclined to yield the right findings that I should be surprised if the findings were not what the researchers wanted to show in the first place. Of course your research shows your therapy is good. You are the ones who decided on the research design in the first place.

Imagine that I offer a group of psychotherapy researchers an unrefusable pile of money to come up with a design that was careful, stringent, rigorous and scientifically pure, a research design to show that a given brand of psychotherapy was no good, ineffective, not at all worthwhile, unsuccessful. I now have two research designs, equal in scientific rigor and stringency, one heavily inclined in favor of the therapeutic approach and one heavily inclined against it.

The test is whether the two designs match, overlap, are similar. Would the proponents of the therapy be willing to use the research design produced by the researchers whose research design was heavily inclined against the given therapy? After all, the two research designs are equal in rigor and scientific stringency. The test is passed if the two designs are similar, if the two sets of researchers come up with the same research design.

It is rare that proponents of a given therapy give their research designs this test. I would bet that virtually every such study would embarrassingly fail this test, provided that I could get them to take the test. The case I am making is that virtually all proponents of a given therapy use research designs that are heavily inclined in favor of producing friendly findings, and that these researchers rarely if ever accept and use the test to determine the extent of their research design preference.

Can identifiable psychotherapies be distinguished from each other in reasonably systematic ways?

There is a great deal of research aimed at seeing whether some particular psychotherapy is any good, and most of this kind of research rests on an underlying quiet, but almost unquestioned, certainty that there really are identifiable psychotherapies that can be distinguished. It is almost essential that seeing whether some psychotherapy is effective means first that there is some kind of psychotherapy to be examined. Does this make sense? Can we identify particular kinds of psychotherapies or does this whole idea fall apart on closer inspection?

Is there really something called behavior therapy or cognitive therapy or cognitive–behavior therapy? Can we even allow for the possibility that there may be no systematic way of identifying anything as a behavior therapy or a cognitive therapy or a cognitive–behavior therapy? 'There may today be no such thing as behavior therapy . . . instead, there may be merely a collection of very different types of therapies that are called "cognitive–behavioral" therapies, but that have no interesting common properties' (Erwin, 1992, p. 152; compare Erwin, 1978).

Behaviorism was introduced and given a rather precise meaning by Watson in 1913. According to Spence, just 35 years later, the meaning of behaviorism became so loose and obscure as to be almost meaningless.

> The term 'behaviorism' may, on the one hand, merely imply a very general point of view which has come to be accepted by almost all psychologists and thus does not point to any particular group or theoretical position. . . . In fact, so far as I know, there are no proponents today of the original Watsonian version.
>
> Spence (1953, p. 571)

It is easy to picture a crowd of psychotherapists at a behaviorist conference, even though some closer examination would probably indicate that most had quite different versions of whatever are the various meanings of behaviorism, and much the same picture holds for what passes for cognitive therapies, humanistic therapies, behavioral therapies and most other so-called families of psychotherapies.

If there really are identifiable psychotherapies, how are they identified and distinguished from each other? If we cannot identify a psychotherapy and distinguish it from others, it seems that we are deluding ourselves by doing research to see whether this non-existent psychotherapy is any good, effective and worthwhile.

Are our category systems more embarrassing than systematic?

Picture someone from outside the field of psychotherapy asking to look at a category system of the various psychotherapies. Instead of being able to hand the person a more or less official category system, we can provide that person with a rather large number of rather different category systems. We should probably have to explain why we have no single, generally accepted, category system.

If that person inquires how many different psychotherapies there are, we can say that there are five or 10, or maybe 10–40 or so, or perhaps 40 to about 100, or even, some say, 200–400 and still counting (Harper, 1975; Parloff, 1976; Goldfried, 1980; Corsini, 1981; Kazdin, 1986). I have first-hand knowledge of the dizzifying number of therapies when I named my approach as experiential, only to find out that there are well over two dozen therapies that also use the word 'experiential' in their official title, and even more that identify themselves as falling within an experiential family (Mahrer and Fairweather, 1993).

The flourishing integrative/eclectic movement can make it an almost impossible task to identify different psychotherapies. By mixing and matching, and by developing new therapies out of existing therapies, the number of therapies can be larger than the number of practitioners.

It seems very hard to do research on some particular psychotherapy if we cannot really identify psychotherapies, if we have no workable category system of the various psychotherapies. Perhaps the whole idea of identifiable, categorizable, different psychotherapies is a sort of happy illusion.

Even if different vocabularies are identified, psychotherapies are not necessarily different

Listen to the terms and phrases therapists use when they talk with each other about psychotherapy, about some case or session they are discussing. It may be possible to see that the words belong to different vocabularies, and even to identify these vocabularies. If the therapist uses terms such as transference, Oedipus complex, superego, penis envy, we can identify a psychoanalytic vocabulary. Terms such as social interest, organ inferiority and lifestyle indicate an Adlerian vocabulary. Words such as archetype, individuation and collective unconscious show that the therapist is using a Jungian vocabulary. If the therapist uses phrases such as cognitive schema, irrational assumption and cognitive permeability, the therapist is probably using a cognitive vocabulary. If the therapist uses phrases such as reinforcement, behavioral contingencies, conditioned response, the therapist is calling on a behavioral vocabulary.

Five therapists may have a session with a single patient, and each may use a distinctive vocabulary in talking about the patient and the therapy: psychoanalytic, Adlerian, Jungian, cognitive and behavioral. Yet being able to identify different vocabularies does not necessarily mean that there are different psychotherapies. How can research be done on some particular psychotherapy if we cannot do a good job of identifying any particular psychotherapy?

Is it feasible to define or identify a psychotherapy by the techniques or methods it is supposed to use?

One way of trying to define or identify a psychotherapy is by means of the techniques or methods that it is supposed to use (Garfield and Kurtz, 1977). The idea is that there are techniques and methods indicated by such tell-tale terms and phrases as empathic reflection, paradoxical intention, interpretation, two-chair technique, homework assignment, self-talk, free association, aversive conditioning, contingency reinforcement and counter-conditioning. If a practitioner uses the two-chair method and a few others, the practitioner is doing gestalt therapy; if the practitioner is doing gestalt therapy, the practitioner will use the two-chair method and a few others. Here are some reasons why it is not especially feasible to define or identify a psychotherapy by the techniques or methods that it is supposed to use:

1. If a method is stripped of its tell-tale label, almost every method seems to belong more to the public marketplace than exclusively to some particular approach (Strupp, 1977; Nichols, 1984; Mahrer, 1989b, 1996/2004). Even if some method is commonly identified with some particular approach, that does not mean the approach has exclusive ownership rights over the method.

   If we take away the label, such as contingency reinforcement or counter-conditioning, most methods were around long before the different therapies came about, and most methods are found in lots of different therapeutic approaches, e.g. well before most of our current psychotherapies were born, what is now called paradoxical intention was carried out. In a review of the history of this method, Hill (1987) cites a report by a physician (Hunter, 1786) in which a patient's impotence was cured by instructing the patient deliberately not to become sexually aroused, and the same method was used in early studies of negative practice (Dunlap, 1928). Once introduced into the field of psychotherapy (Frankl, 1960), it quickly moved from being a logotherapy technique to the public marketplace where it is now found in dozens of different psychotherapies (Fisher, Anderson and Jones, 1981; Weeks and L'Abate, 1982; Madanes, 1984; Dowd and Milne, 1986; Seltzer, 1986). With very few exceptions, when stripped of jargon labels, most methods and techniques preceded the rise of psychotherapies, and most methods and techniques are far more in the public marketplace than exclusively owned by a single approach.

   Suppose that we take a close look at the 100–200 techniques in a dictionary of behavioral techniques (Bellack and Hersen, 1985). It is easy to make a case that many of these techniques were there centuries before there was a behavior therapy, and are found in lots of different psychotherapies. Stripped of their behavioral labels, here are some examples: (a) providing something desirable for doing well; (b) providing something undesirable for doing poorly; (c) controlling what the person attends to; (d) monitoring fluctuations in behavior and states between sessions; (e) having a relatively explicit agreement to carry out some action after the session; (f) deliberately holding one's breath; (g) taking some time out from a stressful situation; (h) relaxing one's bodily musculature; and (i) deliberately stopping certain kinds of thoughts. Whether or not these methods are common in behavior therapies, they probably antedated behavior therapy, and are more part of the public marketplace than exclusively owned by the behavior therapies.

2. If we try to rely on identifying psychotherapies on the basis of the methods and techniques that they actually use, it can be very hard to identify most therapies, or the very existence of most therapies washes away (Lazarus, 1967, 1971; Marmar, 1969; Murray, 1976), or what differences remain tend to seem rather trivial (Goldfried, 1980; Goldfried and Padawer, 1982), e.g. it is commonly presumed that client-centered therapy uses empathic reflections. However, it seems that empathic reflections show up about as much in behavior therapy (Peterson, 1968; Lazarus, 1971; Rimm and Masters, 1979; Morgenstern, 1988). We may conclude that client-centered therapy includes what was formerly behavior therapy, or that behavior therapy includes what was formerly client-centered therapy, or that there is a therapy that relies on empathic reflection and it replaces what used to be called client-centered therapy and behavior therapy.

3. To the extent that a therapy agrees to define itself by its methods: (a) the therapy can be frozen and locked into using those methods; (b) the therapy can have a hard time adding or incorporating new methods (compare Kantor, 1945); and (c) the therapy can risk going out of existence if its original package of defining methods is no longer present. An unfortunate example is psychoanalysis. If it is defined by such original methods as use of the couch, three to five sessions a week, free association, genetic interpretation, analysis of transference, and so on, then, in spite of warnings to uncouple psychoanalysis from its original package of methods (Alexander, 1963; Kutash, 1976): (a) psychoanalysis risks losing the chance of advancing by using new and better methods; (b) there is a solid resistance to using new and better methods; and (c) psychoanalysis faces its own self-imposed extinction by no longer clinging to its original package of methods.

On balance, it does not seem especially feasible to define a psychotherapy by its techniques or methods.

Does defining or identifying a psychotherapy by its encompassing theory work?

A common way of defining and identifying a psychotherapy is on the basis of the larger theory under which it lives. If the theory is behavioral or psychodynamic, the idea is that the psychotherapy is behavioral or psychodynamic. But there are some serious problems.

One problem is that we are not even close to having a reasonably clear way of identifying and acceptably differentiating one theory from another. We cannot even tell if a supposedly new theory is really new. Judging from the self-proclaimed new theories that come out each year, it is hard to differentiate one from another, and perhaps even harder to tell if the new theory is truly new and different from the traditional batch. When it first appeared on the scene, behaviorism was distinguished by an emphasis on observable behavior and a bold rejection of mentalistic notions such as wishes, feelings and all that mentalistic hodge podge. But today's packages of behavior theories have no problem with the whole world of mentalistic notions, including mental disorders and psychopathologies, and almost the whole pot of what had been so justifiably declined. Indeed, virtually everything that truly distinguished behavior theory, when it first appeared, is now gone (compare Garrett, 1996). Theories are about as hard to identify and differentiate from one another as therapies.

A second problem is the belief that, if I can describe how and why change occurs by using the vocabulary of some theory, I must be doing that theory's brand of psychotherapy. If I describe how and why change occurs by using a psychoanalytic vocabulary, I must be doing psychoanalytic therapy. If I use notions of conditioning, my therapy is behavioral. My therapy is cognitive because I say that change occurs by replacing poor cognitions with better ones.

This belief is a problem to the extent that (1) it is simply too easy to describe almost any change using the vocabularies of lots of different theories, (2) almost any vocabulary can be successful in describing almost any change and (3) although many theories may own their technical vocabularies, they rarely enjoy exclusive ownership over the jargon-free ideas referred to by their technical vocabularies.

Picture about 20 psychotherapists, each holding the flag of a different brand of psychotherapy, and each listening to the same audiotaped session. Picture that all 20 agreed that there were some genuine changes. When each practitioner was invited to tell how and why the changes occurred, each could easily do so in their own, relatively distinctive, technical vocabularies. When each was invited to tell how and why changes occurred, but with the challenge that they must do so without using any tell-tale jargon, they managed to do so.

Here are their relatively jargon-free answers. The changes occurred because of: a deeper exploration of self, the fostering of interest in others, the heightening of awareness, getting in touch with one's insides, the therapist's acceptance of the patient, gaining better ways of thinking about oneself and the world, undergoing a meaningful relationship with the therapist, trying new and better actions, having and showing affect and emotion, strengthening control over inner forces, re-education of one's general style of living, appreciating the genius and honesty of the therapist, having more direct contact with whatever was bothersome, releasing the blocked inner self, modifying how one acts and is, softening and reducing the impact of inner forces, accepting inner and outer reality, establishing a helpful relationship with the patient, distinguishing between problematic and better thoughts and ideas, going through an emotional experience that is helpfully corrective, understanding the way the patient sees the world, being able to control actions that are painful or ineffective, gaining faith in a higher force, gaining faith in the therapist's way of seeing things.

It won't work to presume that, if you use some theory's vocabulary to tell how and why change occurs, your therapy is that theory's because (1) it is simply too easy to describe almost any change using the vocabularies of lots of different theories, (2) almost any vocabulary can be successful in describing almost any change and (3) although many theories may own their technical vocabularies, they rarely enjoy exclusive ownership over the jargon-free ideas referred to by their technical vocabularies.

Is it possible to identify a psychotherapy as distinctively integrative/eclectic?

There seem to be several meanings or bases for saying that a psychotherapy is integrative/eclectic, and a case can be made that it is almost impossible to identify a therapy as distinctively integrative/eclectic, even though most practitioners apparently identify their approach as such (Mahrer, 1989b). One meaning of integrative/eclectic is that the practitioner allows him- or herself to move from doing one kind of psychotherapy to another, perhaps using one brand with one patient and another with another patient. This meaning does not even try to declare itself a distinctive brand of therapy.

A second meaning is when a practitioner acknowledges doing psychotherapy in some relatively consistent way, but it is so idiosyncratic that it is hard to parse out which bits and pieces come from which psychotherapies. The therapist acknowledges assembling an approach that is his or her own, but admittedly it is his or her concoction. More than likely, there is a great deal of variation among therapists using integrative/eclectic therapies in this way.

A third meaning is a psychotherapy that declares its identity, proclaims itself a particular brand of integrative/eclectic psychotherapies, and describes its distinctive theory and methods. There are already a fair number of such distinctive psychotherapies. The trouble is that this particular integrative/eclectic therapy faces the same problems as any other supposedly distinctive and identifiable psychotherapy.

A fourth meaning comes from a belief that indeed there is, or can be, a particular kind of psychotherapy that is integrative/eclectic just as psychoanalytic therapy is psychoanalytic and cognitive–behavioral therapy is cognitive–behavioral. There are at least two problems here: (1) we have yet to be told exactly what this integrative/eclectic therapy is so that it can be identified and distinguished from all other therapies; (2) if the first problem can be resolved, whatever emerges as this therapy then faces all the problems that any other therapy already has in identifying itself and distinguishing it from all other therapies.

Whatever the meaning, it is very hard to identify a psychotherapy as distinctively integrative/eclectic (compare Mahrer, 1989b).

A system of identifying psychotherapies when therapists talk about, but do not necessarily do, psychotherapy

We call a therapy psychoanalytic or behavioral or client centered mainly from what a therapist or researcher or theoretician says in talking about the therapy. These labels come from and apply to the psychotherapist who tells how she or he believes change occurs, what this patient's problem is, how the patient got to be the way the patient is. We have labels such as psychoanalytic or behavioral or client centered mainly from our talk about psychotherapy. We can identify solution-focused therapy mainly from the way therapists talk about psychotherapy.

If we were to develop a category system of psychotherapies based on what therapists actually do in their sessions, I doubt if we should end up with labels such as psychoanalytic therapy, behavioral therapy, client-centered therapy, solution-focused therapy, and the like. Suppose that a group of philosophers of science, for example, were to listen to many sessions of many psychotherapists in order to come up with a category system of psychotherapies. If this group were willing to start from scratch, I would bet that the category system with which they come up is very different from the one we have now.

The current category system might identify the distinctive ways that psychotherapists talk about psychotherapy, but it does not come from or really apply to therapists actually doing psychotherapy.

Are there such things as identifiable psychotherapies, distinguishable in reasonably systematic ways?

Doing research to show that some psychotherapy is good, worthwhile, helpful and effective almost takes for granted that we can identify some psychotherapy and distinguish it from other identified psychotherapies. Yet the case is being built that perhaps this is a myth, an illusion. Perhaps there are no such things as implosive therapy or reality therapy or psychoanalytic therapy. If we accept this case, we can have trouble doing research to show that some non-existent psychotherapy is good, worthwhile, helpful, effective.

Proposal for identifying and distinguishing psychotherapies in reasonably systematic ways

Suppose that we set aside our present labels such as implosive or reality or psychoanalytic therapies. I could never understand how my therapy, which I called experiential psychotherapy, could be grouped with other therapies that were also called experiential psychotherapies. When I honestly tried to see if my psychotherapy had much or very little in common with these other psychotherapies, by reading about and listening to tapes of these other experiential psychotherapies, there were some ways I was able to identify my psychotherapy and could distinguish it from most other psychotherapies, however they were labeled.

One way was for me to identify the working goals or objectives of my psychotherapy. There were two, and they applied to just about every session and to just about any person with whom I worked:

1. A working goal or objective for each session was to enable the person to be a qualitatively new and different person, including a deeper potential for experiencing that was discovered in this session.
2. A related working goal or objective is for the radically new person to be free of the scenes, and the bad feelings in those scenes, that were front and center for the old person at the start of the session.

In addition to these two working goals or objectives, my psychotherapy counts on a sequence of four steps to help achieve these two working goals or objectives:

1. To discover a deeper potential for experiencing that is deep inside the person.
2. The person must accept, love, welcome this deeper potential for experiencing.
3. The person must undergo the radical transformation into being this deeper potential for experiencing, within the context of past scenes and situations.
4. The qualitatively new person must taste and sample what it is like to be this qualitatively new person in the context of imminent and forthcoming scenes and situations in the new person's extra-therapy world.

My experiential psychotherapy may be identified as having these particular working goals or objectives and counting on this four-step sequence as the means of attaining the two working goals or objectives. I can tell how similar or different my psychotherapy is from other psychotherapies by seeing precisely what the working goals or objectives of these other psychotherapies are, and what these other psychotherapies count on to help attain their particular working goals and objectives, e.g. there seems to be a psychotherapy that counts on achieving and using a particular kind of therapist–patient relationship and achieving and using a particular kind of patient insight and understanding (Klein, 1970; Blum, 1980; Luborsky, Barber and Crits-Christoph, 1990). Furthermore, this other psychotherapy seems to have working goals and objectives that are quite different from those of my own psychotherapy. Therefore, it seems to me that my psychotherapy is quite different from a psychotherapy that is called psychoanalytic psychotherapy.

I suggest that we think of our present category system of psychotherapies as relatively useless, and that we consider a whole new way of identifying psychotherapies by identifying first working goals and objectives, and then the particular ways and means of helping to attain them. Instead of upwards of 400 different psychotherapies, or four or five big families, we should be able to see just how many distinctive kinds of psychotherapies we currently have. What is more, we should have a relatively careful and systematic way of identifying psychotherapies and of distinguishing them from each other. Until then, I accept the case that there are no such things as identifiable psychotherapies, distinguishable from one another in reasonably systematic ways.

Unfriendly researchers testing the effectiveness of unfriendly therapies

Many researchers pride themselves in the noble myth that they are merely pursuing truth, that they just test hypotheses to see what the truth is. They take the role that they are neutral scientists. Yet these same researchers often point their fingers at target groups, and proclaim that these groups have an ethical and scientific obligation to do the honorable thing if the body of findings says that is what they should do. Sorry, your therapy is no good. Take the honorable action.

These researchers introduce their studies by saying that this therapy makes these claims, holds itself out as a good therapy. Therefore it is the researcher's scientific mission to do the study to check out the claims. Once the results are known, the last part of the report typically talks about implications, including the implication that the therapy's claims are unjustified. Therefore, so the implication goes, the future is not promising for the therapy. The nasty implication is that the therapy should be dismissed, set aside, abandoned.

The truth seems closer to acknowledging that these researchers are not merely after scientific truth. They chose to see whether the therapy was any good. They chose to see whether this therapy really does significantly better than no treatment, or control groups, or placebo therapies, or minimal treatments. These researchers are rarely devout proponents of the therapy. They are researchers dedicated to testing the claims, to subjecting the claims to the kind of scrutiny that can show the claims are not confirmed. They are out to show that the therapy is not all that it is cracked up to be.

Here is the problem. The researcher almost insists that, if the findings show that the therapy is not good, the proponents should give the therapy up, sooner or later, when there are enough of the right studies. If the researcher truly believes this, the researcher might well find out beforehand whether or not the target groups agree, i.e. the researcher should state that, if the findings are negative, non-conforming, non-verifying, there is the probability that these target groups will withdraw this claim, will not do this therapy for that problem, will give up this therapy with those clients, will stop advertising the therapy in these ways. It would be nice if the researcher could get these promises in writing from the target groups.

Here is the core of the problem. If the researcher cannot and does not get these promises, if the probability is virtually zero that the target groups would do any of the honorable things the researcher would want them to do, or if the researcher does not even spell out beforehand what actions should be taken if the unfriendly findings occur, why do the study in the first place?

If the researcher cannot get agreement from the target groups, at least the researcher might be honest in saying beforehand that, if the findings are the way the research is designed to bring about, here are the specific actions that the target groups ought honorably to carry out, but here are the probabilities that the target groups will actually carry them out.

The question the researcher can face is this: 'Why do this unfriendly study if the target constituencies will not agree to do the honorable thing when the findings are in?' The typical answer is that the target constituencies ought to, even though the probability is very low. If that is what the researcher believes, perhaps the honorable thing for the researcher is to say this up front, to be clear about the specific actions the researcher would want the target constituencies to take, to be honest about the probability of their doing so, and perhaps not to do a study with reasons and implications that are largely hidden, covert, unstated and yet rather nasty.

Is it possible for true believers to state and act on reasonable research grounds that involve abandoning their therapy?

Just as it can be much easier to confirm a hypothesis than to disconfirm or refute it, it can be very very hard to do research that convincingly shows that a given psychotherapy is simply not good, worthwhile, helpful, effective. Furthermore, it is almost impossible and unheard of for true believers in some brand of psychotherapy to be willing to set forth the research grounds that they would accept as reasonable and sufficient for them to abandon their therapy. As almost impossible and unheard of as this is, it seems even more impossible and unheard of for these true believers to follow through and dutifully abandon their therapy in the face of those research grounds, provided that the true believers would even have the courage to look seriously at those research grounds.

Put this to the test. Ask Jungian analysts or solution-focused therapists or proponents of any other therapy to accept the test. If they fail the test, as I am willing to bet they would, one conclusion is that it is fruitless and useless to engage in research aimed at showing that a particular psychotherapy is good, worthwhile, helpful, effective, mainly because no amount of research would be accepted by true believers as sufficient for them to abandon their therapy as not good, worthwhile, helpful, effective.

Consider a psychoanalytic proponent holding on to the unconscious, a Jungian analyst grasping the archetype, a rational–emotive–behavioral therapist clinging to the idea of the centrality of ABC, namely that there are activating life events, beliefs that the person has to process these activating events and consequences to holding these beliefs, especially when they are irrational. The test would consist of these proponents stating the reasonable grounds that they would accept as sufficient for them to give up their precious concepts, notions, theories. With the rarest of exception, these proponents would not be likely to put these grounds on the table, and it would be even less likely that they would actually abandon these precious notions and ideas if the reasonable grounds were met.

Hill's (1996) theory and program of dream interpretation consists of three interlocking phases: (1) exploring the dream, (2) gaining insight and understanding of the meaning of the dream, and (3) considering taking action or making changes in one's current life. Consider a study to see if use of all three phases was better than just relying on the first two phases in helping clients to have clearer and better plans for making changes in their current lives (Wonnell and Hill, 2000). Before the study is even carried out, applying the test would mean asking Hill if she would accept negative findings as sufficient for the third phase to be abandoned, or if

she would be willing to state how much of what kinds of reasonable findings would be sufficient to drop the third phase. Although it may perhaps
be possible, it seems unlikely that Hill, or most creators of theories and
programs, would pass this test.

Grounds for abandoning a therapy: weighing up against the initial grounds for establishing and maintaining the therapy

Psychoanalytic therapy did not come about on a whim. Nor did cognitive–behavioral therapy or the various other therapies. Those who
developed the therapy in the first place, and those who were strong proponents thereafter, could almost always point to a body of evidential data
and sound reasons for the therapy. Very few therapies came about and
were maintained on flimsy data and flimsy reasons.

If proponents were willing to take the test, and they tried to state the
reasonable grounds sufficient for them to give up their therapy, these
grounds might be rather simple if the therapy were established and maintained on data and reasons that were simple, light, flimsy. However, most
therapies rest on grounds that are serious, ponderous, and deep, numerous and solid. It would be an almost impossible task to state the grounds
that would be able to oppose the mountain of grounds for development
and maintenance of psychoanalytic therapy, Jungian analysis, cognitive
therapy, or even the notion of an unconscious, the importance of cognitions, the therapist–client relationship, neurophysiological determinants
of behavior, and so on.

Stating grounds for abandoning a therapy or deeply held core concept
can be more complicated than following largely implicit scientific guidelines. One almost certainly has to take into account the history of data and
reasons why the therapy or deeply core concept was developed and maintained. Stating the sufficient findings for abandoning a therapy or
important core concept is almost never done. This is perhaps one reason
why it is so rare.

Are the therapists really doing the therapy well enough so that the findings can show if it fails?

How can you be sure that the therapists are really doing that therapy and
doing it well enough that the findings are capable of labeling the therapy
as a failure, and on its way toward being abandoned? The answer typically goes beyond mere adherence to a manual. Rather, it is common that the
real answer is given by the findings. If the findings are friendly, the therapists must have been doing the right therapy, and doing it well enough. If
the findings are unfriendly, they can be used to show that the therapists
were either not doing the therapy or not doing it well enough. Do not

bury the therapy. Do not even consider abandoning the therapy. It is common to let the findings determine if the therapists were doing the therapy and doing it well enough.

Suppose a researcher wants to show that a particular therapy for pain reduction is indeed effective in reducing pain. The therapy is called psychodynamic body therapy, and it is described as a variant of an affect-consciousness treatment model based on affect-and-script theory and self-psychology, and emphasizing exploration of affect experiences and bodily interventions based on a psychomotor physical therapy (Monsen and Monsen, 1999, 2000). When the researcher selects therapists to do the therapy, it can be exceedingly hard to be confident that they were actually doing that particular therapy and doing it well enough that the therapy might be headed for abandonment if the results were unfriendly.

I have serious doubts that many proponents of particular therapies would read the research design and say: 'I am convinced that the therapists will be doing my therapy, and will be doing it well enough that if the findings come out the wrong way, I am ready to abandon my therapy.'

Would a therapy-friendly researcher attain therapy-friendly findings?

Many researchers like to think of themselves as neutral and objective, and as applying a neutral and objective scientific method in their research. I doubt if this is true for many researchers whose research is aimed at validating their therapy, as showing that their therapy is good, worthwhile, helpful, effective. These researchers are, I believe, less than purely hardly neutral and objective (compare Siegel, 1996). They are doing research to show that their therapy is good and effective, and it is likely that they will succeed in getting the kind of findings they set out to obtain. In other words, researchers who set out to show that their therapy is good and effective hardly qualify as neutral and objective, and I would count on their being able to obtain therapy-friendly findings.

Which research findings would the practitioner be inclined to accept: the researcher's or the practitioner's?

Researchers who do research on psychotherapy have a problem that is probably unique among researchers, at least to a large extent. The problem is that the researcher is in head-to-head competition with the very practitioner whose psychotherapy the researcher studies. The poor researcher has a powerful rival in the form of the practitioner. This is a problem, and the rival is a powerful one, for at least two reasons.

One reason is that the one the researcher is trying to convince is the practitioner whose psychotherapy the researcher studies. This becomes an almost impossible task for the second reason, namely that the practitioner is the researcher's stiffest competitor or rival. The researcher is going to produce research findings. The big trouble is that the practitioner is accumulating research findings every time the practitioner has a session. The practitioner has an incredible amount of evidence that his or her own brand of psychotherapy is good enough to stick with. The practitioner is entitled to trust his or her own cumulative research findings far more than whatever research findings some researcher produces.

The researcher has to convince her- or himself and the practitioner that the researcher's findings are better and are the findings that the practitioner should trust. The researcher must be assured that her or his findings are much better and the practitioner should trust the researcher's findings, even though the practitioner knows much better what it is like to use that therapy for thousands of hours, sees first hand how and where it works, whether the therapy seems good, worthwhile, helpful, effective.

There is less of a problem if the researcher happens to agree with and confirm what the practitioner's findings have been like after using the therapy for thousands of hours. But, suppose that the researcher says that her or his findings show that the therapy used and trusted is, on the basis of her or his findings, not very good? Either the practitioner can bow respectfully, and trust that her or his therapy is indeed not very good, or the practitioner can cock her or his head, raise her or his eyebrow, and wonder how this rank outsider, this 'researcher', can dare to presume that her or his research findings are more to be trusted than the practitioner's own impressive body of research findings. Has the practitioner been a naïve idiot, trusting that her or his therapy was good when the researcher is holding out a small plate of research findings showing that the practitioner has been mistaken all along?

The researcher has a massive problem in trying to convince the practitioner that the researcher's findings are somehow superior to and better than the practitioner's own huge body of research findings.

Conclusions, serious problems and suggestions

The previous chapter was about research aimed at showing that psychotherapy in general was good, worthwhile, helpful, effective. The present chapter deals with research aimed at showing that a particular psychotherapy is good, worthwhile, helpful, effective. Do these two chapters overlap to such an extent that they ought to be combined into a single chapter? The answer leans toward no when we compare the serious problems in each, and see that each reason seems to be accompanied by its own relatively distinctive set of serious problems.

The concluding case is that there can be some serious, and distinctive, problems that go with doing research to show that a given psychotherapy is good and effective. Even further, the case is that these problems can be serious enough to block the chances of doing this kind of research successfully, perhaps even to dissuade researchers from doing this kind of research in the first place.

Especially for researchers who can appreciate the seriousness of these problems, the suggestion is for these researchers (1) to take some time out from doing research for this reason, and instead (2) to do their best to help resolve these serious problems.

Solving these problems can help remove many of the roadblocks for researchers who are ready and willing to acknowledge the serious problems, and who are nevertheless intent on doing research for this reason. However, there can also be a greater bonus, in that solving these problems may also help to nudge the field toward a revolutionary leap forward. Here is a summary of some serious problems in doing research for this reason:

1. Doing research for this reason may culminate in stamping a given therapy as good or worthwhile, but this alone may be regarded as seriously inferior to a much more stringent assessment of the therapy's explicit goodness and worth. The serious problem may be stated as follows: 'How can research determine the explicit likelihood, the degree of probability, of obtaining what explicit identified kind of change in regard to what explicit identified kind of problem or issue?'
2. Doing research to see if a given therapy is good or effective is inclined to mask or overlook exceptional instances of exceptional extraordinary change. A serious problem may be stated as follows: 'How can research flag exceptional instances of exceptional extraordinary change?'
3. Judgments of a given psychotherapy as good or effective can often de-emphasize or omit differences in the judgments of the various stakeholders. Although it can be relatively easy to acknowledge that judging a given psychotherapy as good or effective can vary with the judgements of various stakeholders, a serious problem may be stated as follows: 'How can researchers identify, determine and incorporate significant differences in the judgements from the perspectives of: (a) the initial client and the significantly changed client; (b) relevant people in the world of the initial client, and the relevant new people in the

world of the significantly changed client; (c) those with a professional or financial stake in a particular direction of change, including the therapist, referral agent, departmental or administrative unit, clinic or agency, and those who pay for the psychotherapeutic services; and (d) researchers who are invested in getting friendly findings?'

4. Doing research for this reason generally involves an initial diagnosis of a mental disorder or identification of a problem or difficulty, and a presumption that the initial mental disorder, problem or difficulty typically continues as the focus of treatment throughout treatment, and is to be evaluated or assessed when treatment is completed. A serious problem may be stated as follows: 'To what extent, and under what conditions, is the initial focus of therapy understood, presumed, or thought of as (a) persisting over the course of sessions, or (b) understood, presumed, or thought of as being eminently replaceable by a series of substantially different ones from session to session over the course of therapy?' This third reason for doing research on psychotherapy would probably find the persistence of an initial diagnosis or problem to be friendly, and the changeability of the focus to be a serious road block.

5. When the focus is psychotherapy in general, as in Chapter 2, a problem is how to devise and use a worthy plausible alternative for psychotherapy in general. When the focus moves to a given psychotherapy, a substantially different but equally serious problem may be framed as follows: 'How can a researcher provide a plausible alternative that (a) is not a rival psychotherapy, (b) bears sufficient resemblance to take the place of the given psychotherapy and yet (c) lacks the effective ingredients of the given psychotherapy?'

6. Doing research for this reason may be understood as almost requiring a presumption or firm belief in there being different kinds of psychotherapies. For both true believers and skeptics, for both researchers and the many groups with stakes in this issue, the serious problem may be framed as follows: 'On what explicit grounds can a case be made for or against the existence, identification, and differentiation of a range of supposedly different kinds, types, schools or brands of psychotherapies?'

7. Proponents of the given psychotherapy may welcome the findings as friendly and reassuring, or find the findings unfriendly and bothersome. Therein can lie a serious problem: 'How can research on whether a psychotherapy is good, worthwhile, helpful, effective, be taken seriously if proponents are unwilling or unable to state evidentiary grounds that they would honor as sufficient for the proponents to accept a conclusion that their psychotherapy is not good, worthwhile, helpful, effective, and to be ready and willing to abandon it?'

8. The final problem is beginning to look familiar. If the researcher does research to show that this particular psychotherapy is good, worthwhile, helpful, effective, the study is not especially designed for, nor is it especially likely to discover more and more of what psychotherapy can accomplish, nor how to accomplish these things better and better. This problem can become a serious problem for those who value such a reason, and who see that this is not included in the various reasons for doing research on psychotherapy.

CHAPTER 4

Is this psychotherapy more helpful and effective than that psychotherapy for this particular problem/disorder?

The third reason for doing research was to show that some particular psychotherapy is indeed good, worthwhile, helpful, effective. A fourth reason goes beyond the third reason in at least two main ways:

1. It compares two or more psychotherapies with each other.
2. It compares them on something particular, namely their relative ability to do something helpful and effective for a particular problem or mental disorder.

The case is that this reason for doing research on psychotherapy is accompanied by its own relatively distinctive package of serious problems. The intent is to describe these serious problems at a sufficiently concrete level that they can be worked on, studied, solved. Describing serious problems at a vaguely general level may accurately classify them as design problems, researcher bias problems or epistemological problems, but such general classifications may not be especially helpful in studying them to find solutions. It can be easier to solve the problem of adding two plus three by identifying the problem as the sum of two and three, rather than classifying the problem as one of addition.

The most popular question in the field of psychotherapy research

Perhaps the most popular phrasing of the popular psychotherapy research question is: 'What treatment, by whom, is most effective for this individual with that specific problem, and under which set of circumstances?' (Paul, 1967, p. 111). Variations on this wording include the following: 'Is one form of therapy (e.g., "behavior therapy") more effective than another (e.g., "psychotherapy")?' (Kazdin and Wilson, 1978, p. 105). 'What treatment administered by which therapist is most effective for what problem in which patient?' (Kazdin and Wilson, 1978, p. 106). 'What kinds of therapists administering what psychotherapeutic treatments to what kinds of patients produce what kinds of perceived effects, both immediate and ultimate?' (Fiske, 1977, p. 24; compare Marmar, 1976; Parloff, 1979).

Inspirational reason for those who are true believers in the giant matrix

Some researchers look up to a research heaven in which there is a giant matrix of kinds of treatments, kinds of problems and mental disorders, kinds of patients, kinds of circumstances and treatment effectiveness. Hordes of careful researchers carefully fill in the ever-fewer empty cells until all the researchers are called to witness the giant matrix that heralds the field of psychotherapy reaching the plateau of a true and mighty science (Beutler, 1986, 1991; Beutler et al., 1993).

However, even though the spirit of this reason for doing research is appealing, the story can be much less appealing when you take a careful look at the actual categories that make up the rows and the columns of the giant matrix. To do research for this reason, or to pay attention to the findings, you really ought to believe in the specific variables that make up the cells. Here is a serious problem because many researchers, theorists and practitioners do not necessarily cherish notions such as various coping styles, internalizers and externalizers, reactance potential, reciprocal altruism, object cathexes, and dozens and dozens of specific cell entries that make up such a giant matrix. Experiential researchers would decline these notions. So would many other researchers and consumers of this kind of research.

Which competing constituency provides the researcher?

When two or more therapies compete with each other to see which is best, there is almost always a researcher. Which of the competing therapies picks the researcher?

If Jungian therapists and cognitive–behavioral therapists find themselves interested in seeing which one is better for this or that, which side gets to pick the researcher? If a researcher decides to see if Jungian therapy or cognitive–behavioral therapy is best, is the researcher a graduate of a Jungian Institute or a teacher of the required course in cognitive–behavioral therapy, or does the researcher have a part-time private practice of cognitive–behavioral therapy?

Researchers like to talk about being scientific, unbiased, unprejudiced, going by the findings, being objective. They play this tune whether they work for a particular pharmaceutical company, aircraft firm or psychotherapy research team. Is it permissible to wonder whether researchers tend to get the kinds of outcomes that it is important for them to get?

Choosing a researcher, or accepting a researcher's conclusions, is very much like choosing a lawyer, or accepting a lawyer's conclusions. It helps to know for whom the lawyer or researcher works, or what the lawyer's or researcher's card-carrying affiliations are.

When a researcher announces that she is intending to compare these two therapies to see which is better for this or that, it is likely that the researcher will (1) insist on her scientific neutrality and objectivity, and (2) be holding the hand, under the table, of one of the competing therapies. Almost without exception, researchers are inclined toward one of the competing contestants.

Consider three constituencies that are going to be compared. One is therapists who believe that they are far better than computer therapies. A second consists of computer lovers who would love to show that computer therapies do at least as well, if not better, than most therapists. The third constituency is more political and diplomatic. It believes that therapies are, of course, just excellent, and that computer therapies are also good, provided, again of course, that they are monitored and overlooked by professional psychotherapists.

Suppose that a researcher for each constituency hands in a research proposal. Even before the research is done, notice how the design of the third constituency strongly favors the third constituency in which the professional psychotherapist is also involved in managing and overseeing the computer therapies (Jacobs et al., 2001):

1. A therapist-type person conducted an intake assessment and guided the person in identifying some problems to work on.
2. In the computer therapy, there still was a therapist who instructed on use of the program, reviewed the printout of each session with the person, helped the person focus on the problem and answered the client's questions, in each session.

Given the constituency that the researchers represented, it is understandable that the conclusion had high goodness of fit with the spirit and aims of the constituency:

> We urge psychologists to be receptive to interactive computer approaches, viewing them as a new tool in our armamentarium to be used creatively in conjunction with professional assistance.
>
> Jacobs et al. (2001, p. 96)

The chances are high that the conclusions would have been quite different if the researchers represented a constituency that professional psychotherapists are far better than computer therapies, or that computer therapies are far better than professional psychotherapists.

Agreement on what to treat and how to determine what to treat: contesting therapies have a hard time

Picture four or six therapies sitting around, talking friendly, and one suggests that they have a contest to see which is the best. So far, so good. The trouble comes when they try to figure out what they shall treat, work on, try to do something about. Here is where the trouble starts.

First, they cannot agree on the terms each uses to name what each believes it can treat, work on. One suggests that they compete to see which is best at treating mental illnesses and diseases and disorders, and they could select one such as bipolar or paranoia or borderline or something. Those terms don't even make any sense to a few of the therapies.

One suggests that they compete to see which is best at treating a weak ego. No agreement. Another therapy suggests a self-defeating conceptual schema. Some therapies frown because that phrase makes no sense to them. Another suggests seeing which is best at treating identity diffusion. They laugh. One wonders if the other therapies want to compete over women who are out of touch with their feminine strength. Everyone groans. There is a problem because they cannot even find any set of words that makes sense to all of them.

The conversation gets serious. One therapy asks how the others ever arrive at what to treat or work on with a person. Can the therapies even agree on how to determine what they treat, what they work on?

One therapy says that the therapist gets a lot of information and then decides what to treat, e.g. with one patient the therapist decided that the thing to work on was that the patient got tense whenever some boss or authority got tough with him or was even talking directly to him. The other therapies agreed that the description was all right, but not all of the other therapies trust the therapist as the one to make the decision. Too many problems here. A few of the therapies relied on this way, but those that didn't just simply didn't place that much trust in the therapist being the one to make the decision.

The defensive suggestion was that the patient is the one to name what therapy is to work on. However, the therapies were too seasoned for that one. If the patient mentions a lot of things, and one happens to be something a particular therapist gets all excited about, that therapist can proclaim: 'He said he had trouble taking his wife seriously.' The other therapies shake their head. They all know how therapists are marvelously selective at picking out and emphasizing what they want to hear.

But suppose the patient mentions it even before therapy, like on a checklist, or a question about what the client wants therapy to treat? Wouldn't that be all right? Picture the patient writing down something on a piece of paper. Here is what I want to work on. I pull out the hairs in my eyelashes and it is getting embarrassing. I hate the kind of work I do, but I can't get out and jobs are hard to find. All the therapies lean forward. If the patient can be reasonably free to identify just what concerns her, troubles her, makes her feel bad, maybe there can be a contest to see which therapy is best.

But again there is a problem. The therapies reluctantly agree that most patients would have a hard time identifying something without the therapist's help. But the therapies do agree that, if they are to have a contest, it should be the patient, not the therapist, who has the much larger hand in determining what the therapy is to treat.

The therapies begin to wonder whether psychodynamic therapists are restricted to competing with like-thinking psychodynamic therapists, and existential therapists are restricted to competing with like-thinking existential therapists, and so on. That spoils the fun.

The experiential therapy adds a few more problems to the contest. One is that the experiential therapist works on a rather specific thing, namely a painful scene in which there is a painful feeling. The painful scene is to be relatively concrete and specific. And the therapist shows the person how to find this scene. It takes some work to find the painful scene of painful feelings. The other therapies shake their heads.

What is more, these scenes of strong feeling may include positive feelings that feel wonderful. More shaking of heads.

Furthermore, these scenes of powerful feeling are determined at the beginning of each session, not just once before treatment is started. The other therapies at the table keep shaking their heads.

The experiential therapist goes on. But the scene of painful feeling is only one thing that the session works on. The session also tries to discover what lies deeper in the person, and to show the person how to become a qualitatively new person, based on the deeper thing that was discovered in this session. The therapies decide to play cards instead of having a contest to see which is better at doing therapy.

When lots of therapies honestly consider how to have a contest to see which is best, they can have a very hard time agreeing on precisely what they are to work on, to help change. Maybe it is impossible.

Limitation of contesting therapies: those who agree that the winner is best at treating the mental disorder or problem

To compete, the competing therapies ought to agree that they are competing to see which is best at treating the mental disorder or problem. If a particular contest is announced, what proportion of therapies would be interested in seeing whether they are best at treating mental disorders or problems, or that particular mental disorder or problem? My guess is that the contestants would include far less than 50 per cent of the available therapies.

Do contesting therapies agree that mental disorders and problems are real things rather than figments of collective imagination?

Contesting therapies would probably be limited to those therapies that truly believe in the objective real existence of things such as schizophrenia, inadequate self-concept, lack of assertiveness, poor internal control, borderline condition, seasonal affective disorder. When all mental disorders and problems are objectively real, they can be diagnosed before the contest, and the winner can be declared after seeing how each contestant did at treating the mental disorder or problem.

The contestants would not include all those therapies that believe psychotherapy has fabricated the whole illusory list of mental illnesses, diseases, disorders and problems, none of which can actually claim real objective existence. 'Psychotherapy is the only form of treatment which, at least to some extent, appears to create the illness it treats' (Frank, 1982, p. 8; compare Szasz, 1961; Taylor, 1973; Haley, 1986; Gergen, 1994; Mahrer, 1996/2004, 2004).

Researchers can create the illusory aura of the objective reality of mental disorders and problems by the diversionary tactic of devising hundreds of tests, measures, inventories, questionnaires, scales, of unreal things such as schizophrenia and extraversion, and then proudly pointing to the scientific merit of these 'measures'. The public relations reasoning is that, for example, because these measures have uncontested reliability and validity, what these measures measure must therefore be objectively real, even though collective agreement may please reliability but is far from upholding the validity of things such as schizophrenia and extraversion and all the other mental disorders and problems.

Researchers can give the impression that mental illnesses and diseases are real by doing all sorts of studies on the kinds and types of mental illnesses and diseases. If you skip doing research to see whether mental illnesses and diseases are real, and instead you do research on the various kinds and types, you are inadvertently and indirectly confirming the reality of mental illnesses and diseases. Don't study if there are really things such as centaurs, elves and goblins. Instead, do research on the various kinds and types of centaurs, elves and goblins. This is a clever ploy. Of course there is such a thing as schizophrenia. Look at all the studies of the various kinds and types of schizophrenia.

Klonsky (2000) has reviewed studies based on the presumption of the standard diagnostic system of personality disorders, and he proposed an alternative classification system of personality disorders generated by a different body of studies. The problem is that, regardless of which body of studies wins, each salutes its own favorite classification, and the idea of there being personality disorders or mental illnesses and diseases wins inadvertent and indirect support. The clever ploy is to do research on the kinds and types and classifications of unreal, fanciful, imaginary things such as personality disorders, mental illnesses and diseases, and thereby perpetuate and strengthen the implicit notion that there really are things such as personality disorders, mental illnesses and diseases (Mahrer, 2000b, 2004).

Do contesting therapies agree that mental disorders and problems exist independent of the various psychotherapies?

Very few psychotherapies would probably enter a contest to see which is best at treating melancholia, or miasma, or a wandering womb, or Drapetomania. The therapies that treated these mental disorders and problems have floated out of existence together with the notions and ideas that created them in the first place. In the same way, not all therapies today would enter a contest to see which therapy is best at treating dysthymia, lowered perceptual defence, ego diffusion, erotomania, self-depletion, schizophrenia, cognitive rigidity, a punitive superego, bipolar disorder or attention deficit hyperactivity disorder. These therapies know that all these mental disorders and problems are the personal creations of a particular family of psychotherapies who may well enter the contest.

Many psychotherapies are convinced that mental disorders and problems simply exist, over and above the various psychotherapies. The contest is then between treatments with different notions of what caused and what can cure the mental disorder or problem. 'Different metaphysics result in the framing of different kinds of problems: "What sin or demonic possession caused this speaking in tongues, and what penance or prayer can remedy it?" versus "what physiological problem caused this delirium and what physical–chemical intervention can remedy it?"' (O'Donohue, 1989, p. 1465). The contest is probably restricted to therapies that create and believe in delirium and speaking in tongues.

Do contesting therapies agree that what is diagnosed/assessed before treatment is what should be checked afterwards?

To have a contest to see which therapy is better at treating some mental disorder or problem, the contestants ought to agree that whatever they set out to treat is what is checked out to see which therapy won at the end of the contest. Before the treatments start, the contestants have to agree that they all are treating a borderline disorder or a depressive disorder or a problem of insomnia or an inability to tolerate stress. And they all should agree that the mental disorder or problem has clear-cut stability and duration so that what determines success is what was diagnosed and assessed before treatment and is to be checked out at the end of the contest. It would not be a contest if a whole new diagnosis and assessment were to be done at the beginning of each session or every so often during the contest.

Only certain therapies would probably enter the contest in the first place. The contest would not be for those therapies for whom it is simply inappropriate to believe that whatever happened to be the focus of therapeutic work in the initial session is always or even often or even likely to be the focus of therapeutic work in the final session.

Do contesting therapies agree on how to determine who wins the contest?

In most contests, there are relatively clear rules for determining who is the winner. But this is not necessarily the case in contesting therapies. One problem is when contestants may agree on what the general mental disorder or problem is, but there is disagreement on what the specific target issue is for their specific patient and therefore on what each therapy tries to achieve by the end of treatment, e.g. all contestants may agree that their patient falls under the general category of borderline, but one contestant identifies the target problem as the patient creating serious disturbances in the family, and success is when the patient's condition is such that the family system is once again stable, intact and harmonious. For the second contestant, the borderline's target problem is being victimized, and success is when the patient attains a state of standing up for herself, self-empowerment, autonomy. A contest is not much of a contest when the contestants run off in different directions, even though they started from the same starting line.

A second problem is when the contestants agree on what the mental disorder or problem is, but not on what determines who wins, e.g. all the contestants may agree that the problem is terrible guilt over masturbation, but winning, for one contestant, is replacing masturbation with sexual intercourse, a second aims at acceptance of the guilt feelings and a third knows that winning is when the patient feels comfortable masturbating.

It is likely that each contestant would declare itself the winner and regard its rivals as failures, and the contest organizers would have to have a committee meeting to figure out what went wrong and what to do.

A third problem is when the contestants have altogether different ideas about what the contest is to be. A professional boxer, a politician, a gymnast and a basketball team have their own versions of what a contest should be, but it would be whimsical to picture negotiations for a single contest to decide who is the better professional boxer, politician, gymnast or basketball team. In the same way, it would be almost impossible for there to be a contest between Beck's cognitive therapy (Beck, 1967, 1976; Beck et al., 1979) and Mahrer's experiential psychotherapy (Mahrer, 1996/2004). Beck might say that his approach can do better in treating depression. Mahrer might say that his therapy is better at discovering the deeper potential for experiencing each session, enabling the person to become a qualitatively new person, based on this deeper potential, and enabling the new person to be free of the painful situations that were front and center for the old person in the session. The contest organizers would probably have a hard time finding a contest in which they could honestly compete.

A fourth problem is: 'Who gets to decide on what the actual rules are to be for the contest?' For example, precisely what is the indication of who wins? A great deal of negotiation may well occur around this question. 'Who gets to decide whether the judges are or are not to include the researchers, and just who the judges are to be?' Truly unbiased judges are perhaps so rare that they may be the invention of researchers who really favor one of the contestants (Siegel, 1996). Is the winner to be declared after a single showdown, four out of seven, some unnamed number of studies?

In general, it seems that these kinds of contests are limited to those therapies that agree that the winner is the one that is best at treating the mental disorder or problem, that agree on the real meaning of mental disorders and problems, and that agree on the contest rules and regulations. Not all therapies are potential contestants. Many therapies are excluded from competition.

Which therapy gives the more valued package of additional gifts?

John and Janine started their sessions with bad feelings of being in recent scenes where the feeling was of being victimized, intruded into, violated. Both had small apartments that had been broken into, robbed. The situations were similar and the painful feelings were similar. After one session, the painful feelings were essentially gone. Each had a wonderful session, although John had an experiential session and Janine had a session of integrative therapy.

However, after her session, Janine was essentially the same person she had been before the session, except that the painful feelings were largely gone. In contrast, John had discovered something much deeper, a hidden deeper potential for experiencing, and became a qualitatively new and different person who now included that deeper part of himself. John emerged as a new person, one who was also free of that painful feeling of being victimized, intruded into, violated. In regard to the fate of the painful feelings, both sessions were comparable. However, in terms of the additional gifts, John's session may be judged as providing a more valued package of additional gifts.

Most comparisons of therapies concentrate on a single common target. Is there a desirable change in the symptom, in the depression, in the premature ejaculation, in the lower back pain, in the fear of being in enclosed places, in the hidden little angers at the person one lives with, in the stealing of silverware from restaurants? The suggestion is that a more powerful way of comparing therapies is to widen the scope of what is compared. Yes, each of the therapies helps bring about comparable good changes in their common target. If we widen the scope, which therapy also provides a set of bonus changes? Look at the larger package of valued changes. Although several therapies provide essentially similar changes on their common target, the suggestion is that the superior therapy is the one that provides the more valued package of additional gifts.

If findings are equivocal, should the conclusion be 'neither' or 'either'?

There are loads of studies comparing whether this treatment is better than that treatment for treating this mental disorder or problem. Often the studies do not clearly favor one as the uncontested winner. Sometimes most of the studies are equivocal. Sometimes there are studies favoring one psychotherapy and other studies favoring the rival psychotherapy. When the studies are equivocal, is the conclusion that neither wins or that both win? Depending on whether the conclusion is 'either' or 'neither', a case can be made for using either psychotherapy or neither psychotherapy for that particular mental illness or pathological problem. The difference in what conclusion is drawn can make for either a serious practical difference or essentially no differences at all.

Do contesting therapies not include therapies for everyone, or therapies with particular aims and goals?

At least two kinds of therapies would be unlikely to show up at the contests. One group includes therapies that might be described as relatively all-purpose therapies, appropriate for just about everyone, therapies that are not specially for this or that mental disorder or problem. Here might be included therapies such as psychoanalytic therapy, Daseins analysis, psychodynamic therapy, Adlerian analysis, Jungian analysis, Gendlin's focusing, Mahrer's experiential psychotherapy, gestalt therapy, solution-focused therapy, meditation, and others.

A second group, probably overlapping, of therapies that would probably not be among the contestants are those with aims and goals that are peculiar, i.e. their aims and goals do not quite fit in with the traditional goals of treating mental disorders and what is regarded as standard psychological problems, e.g. Mahrer's experiential psychotherapy has two goals, neither of which quite fits in. One goal is for the person to be able to be a qualitatively new person, including the deeper potential for experiencing that had been accessed in this session. A second goal is for the new person to be free of the painful scenes and painful feelings in the scenes that were front and center for the old person in this session. Most of the eligible contesting therapies would find these two aims and goals as outside what they ordinarily know as therapeutic aims and goals suitable for the contest. They are probably right.

Typically, some studies favor one treatment, some favor the other, and in some you just cannot tell which is better. What kinds of conclusions may be drawn? Meehl (1978) points out that reviewers usually count up the studies favoring each and conclude that one is superior if it won in at least 60 per cent of the studies.

Consider a body of studies in which 10 favor one treatment, 10 favor a rival treatment, and all 20 are of relatively equal weight in terms of soundness. What conclusion seems most fitting? One conclusion may well be that neither treatment is superior. A different conclusion is that either or both treatments seem to be equally successful and effective. When a body of findings seems to be equivocal, the conclusion may well be 'neither' or 'either' (compare Erwin, 1978; Meehl, 1978; Erwin and Siegel, 1989). And which conclusion you draw can have considerable practical consequences for the rival treatments. The mere presence of an equivocal body of studies leaves you with two different but practically important conclusions: neither rival is superior and either rival is choosable.

If a therapy is better, is it necessarily any good?

There is something rather deceptive in doing research to tell which therapy is better than its rival in treating some mental disorder or problem. The easy impression is that the winner, and even its close rival, are pretty good. But this impression is more clever and deceptive than fully straightforward. It may be that the winner is a fine treatment, but this kind of research tells which treatment is better, and not at all whether any of them is any good. They may all be fine, they may vary a great deal or, as I usually suspect, none of them is any good. It is simply an error to conclude that the winning treatment is a good one, even though this is a common conclusion that is drawn.

Suppose that there are 2000 lottery tickets, that Louis has 50 tickets and Louise five tickets. Although it may be shown that Louis has better chances than Louise, neither has a very good chance of winning the lottery (compare Erwin and Siegel, 1989). Our research commonly shows that a Louis therapy is better than a Louise therapy, and the spin put on the conclusion is that the Louis therapy must be pretty good, even though a more sensible conclusion is that both are pretty ineffective. Wait till a Laura therapy comes along, with 1800 lottery tickets.

Common research mind-set: assumption that practitioners adopt the researchers' mind-set, so researchers fail to study the real reasons for practitioners' actions

Researchers generally have a collective mind-set that assumes that practitioners should think in terms of the researchers' own distinctive mind-set. Accordingly, researchers do their research magic, conclude that this therapy or program or method is better than the studied rivals, and therefore practitioners should adopt and use the research-approved therapy or program or method.

In other words, practitioners should do what they do because of the distinctive mind-set of researchers. In still other words, researchers believe that their mind-set is superior and should be adopted by practitioners.

As a result, researchers generally fail to study the real reasons why psychotherapists usually do what they do. Their mistake is to study the wrong reasons (compare Chalmers, 1982). Their egregious and perhaps colossal blunder is to assume that practitioners must have the researchers' mind-set.

Imagine that the situation is reversed, and practitioners assume and insist that researchers adopt the practitioners' collective mind-set. The reasons for adopting and using a given therapy or program or method must of course be the practitioner reasons. It is almost unthinkable that researchers would respectfully follow the practitioner mind-set. But most researchers find it unthinkable that practitioners would decline to follow the researchers' mind-set! This, I believe, is a colossal blunder, an arrogant and egregious blunder, and yet it is, I believe, a blunder committed by most researchers who thereby fail to study the real reasons why practitioners do what they do, and continue to look at psychotherapy in terms of a collective mind-set that is often quite different from that of most practitioners.

Does this reason for doing research collapse if there are no distinguishable psychotherapies?

The third reason for doing psychotherapy research was described as seeking to show that some particular psychotherapy was indeed good, worthwhile, helpful, effective. In discussing this reason, a question was posed: 'Are there such things as identifiable psychotherapies, distinguishable from one another in reasonably systematic ways?' The answer was that a fairly good case can be made for a 'no' answer. If we transfer this answer to the present reason for doing psychotherapy research, it seems that this entire reason for doing research collapses if there are no distinguishable psychotherapies to compete with each other. It seems that this whole reason for doing research ought to be on hold until we are confidently able to identify genuinely different psychotherapies.

Use a specific psychotherapy rather than a big loose family

Even though it is almost impossible to identify psychotherapies as distinguishable, researchers manage to do it easily, decade after decade. I don't think it is possible, but researchers routinely identify a psychotherapy and try to show that this psychotherapy is better than that one for this illness or disorder or pathological problem.

One trouble is that researchers usually use big families in their studies. Researchers study 'humanistic' therapies and 'behavioral therapies', 'psychodynamic' or 'cognitive' or 'integrative/eclectic' therapies. These are huge families where there can be more differences within the family itself than between the family and most other families.

If the researcher claims that humanistic therapy is better than cognitive therapy for this disease or pathological problem, the dozens and dozens of different humanistic therapies might be quiet, accepting the gift with thanks. However, the various members of the cognitive family, or of any other family that is unhappy with the findings, can and do easily raise some serious objections.

One objection is that my therapy was not fairly represented by the family. The researcher studied the big loose family of 'cognitive therapy', but that was not my particular cognitive therapy. Just because 'psycho-dynamic' therapy did not do well, that has nothing to do with my therapy because I do Adlerian therapy. Just because the researcher studied inte-grative/eclectic therapy, the findings don't apply to me because I do a particular brand of integrative therapy. The findings were supposed to apply to 'experiential therapy', except that there are about four dozen or more quite different members of the loose family, and the therapists were nowhere near to doing my particular experiential psychotherapy.

The other side of this objection is that it would make more sense for researchers to abandon trying to study big loose families, and instead to try to study explicit brands of psychotherapy, provided that any can be well identified and have a fair constituency of practitioners.

Official approval of the specific psychotherapy and the psychotherapists

Even when the researcher tries to study explicit psychotherapies, it is researchwise to get official approval that the specific psychotherapy real-ly qualifies as the designated psychotherapy. Too often, the leading proponents of an explicit psychotherapy dismiss the study as not really representing classic psychoanalysis or a particular form of client-centered therapy, or the official rational–emotive therapy or the formally acknowledged gestalt therapy.

It would seem helpful to researchers if the proponents of given psy-chotherapies would spell out what would be acceptable to conclude that the researchers were really studying the explicit psychotherapy, and that the therapists were really doing that explicit psychotherapy. The use of manuals may be a step in this direction. Then researchers could be some-what assured that they had official approval that they were studying the explicit psychotherapy and that their therapists were really doing that explicit psychotherapy.

Do research findings count for much in big league competition?

Task forces put a great deal of weight on research findings in seeing which therapy is better for this or that problem or mental disorder, in putting a research-approved stamp on a therapy as research validated, research supported (Task Force on Promotion and Dissemination of Psychological Procedures, 1995; Chambless et al., 1996, 1998; Chambless and Hollon, 1998; Chambless and Ollendick, 2001). In the competition for research approval and support, most therapies respect research findings.

On the other hand, the scene can look quite different when the competition is not among the various psychotherapies, but between the field of psychotherapy and biological psychiatry, i.e. drugs. 'If clinical psychology is to survive in this heyday of biological psychiatry, APA must act to emphasize the strength of what we have to offer – a variety of psychotherapies of proven efficacy' (Task Force on Promotion and Dissemination of Psychological Procedures, 1995, p. 3) – in other words, 'to summarize what was known about the effects of the panoply of drugs and psychotherapies for each major disorder' (Seligman, 1995, p. 966).

In the big leagues, the competition is not so much among the various psychotherapies, but between the field of psychotherapy and the 'healthcare system', and the stakes can be exceedingly high. Winning can mean being included; losing can mean being excluded. 'If we do not promote and disseminate existing evidence for the efficacy of our psychological interventions, then we will put psychotherapy at a severe disadvantage and risk a substantial deemphasis if not elimination of psychological interventions in our health care delivery system' (Barlow, 1996, p. 237; compare Barlow, 1994). In the big leagues, the competition can be fierce and the stakes can be exceedingly serious.

The question is whether the contestants in the big leagues play by the research rules that researchers use in competition among the various psychotherapies. It seems more likely that biological psychiatry and drug companies count much more on the big league power of marketing specialists, lobby groups, public relations and power politics. Doing research to see which psychotherapy is best for some problem or disorder may not count for much in the high-powered, high-stakes competition of the big leagues, where research findings may prove to be insignificant, whatever they are, and where the field of psychotherapy may have to complement research finding with high-powered politics.

Conclusions, serious problems and suggestions

This chapter featured doing research to compare treatments to see which is better for a given psychological problem or mental disorder. This reason departs from the reason featured in the previous chapter, namely to see if some given therapy were good, effective. This chapter invites the good and effective therapies, as well as any others that wish to compete, to enter a contest to see which is best in treating the particular problem or mental disorder.

The concluding case is that this reason is so fraught with its own distinctive cluster of serious problems that doing research for this reason may as well be set aside, or at least postponed, until the serious problems can be resolved.

Accordingly, the suggestion is for interested researchers, and anyone else who might be willing, to take some time out in order to solve these serious problems. Solving these serious problems not only would help to open the way for doing research for this reason, but may well offer a bonus of helping to nudge the field of psychotherapy into a revolutionary step forward. Here is a summary of some of these serious problems:

1. One serious problem has already been identified in its general form, namely how to make a case for or against the existence, identification and differentiation of presumably different kinds, types, schools or brands of psychotherapy. With regard to the present reason for doing research, the general problem can be seen as taking a more explicit form: Can designated therapies be shown to differ significantly from one another in regard to their in-session procedures, operations and intended changes? If therapies are to be compared with each other, how can the competing therapies be shown to be significantly different, not so much in their philosophies, theories and vocabularies, but in their actual and specific in-session procedures, operations and goals?

2. If therapies are to compete with one another, how can proponents of the competing therapies authorize and agree on the rules of the contest, the design and methodology of the research, and the criteria for determining the outcome of the competition? This can be a serious problem that is commonly minimized or overlooked in many such competitions.

3. Competition between therapies virtually requires agreement on what they are aiming at treating, and on the changes they are trying to achieve. The clearer it becomes regarding precisely what the competing therapies are treating, and the consequent changes they are trying to achieve, the clearer becomes a serious problem: 'To what extent is this reason for doing research limited and restricted to therapies that share similar treatment targets, aims and valued changes, thereby effectively excluding all other psychotherapies and all other therapeutic aims, goals and valued directions of change?'

4. Doing research for this reason may lead to a conclusion that one treatment is better than its rivals in treating a particular problem or mental

disorder, but this kind of conclusion pays little or no attention to a serious, two-sided problem: (a) How can it be determined that the winning treatment is itself a superior treatment, a moderately effective treatment or an inferior treatment that is nevertheless better than its even more inferior rivals? (b) What are the gold standard criteria for determining that competing treatments are superior, of moderate capability and effectiveness, or relatively inferior as a set of competitors?

5. Although it may be reassuring for researchers to believe that practitioners ought to adopt or abandon a given psychotherapy on the basis of research findings, this common researcher mind-set sheds little if any light on a serious problem with two sides: (a) What are the 'real' determinants of practitioners adopting, maintaining, revising, integrating or abandoning their particular psychotherapy? (b) Do research findings play a major, moderate or minor role among these 'real' determinants?

6. In the practical and real world of competition for power, prestige, money and the provision of consumer services, a serious problem may be framed as follows: How can the profession and science of psychotherapy effectively compete with the medical establishment and the pharmaceutical industry, with their vast marketing and public relations resources, their powerful legal and lobby groups, their deep pockets for research and development, their advertising and media specialists? How effective or ineffective is mere psychotherapy research against these other high-powered resources in the practical and real world of competition for mental health power, prestige, money and the provision of consumer services?

7. As with the previous three chapters, the final serious problem is that this reason for doing research on psychotherapy seems to bring us slightly or no closer to learning more and more of what psychotherapy can help accomplish, and to learning better and better ways of helping to accomplish what psychotherapy can help accomplish.

CHAPTER 5

Is this particular in-session thing connected with successful post-treatment outcome?

Chapter 1 concentrates on doing research to show that this kind of psychotherapy thing goes with that kind of psychotherapy thing. This chapter concentrates on doing research to show that this in-session thing is connected with successful post-treatment outcome. If you are high above the various reasons for doing research on psychotherapy, it might look as if the present reason belongs under the first reason because the present reason studies one class of psychotherapy things and its connection with another class of psychotherapy things – in-session things and post-treatment things.

On the other hand, the case for having two separate chapters is that the two packages of serious problems differ, i.e. there is little or no significant overlap between the serious problems that accompany the first reason for doing research on psychotherapy and those underlying the present reason for doing research on psychotherapy.

Doing research for this reason is usually called process-outcome research because it looks at the connection between this particular in-session or process thing and successful post-treatment outcome (e.g. Stiles, 1982, 1988; Beutler et al., 1986; Orlinsky and Howard, 1986; Shoham-Salomon, 1990).

What are these in-session things? Typically, researchers study at least three kinds of in-session things:

1. Things can refer to relatively specific techniques or methods such as empathic reflection, the two-chair technique, symptom prescription, interpretation, reframing, blocking technique, double-bind method, flooding, self-talk, contingency management technique, playing the projection, focusing, aversive control, modeling, confrontation, thought stopping, refutation.
2. Things can refer to characteristics of the therapist or patient such as age, cultural background, social class, gender, nature and extent of patient motivation, degree of psychopathology, religion, family and support structure, intelligence.

3. Things can refer to the way that therapist and patient are with each other, such as the nature and degree of transference, helping relationship, real relationship, working alliance, mutual co-operativeness, liking and respect, openness and honesty, the professional and personal roles played out by therapist and patient.

Doing research for this reason can be appealingly straightforward. You can see whether some particular thing, e.g. empathic reflection, is connected with a successful post-treatment outcome, or which of several things, e.g. empathic reflection or interpretation, is better connected. On the other hand, you can see whether a whole package of things is connected with successful post-treatment outcome. Perhaps the first and most well-known formulation of such a package was Rogers' (1957) formulation of the necessary and sufficient conditions for bringing about successful and effective therapeutic change. But there were other attempts to see whether some package of things is the key to successful treatment outcome, some around the time of Rogers' famous formulation (e.g. Wolberg, 1954; Hobbs, 1962) and others somewhat later (e.g. Strupp, 1973, 1974; Beck, 1987).

In general, it was and is quite popular to see whether there are connections between some particular in-session things and successful post-treatment outcome. According to Orlinsky (1994), there were about 2400 such studies between 1950 and 1994, and the rate is probably still increasing.

Can research be done that allows the conclusion that this thing actually helped to achieve a successful post-treatment outcome?

Suppose that some patients had 20 or 50 or 100 sessions, and you did research to see whether some specific thing, or set of things, was especially connected with a successful post-treatment outcome, actually helped to bring it about. Can you conclude, with a reasonable sense of confidence, that it was the therapist's fine self-disclosure in the sixth session, or the therapist's use of thought stopping in sessions 5, 7, 13, 14 and 19, or the use of fine empathic reflections in most of the sessions, that helped bring about the gratifying post-treatment outcome? It seems very hard, almost impossible, to conclude that any particular thing, or set of things, accounted for whatever you use as an indication of successful post-treatment outcome (Kazdin and Wilson, 1978). There are at least three problems here.

One of the problems is that there are simply far too many other things, say somewhere between 10 000 and near infinity of other possible in-session things and combinations of things, that might help to account for the post-treatment outcome. The design has yet to be invented that can allow a researcher to conclude that the therapist's use of thought stopping in five of the 50 sessions was the thing that was connected with the good post-treatment outcome. Far too many other things happened before the thought stopping, during and in between the thought stopping, and after the thought stopping. This brings us to a second problem.

Researchers like the idea of using control groups to control for everything but what they suspect is the thing that is connected with successful post-treatment outcome. If the researcher suspects that the key element is the therapist's self-disclosure, precisely what would the researcher control for? Would it be self-disclosure, or would it be self-disclosing under particular in-session conditions, and in these particular ways, or would it be the kind of relationship in which both therapist and patient disclose special things about themselves, and under particular conditions? And what would the control therapists do that would be solidly comparable and yet different from self-disclosure? I doubt if the control therapist could really offer everything but the therapist self-disclosure in any but the crudest way.

A third problem is that this reason for doing research is based on the idea that the in-session thing itself is connected to the post-treatment outcome. This leaves out the common likelihood that the in-session thing is more connected to something else or to a larger package, and it is this something else or the larger package that is perhaps connected with the post-treatment outcome, e.g. suppose that the investigated thing is a method or technique that helps to attain step 2 in a three-step sequence that is connected with post-treatment outcome. If the method is taking deep breaths and saying it with strong feeling, it is not especially the technique that is connected with outcome, but the three-step sequence of which that particular technique is but a small part. Nor would controlling for that technique work, or even systematically removing bits and pieces, if there are packages of methods and techniques for achieving each of the steps.

All in all, it seems almost impossible to do research that allows you to conclude that this thing actually helped to achieve a successful post-treatment outcome.

How can researchers show that this in-session thing is connected with successful outcome?

Researchers can almost always show that this in-session thing is connected with good outcome. Start with some in-session thing that seems promising and use a little cleverness. Modify what you have selected. Alter it a bit here and there. Be persistent in trying this or that variation. Include a fairly large number of possible candidates. The payoff is frequently successful. For example, suppose that the researcher starts with the general idea that the therapist–client relationship is related to successful outcome. An entire program of studies can be generated by examining the different kinds or components of the therapist–client relationship, e.g. the working relationship or alliance, the transferential relationship or the real relationship. Break these down further by including the various elements that make up each of these three kinds or components of the therapeutic relationship. Include the different patterns of how all of these can play themselves out across treatment, e.g. linear patterns, quadratic patterns, curvilinear patterns. Add in the various approaches to treatment, perhaps five to ten different orientations. Make sure there are different meanings of outcome, including follow-up outcomes. Select a variety of ways of measuring each of the dozens of variables that are studied.

There are other clever ways of showing that your favorite in-session things are indeed connected with successful outcome. Suppose that you come across studies that are not friendly to the idea that the therapist–client relationship is connected to successful outcome, or that your own findings are not especially friendly. For some researchers, this is more of an opportunity to be clever than it is discouraging. Modify the research design. Change the procedure. Use different statistics. Use different measures. Refine the methodology. Do the study the way it ought to be done to get the findings you want to get.

With a little ingenuity, the researcher will almost assuredly come up with some findings that can be said to show that selected favorite in-session things are indeed related to good outcome.

What grounds would be sufficient for proponents to concede that their favorite thing is not connected with successful post-treatment outcome?

A method or technique is typically connected with successful post-treatment outcome mainly because its proponents believe that it is. You really don't need to convince those who are already true believers, but this kind of research would show the power of true science if it could convince those who already believe in some in-session thing that it is not connected with successful post-treatment outcome. Here is the question that researchers might well borrow from Popper (1972a, 1972b, 1980) and put to proponents of the thing to be studied: 'What would be the reasonable research grounds that you would accept as sufficient to concede that your method or technique is not connected with successful post-treatment outcome, and for you then to conclude that the method or technique should be abandoned?'

Consider methods or techniques such as empathic reflection, interpretation, the two-chair technique or looking for the client's cognitions. Consider a study to determine whether the kind of emotion and the intensity of the emotion can be recognized in a psychotherapy session (Machado, Beutler and Greenberg, 1999). Are proponents prepared to state the grounds that would be sufficient for them to dutifully and honorably abandon empathic reflection, interpretation, the two-chair technique, looking for the client's cognitions, or identifying the nature and the intensity of emotions? I doubt if they would be willing either to state the sufficient grounds or to abandon these methods and techniques if those grounds were presented to them. It seems that these are grounds for not even doing the study in the first place.

Many psychotherapists have a strong belief that over a series of sessions increasing client insight can and does lead to reduction in symptoms. Picture a study in which clients in psychoanalytic counseling were asked, after sessions, to write down what was important in the session, how and why it was important; then judges judged whether or not what the clients wrote indicated insight. The aim of the study was to see whether increasing client insight does indeed relate to a reduction in symptoms (Kivlighan, Multon and Patton, 2000). Suppose that the findings are unfriendly. How likely is it that true believers would dutifully give up their true belief that increasing client insight can and does lead to a reduction in symptoms? I seriously doubt if most true believers would give up their true belief even if the researchers said this conclusion follows from the findings, or even if two studies or 20 studies turned up with unfriendly findings. If true believers are not prepared to do the scientifically honorable things, why does the researcher do the research in the first place?

It is common for therapists to give their interpretation or meaning to something about the clients, something like their symptoms, their intrapsychic dynamics, their ways of thinking, their dreams. A study may set out to show that therapists' interpretations of the early childhood meaning of a dream may well be considered and accepted by the dreamers, especially if the interpretations are preceded by a sensible rationale (Mazzoni et al., 1999). The design had the clinician 'suggest to participants that the dream was the overt manifestation of repressed memories of events that happened before the age of 3 years. To be specific, the dream interpretation suggested to the participants that the dream was indicative of a difficult childhood experience, such as getting lost in a public place, being abandoned by one's parents, or being lonely and lost in an unfamiliar place' (Mazzoni et al., 1999, p. 46).

On the basis of the findings, the authors discussed the influence of therapists' meanings and interpretations, especially under conditions where the therapists offer sensible rationales for their psychological meanings and interpretations of dreams and similar clinical material. Before this study arrived at its findings, before a group of related studies arrived at their findings, picture all the therapists in the world being asked if they agree to abandon giving their meanings and interpretation to dreams and other clinical material if the findings are unfriendly. What proportion of the therapists would agree and actually honor their commitment? There may be the usual special exceptions, but the researchers might have found something else to do if they had asked therapists, before the study, if they were prepared to do the honorable thing if the findings were unfriendly.

It is virtually non-existent for proponents to be asked if they would agree to honor the findings of a given proposed study or group of studies, and give up what they are proponents of, provided that the findings are unfriendly. I do not know of many or any studies where proponents first look at the design and agree that if the findings are unfriendly the proponents would give up empathic reflection, interpretation, the two-chair technique, looking for the client's cognitions, identifying the nature and intensity of emotions, or getting at the meaning of dreams. Consider a study, cited earlier (Hill et al., 2000), that starts with the idea that proponents of dream interpretation trust that dreams can be valuable and special, and can add something unique and special to psychotherapeutic work. The study used a design to see whether dreams were indeed special and unique, or if they added little or nothing beyond the three-step sequence used in the study to work with a particular approach to making sense of dreams. A problem is that such studies are carried out as if proponents of what is studied are to give up what they value if the findings are unfriendly, but they rarely if ever inquire whether the proponents agree beforehand that they will give up what they value if the findings say that it is the honorable thing to do.

Most studies do not start by having proponents of some in-session thing put into words the sufficient evidential grounds. Indeed, there are few if any of these studies. It begins to look as if proponents of studied in-session things might perhaps acknowledge friendly findings, but have plenty of good reasons for simply ignoring findings of studies that failed to ask proponents beforehand what the findings would have to look like for the true believers to take the findings seriously.

Findings that some in-session thing is not connected to desired post-treatment outcomes tend to get the attention of researchers and practitioners who do not use that in-session thing anyhow, who prefer some alternative or rival in-session thing, or who already believe that the in-session thing is probably not connected to the desired post-treatment outcome.

Doing research for this reason may be fun and publishable, but it is almost fruitless to try to get proponents of some favorite method or technique to state the grounds that would be sufficient for them to abandon any treasured method or technique dear to the hearts of its proponents. Picture psychoanalytic therapists being shown lots of serious studies, all abiding by the grounds that the psychoanalytic therapists stated would be sufficient, a picture that is almost impossible to picture; then picture the whole group dutifully abandoning interpretations. Don't hold your breath.

On what grounds do researchers select that particular in-session thing to study?

Suppose that the researcher intends to see whether some in-session things are connected to an outcome of a significant reduction in some emotional state such as anger, anxiety/stress or depression. How do they select the particular in-session things they will study? They can claim that they are neutral, and that a body of studies has suggested that this particular in-session thing is connected with favorable outcome. They can also claim that they have some reason to believe that some particular in-session thing is connected to favorable outcome.

It is usually rather clear that the researcher does or does not believe that that particular in-session thing is connected with a favorable outcome. Indeed, the most common grounds for selecting that particular in-session thing, out of all possible in-session things, is that the researcher is inclined toward believing that it is indeed connected to the favorable outcome. So the researcher studies in-session things such as the desensitization method, the replacement of ineffective with more effective cognitions, the achievement of significant insight and understanding, or whatever the researcher already believes is connected with favorable outcomes.

If researchers choose favorite in-session things, it is unlikely that unfriendly findings would lead the researchers to abandon those favorite things. They chose them for a reason. Unfriendly findings would probably not be sufficient for the researchers to abandon them.

Should the in-session thing be different from the outcome, rather than an in-session preview of the post-treatment outcome?

The rationale for this reason for doing research may be illustrated as follows: if the target post-treatment outcome is that the person no longer has headaches or tries to kill himself, the in-session thing is something that might be thought of as helping to bring about such welcome post-treatment changes, and the something is different from the post-treatment outcome. However, in many studies, the in-session thing is virtually the same thing as what is later called the post-treatment outcome. When this happens, and it happens quite often when you take a close look at what precisely is assessed as post-treatment outcome, the study has done little more than point toward an in-session cameo appearance of what will later be called the post-treatment outcome.

Suppose that the outcome consists of indications that the client says she felt that therapy helped, and the in-session thing turns out to be the therapist encouraging the client to say that therapy is helping. Outcome consists of the client saying or indicating that she feels better, and the in-session thing is mainly the therapist eliciting the client to say that she is now feeling better. Outcome measures something called experiencing, and it is shown to connect with in-session instances of the client experiencing. Outcome consists of the client now thinking differently, and the in-session thing is the client doing what the therapist wants by thinking in a different way. Outcome shows that the client has insight and understanding, and the in-session thing consists of the therapist telling the client what the insight and understanding of the client are to be, and the client shows that she dutifully has that insight and understanding.

It is often hard to distinguish what is the outcome and what is the in-session thing because they commonly overlap so much with each other, e.g. can you tell which of these belong to outcome, and which belong to in-session things?

1. The client is to indicate whether there seems to be some change in him- or herself and, if so, what it is.
2. The client is to indicate whether there is a change in what seems hard to be or do, or in the client being too much this way or that way.
3. The client is to indicate how distressing this and that seem to be.

Although a case can be made that each may serve as outcome or in-session things, the first one was used as an in-session thing and the other two were used as outcome (Kivlighan and Arthur, 2000). In general, in-session things and outcome all too often seem to come from almost the same pot, with the in-session things being a preview or sample of the outcome.

Consider a study in which the in-session thing includes working on a dream and concluding with a focus on changes that the client would now be inclined to make in his or her current life, and the actions to be taken in making those changes. What is the outcome? The outcome consisted of writing an answer to this question: 'Based on this dream interpretation session, what changes would you like to make in your current life, and how would you go about making those changes?' (Wonnell and Hill, 2000, p. 374).

Consider a study of the relationships between therapeutic alliance development over sessions and treatment outcome. Therapeutic alliance ratings and outcome assessment both consisted of clients' answers to questionnaires, and a closer inspection indicates that, for example, clients indicating that they and their therapists agree on what therapy is to work on is part of an indication that therapeutic alliance is high, and clients indicating that they trust others is part of an indication that therapeutic outcome was successful (Kivlighan and Shaunessy, 2000). In other words, the two questions virtually tap the same thing, even though one is called therapeutic alliance and the other successful outcome.

In general, it seems rather weak for both the outcome and the in-session thing to be virtually one and the same, and it is all too common that this is the case in many studies.

Use of clients with a strong commitment to this explicit method working with this explicit problem

At one extreme are therapies that take all comers and count on some special methods as being helpful for most clients. 'Of course, some clients are inappropriate or unsuitable, but I rely on methods of careful empathic listening, getting at core cognitions, and opening up of bound affect. It works for most of my clients.' At the other extreme are therapies that work mainly with clients who have a strong commitment to the explicit method or methods of this therapy working with that explicit problem.

Picture an advertisement that announces free therapy for clients who remember little or nothing of their early childhood and who want to be hypnotized to recover those childhood memories. Picture an advertisement that announces free feminist therapy for women who have trouble standing up to the man with whom they live, and who want to develop their own empowerment, their own assertiveness, strength, their own tough-talk capability. Picture that the free therapy starts with training programs in the explicit methods and how they work to resolve the explicit problem, and that the clients who are accepted into treatment are those with impressively high confidence in and commitment to this explicit method for this explicit problem.

Suppose that your therapy is for resolving childhood traumas, and that the emphasis is on the method of re-experiencing the traumatic memory and the method of expressing the related emotions. The research you do will have a higher likelihood of showing that your methods work if you start with clients who come for treatment of the explicit problem and who are screened to find, and treat, those who have a strong commitment to your explicit methods working with their explicit problem. Offer them free therapy, and make sure that a 'criterion for suitability was client agreement with the treatment focus on re-experiencing trauma memories and emotional expression' (Pairio and Patterson, 1999, p. 345).

Be careful in choosing your research design and in what you say in your conclusions. You can stack the research cards in your favor if you start with clients with a strong commitment to your explicit method working with that explicit problem, and your research design and conclusions can either acknowledge or hide the probable importance of the strong commitment.

Weak evidence if both the in-session thing and the outcome are reflections of a friendly disposition toward therapy

You may believe that you are studying the relationship between this in-session thing and outcome; however, a better case is that you are merely tapping a generally friendly or favorable disposition toward therapy. The in-session thing and the outcome are then both an expression of being favorably disposed toward therapy. You are essentially showing that a favorable disposition toward therapy can show itself in both an in-session thing and outcome. In essence, you are merely tapping into and measuring a favorable disposition toward therapy.

Consider a study in which the in-session things include the client's impression of feeling understood, ease of communication, feeling that the doctor was concerned, feeling helped. The outcome consisted of asking the client a single question, three months after the final session: 'Generally speaking, has there been any change in how you are feeling emotionally compared to three months ago? (Please tick one), with response alternatives "feel better now", "feel worse now", "no change"' (Cape, 2000, p 388). It is easy to see both the in-session things and the outcome as reflecting the clients' favorable or unfavorable disposition toward therapy. It is easy to see the study as reflecting the persistence or change of the clients' favorable or unfavorable disposition toward therapy.

Comparison of several in-session things: are contestants satisfied that the selected post-treatment outcome is a fair test of who wins?

Suppose that the contest is to see whether focusing or Adlerian interpretation is better connected to post-treatment outcome, or that there is a larger group of contestants including flooding, two-chair technique, self-talk, guided imagery, empathic reflection, and a few others. Imagine their agents at a meeting to discuss the specific criteria to decide who is to be crowned the winner.

The agents for focusing will probably argue for use of the experiencing scale, and this is understandable because the experiencing scale favors focusing and was developed by the focusing people. On the other hand, the agents for Adlerian interpretation would probably press for the winner to be decided on the basis of Adlerian heightened social interest. And agents for each of the other contestants can be expected to lobby hard for their own favorite tests.

Some promoters are inclined to use a post-treatment outcome that they think is blandly all-purpose, such as the Minnesota Multiphasic Personality Inventory or some supposedly universal questionnaire. But the problem is that either few if any of the contestants are really happy about that particular way of determining the winner, or few if any of the contestants accept that as their serious outcome indicator and therefore do not take the findings very seriously.

The net result is that, even though the researcher may be satisfied with the particular criterion for who wins, most of the contestants were never asked or did not give their approval, and therefore most contests are not generally recognized as fair by the contestants and their constituencies.

Conclusions, serious problems and suggestions

Chapter 1 focused on research aimed at showing that this kind of psychotherapy thing goes with that kind of psychotherapy thing. In one sense, what is ordinarily known as process-outcome research, the focus of the present chapter, can be thought of as merely a special topic within the larger aim of seeing whether this psychotherapy thing goes with that psychotherapy thing. There is some overlap and a case can be made for this.

However, in another sense, research aimed at showing that this particular in-session thing is connected with successful post-treatment outcome warrants its own chapter because (1) instead of being free-ranging and generally unconstrained, the connections are restricted to a class of in-session things that may well be tied to post-treatment outcome, and to a second class of post-treatment outcome things; (2) the connections virtually call for a status of causal determinants so that the in-session things can at least claim to have a substantial causal connection to post-treatment outcome; and (3) the serious problems associated with doing research on the connections between in-session things and post-treatment outcome things are substantially different from those associated with doing research for the reason discussed in Chapter 1.

The main conclusion is that doing research for this reason is associated with its own distinctive set of problems that are sufficiently serious, sufficiently impeding and blocking, so that at least some researchers are warranted to postpone further research for this reason until the serious problems can be resolved.

The suggestion is for interested researchers to take some time out so that they and others can solve these serious problems. Not only would solving these serious problems help remove some serious road blocks for those interested in doing research for this reason, but also the solutions would seem to have a good chance of inching the field in the direction of a wholesale revolution. Here is a summary of some of these serious problems:

1. One serious problem may be framed as follows: 'How can a researcher be reasonably confidant that this given change is the outcome or consequence of that antecedent or package of antecedents?' This can be considerably less of a problem when the significant change is an in-session event, and the antecedents are thought of as closely preceding the consequent in-session change. On the other hand, the problem can become frustratingly serious when the consequence is the commonly understood outcome of a program or series of sessions, and the antecedent causal determinants are thought of as lying somewhere in an ever changing sea of intertwined packages and pools of preceding variables, determinants, factors, causes, influences and continuously fluctuating conditions.

2. For most psychotherapies to be carried out over a series of sessions, most psychotherapists, clients and researchers may be thought of as almost requiring a residual faith, belief, confidence or expectation that certain elements of the therapy can be favorably connected with the valued outcome. Accordingly, a serious problem may be worded as follows: 'How can researchers isolate, identify and assess the role of their own, the therapists' and the patients' residual faith, belief, confidence or expectation that the selected elements of therapy are connected to the desired outcome?'

3. Most proponents have a reasonably heavy investment in believing that their favorite in-session things are indeed connected with successful post-treatment outcomes. Accordingly, the serious problem may be stated as follows: 'Can researchers, practitioners and theoreticians name the reasonable grounds they would accept as sufficient for them to concede that their precious in-session thing is not connected with successful post-treatment outcome, and their precious in-session thing is therefore to be dropped from their therapy?' Until this test can be successfully applied and passed, much of the very basis for doing research for this reason may be thought of as having dissolved.

4. For many in-session things, a reasonable case can often be made that they are qualitatively different from the post-treatment outcome, and that they can be understood as causing, as helping to bring about, as

leading to the occurrence of the post-treatment outcome. However, there are many other instances in which a serious problem can be framed as follows: 'How can a connection, especially a causal connection, be attributed to an in-session thing that can be shown to be a cameo or preview appearance of what is later heralded as a successful post-treatment outcome?' This serious problem does not seem to be resolved by attempts to dress the in-session thing and the post-treatment outcome in what can appear to be different terminologies or conceptual explanations.

5. Once again, a thematic serious problem is that this reason for doing research is apparently neither designed for, nor especially useful for, learning more and more of what psychotherapy can accomplish, or in learning better and better ways of helping to accomplish what psychotherapy can accomplish.

CHAPTER 6

Are these things common across successful, effective therapies?

The question that this research seeks to answer is something like this: 'What factors, ingredients, elements seem to be common across successful and effective therapies?' The idea is that, if we knew what factors, ingredients or elements were common, maybe therapies could become more successful and effective by incorporating them or more of them, or by enlarging their use of these common factors, ingredients, elements.

It seemed so self-evident that this kind of research would probably have constructive payoffs that early researchers had already begun doing this kind of study well before 1936, when Rosenzweig presented his overview of what he felt were the common factors across successful and effective psychotherapies. Researchers have been looking for the common factors, ingredients and elements ever since (e.g. Shaffer and Shoben, 1967; Stiles, Shapiro and Elliott, 1986; Frank, 1971, 1973, 1982; Kazdin, 1979; Goldfried, 1980; Beutler, Crago and Arizmendi, 1986; Karasu, 1986; Horvath and Symonds, 1991; Hill, 1992; Prochaska and DiClemente, 1992).

Thinking in terms of identifiable different psychotherapies

In several of the reasons for doing research on psychotherapy, the presumption is that there are identifiably different psychotherapies. This can rise to the level of a serious problem when a case is made for serious questioning of whether there are genuinely different psychotherapies, or whether some carefully systematic way is needed to identify psychotherapies and be able to distinguish them from each other.

Suppose that we accept that this problem can also apply to this reason for doing research. However, suppose we take a step further and consider that this problem recedes in importance and is overshadowed by even more serious problems that are directly tied to this present reason for doing research, serious problems that constitute a distinctive package of serious problems in this reason for doing research on psychotherapy.

Given that this reason presumes identifiable different psychotherapies, what are the serious problems that are relatively unique to doing research for this reason?

Would the therapy get better or worse if it incorporated common elements?

It is almost taken for granted that the more a therapy incorporates these common ingredients of successful therapies, the more successful the therapy should become. If there are five or six common ingredients, and a therapy includes only one or two, incorporating more ingredients should increase the therapy's effectiveness. If a therapy includes only a little bit of a common ingredient, including it to an optimal degree should help its successfulness. This way of thinking is supposed to apply to successful therapies and also to those that are less successful.

But there are at least a few considerations which suggest that, if some therapies incorporate supposedly common ingredients of successful therapies, those therapies would probably get worse! One consideration is that adding the common ingredients might well destroy the very structure of the therapy itself, e.g. if one common ingredient is a particular kind of therapist–client relationship, therapies such as experiential psychotherapy and classic psychoanalysis would probably no longer exist if they became therapies that featured a drastically alien kind of therapist–client relationship. For many therapies, the choice is almost between keeping your identity and exchanging your identity for one that is defined by the common ingredients.

A second consideration is that, if a range of successful therapies all incorporated ingredients that were found to be common, a case can be made for the less successful therapies possibly getting better, and the top successful therapies probably getting worse. Putting these two considerations together, it seems that, if therapies allowed themselves to take healthy doses of common ingredients, there is a real danger that many or most of them may well get worse, not better.

Is the therapy more successful and effective if is has more of this common ingredient?

The common meaning of a common ingredient is that it is judged as a characteristic in many therapies that are considered successful and effective. A somewhat different meaning, one that would seem a little more impressive, is that a common ingredient is one that is correlated with a degree of success and effectiveness, i.e. (1) therapies that had a little, a moderate amount or a large amount of the common ingredient would have a little, a moderate or a high degree of success and effectiveness, and (2) if a therapy reduced or increased the amount of the common element, its success and effectiveness would be correspondingly lowered or raised.

This would be impressive, but I know of no respectable body of studies here. If there were, lots of practitioners would have good reason for adding the right amount of that common element to their therapy, provided the practitioners valued whatever specific meaning of success and effectiveness was used in the non-existent studies.

Why search for common ingredients if the therapeutic aims and goals are quite dissimilar or quite similar?

This kind of research studies therapies that are successful and effective, but the researcher almost has to make a decision to include therapies with actual, practical, working aims and goals that tend to be either quite dissimilar, ranging all over the place, or quite similar. The therapies may all be successful and effective, but at what – at helping to accomplish what aims and goals?

If the therapies have practical, working aims and goals that are quite different and range all over the place, the commonalities that are found would probably be rather (1) meaningless, trivial, vague and (2) unhelpful to the therapies that are studied. Picture the commonalities that might well be found in therapies, some of which are developed to help patients reduce weight, some to reduce annoying voices in the head, some to enable an accident victim to take pills to reduce pain, and some to help express long-suppressed anger toward an abusive parent. Not only would the supposed commonalities probably be meaningless, trivial and vague, but it is likely that the strength of each treatment, its very ability to be successful and effective, would suffer if it honestly incorporated whatever commonalities were supposedly found.

If the therapies have practical, working aims and goals that are very similar or even identical, the commonalities would probably either (1) be meaningless and trivial, if the therapies themselves are very similar, or (2) mask and lose genuinely alternative ways of helping to achieve the particular practical, working aims and goals. Picture two quite different therapies that are both successful and effective at freeing a person of seriously troublesome stuttering and stammering. The acknowledgment that here are two ways of accomplishing this aim and goal, that they offer useful and genuine alternatives, would be defeated and lost if the commonalities that would probably be found were used to change, and probably harm, each of the solid alternatives. If, on the other hand, the two therapies were quite similar to one another, then whatever commonalities might be found would probably be meaningless and trivial to the further development of the therapies. Whether the therapeutic aims and goals are quite dissimilar or quite similar, it seems essentially fruit-less, meaningless, trivial, vague, or even unhelpful and self-defeating to search for and try to use common ingredients.

Are commonalities doomed if you plunge to a low level of minuscule triviality or rise to a high level of meaningless generalization?

If you are determined to find commonalities, you can find some, espe-cially if you just look for commonalities, and you are not particularly concerned with how to use whatever you find. Most likely, many of the commonalities you find will be relatively trivial or meaninglessly vague and general.

You will probably find some commonalities by probing down to the level of minuscule triviality, and the commonalities you find will probably be minuscule trivialities concerned with such things as ratios of pronouns to inactive verbs, correlations of pupillary dilatation and dyadic gaze phase, voice quality striations, constriction of alpha waves, curvilinear relationships of speech rate and postural lean. The search for commonal-ities is assured success if it descends to a low enough level of minuscule triviality.

At the other end, you can virtually be assured of finding something common across successful therapies if you rise to high enough levels of generalization. Then successful therapies can be found to share such meaninglessly general commonalities as thematic verbal content, interac-tive respect, a mutual relationship, phases of therapeutic movement. The higher the level of abstraction, the more likely it is that commonal-ities can be found, and that the commonalities will be meaningless generalizations.

If you stoop to low enough levels of minuscule triviality or rise to high enough levels of absurd generality, your search for commonalities is almost doomed to success – and also to being essentially useless.

Success for most approaches: is this ensured with a friendly and non-threatening, generalized common factor?

Carl Rogers and his co-workers are generally credited with elevating the therapist–client relationship into the centerpiece of a great deal of research on the therapist–client relationship as a major common factor. It is generally acknowledged today that the therapist–client relationship is indeed a major, if not the major, common factor.

In terms of politics and public relations, it seems that Rogers would have been more successful if he had simply presented the therapist–client relationship as a generalized common factor, and done so in a way that made most approaches smile in friendliness and without being threatened to any real extent. He didn't. Instead, in his research and in his classic setting forth of 'the necessary and sufficient conditions of therapeutic personality change' (Rogers, 1957), he made some choices that may have been questionable. As a result, his particular version of the therapist–client relationship failed to win approval from about two decades of research on his particular formulation.

One choice that Rogers made was to identify a particular kind of therapeutic relationship. He identified a relationship in which the therapist offers genuinely felt empathy and unconditioned positive regard or non-possessive warmth, and where the client receives and values this. Rogers would perhaps have done better in naming a common factor by just mentioning a generalized therapeutic relationship, instead of going ahead and identifying a particular one.

A second choice Rogers made was to minimize the importance of therapeutic techniques by saying that we are in the service of establishing and maintaining the relationship. 'The techniques that therapists employed, whether reflective or interpretive, were of little account except insofar as they invested the therapeutic relationship with these growth-facilitating qualities' (Orlinsky and Ronnestad, 2000, p. 843). Perhaps it would have been more politically wise just to say that the relationship was the important common element. Trivializing techniques was an unfriendly move for therapists who swore by their precious techniques.

A third choice was that Rogers asserted that his particular kind of therapeutic relationship was for all therapies, not just the client-centered therapist. In terms of public relationships this may have been a bad move. It meant that all therapies were to use the client-centered methods with the therapist in the role of the empathic, genuine, unconditionally positively regarding person. That did not go too well with many therapies.

If you want to name a common factor, identify one that is sufficiently generalized so that most therapies can nod their heads in agreement, and few if any therapies would be threatened. Call it 'the therapeutic relationship'. Call it 'the working alliance'. This is essentially what Bordin (1948, 1979, 1994) did, and it worked. Most therapies found this proposed common factor friendly, acceptable and non-threatening.

Losing out on worthy differences

Looking for commonalities usually means taking a look at a number of therapies that are successful and effective at attaining some goal, some change, some good outcome. The problem is that such a search overlooks finding worthy differences among the therapies, worthy because either the differences might well identify alternative ingredients or ways of helping to achieve success, or they may well help to explain what might be useful and workable about the common ingredients.

These worthy differences tend to be lost by the sheer emphasis on looking for commonalities. Also, it is likely that the search stops when it either succeeds or fails to find commonalities. It might perhaps be more profitable if, in either case, the search would keep looking for worthy and worthwhile differences in therapies that are successful and effective.

Study of 'relationship' and 'technique' depends on your mind-set

One mind-set is that the whole is made up of the sum of its parts. According to this mind-set, the mind plus the body equal one, mental factors plus bodily factors account for and explain the phenomenon in question. If a person has a headache and it is found to be 80 per cent neurophysiological, it must be 20 per cent psychological. If the neurophysiologist finds solid neurophysiological reasons to account for the headache, why refer the patient to the psychologist or the psychiatrist? If there seem to be little or no neurophysiological reasons to account for the headache, refer the patient to the psychologist or the psychiatrist. Here is a common way of thinking, a common mind-set.

In studying common factors, this mind-set tends to reason that outcome is generally a function of 'relationship' factors and 'technique' factors. Sophisticated research versions of this common mind-set hold that, if 20 per cent of the statistical variance can be attributed to the relationship, the remaining 80 per cent of the variance must be accounted for by technique factors plus unknown factors. Accordingly, a research study on common factors may report that 20 per cent of the variance can be attributed to the relationship, 45 per cent to techniques, and the remaining 35 per cent to unknown factors.

Now let us turn to a quite different mind-set in which an event or phenomenon may be understood as open to description and understanding from various relevant modes of understanding and description. A headache may be open to understanding and description physiologically, chemically, sociologically, neurologically, economically, politically, from a psychoanalytic approach, an Adlerian approach, a Jungian approach, a biological viewpoint, an anthropological viewpoint, and so on and on. Furthermore, each mode of description and understanding may conclude that it is able to do a full and complete job of description and understanding, a fair job or a poor job (Mahrer, 2004).

According to this mind-set, the headache may be fully or slightly described and understood neurologically, and psychoanalytically and sociologically and anatomically and culturally and biologically and psychologically, and so on and on. With regard to common factors, in this mind-set, the outcome may be fully open to description and understanding in terms of both the relationship and techniques, or the outcome may be slightly open to description and understanding in terms of both relationship factors and technique factors, and the same thing may hold for unknown other factors. It is your particular mind-set that goes a long way in determining whether your way of studying how much results from relationship factors and technique factors is sense or nonsense. Each mind-set may well find the other mind-set's conclusions to be sense or nonsense.

Is a psychotherapy still that psychotherapy if it incorporates a substantial number of the common elements?

The idea is that, if this particular psychotherapy incorporated the common elements, this particular psychotherapy would get better. Incorporating common elements usually means more than just talking about psychotherapy in some different way, using a different language. It usually means adding some quite tangible elements that are common in successful and effective psychotherapies.

Suppose that a particular psychotherapy sees itself as actually having very little of the 'common elements' kind of therapist–client relationship, and it faces the job of incorporating a substantial portion of this kind of therapist–client relationship. Suppose that the psychotherapy has little or nothing of a particular technique or method that the research shows is a common element. The problem is that, if the psychotherapy actually incorporates the common elements, it is in danger of no longer being the psychotherapy it was. Indeed, the danger is that the psychotherapy will lose its identity, or much of it. I can think of several psychotherapies that would therefore have good reasons to decline incorporating common elements, except for perhaps a slight token here and there.

A belief in a common, single, grand megatherapy

Suppose that this line of research points toward four to seven common factors or ingredients of successful and effective psychotherapies. Then what? The invitation is for most psychotherapies to incorporate the four to seven common factors or ingredients, e.g. suppose that one is a particular kind of helping alliance: most psychotherapies are invited to include the helping alliance, and this means not only the particular procedures, techniques and methods that define the helping alliance, but also the supporting notions and ideas that provide the foundation for the helping alliance.

As most psychotherapies incorporate the common procedures, techniques and methods of the four to seven common ingredients, together with their common underlying notions and ideas, these psychotherapies would probably move, little by little, toward giving up their individual identities, and blending into a single grand megatherapy. In other words, finding and incorporating common ingredients is an effective way of starting from a large number of different psychotherapies and blending them to become a single grand megatherapy. In yet other words, for those who believe in the development of a single grand megatherapy, the search for common ingredients is a very worthwhile avenue.

Conclusions, serious problems and suggestions

Doing research for this reason can be appealing in large part because it rests on an apparently sensible idea that, if there are common elements in successful and effective therapies, featuring, enhancing and highlighting these prized common elements can help to improve and advance the success and effectiveness of the therapies.

However, one way of analyzing this reason supports a case that doing research for this reason is accompanied by a relatively unique set of serious problems. Furthermore, the case holds that the problems can be sufficiently serious to postpone, take time out from further research of this kind, until these serious problems can be resolved.

Accordingly, the suggestion is for interested researchers, and others, to put their attention to solving these serious problems. Not only can solving these serious problems help to remove some frustratingly effective road blocks, for those interested in doing research for this reason, an additional bonus is that the field of psychotherapy is nudged in the direction of a revolutionary shift forward. Here is a summary of some of these serious problems:

1. A serious problem is that significant incorporation, addition or heightening of common elements and their accompanying conceptual baggage can lead to: (a) a loss or wrenching change in the identity of the host psychotherapy; (b) the evolution of a single grand megatherapy; or (c) a regression to the mean on the part of the more successful therapies.

2. The search for common elements can lead to an appreciation of a serious problem that may be worded as follows: 'To what extent do improvement and advancement in a psychotherapy include substantial change in the very nature, content and identity of the psychotherapy?' If the common element is trivial, its inclusion may have little or no significant effect on either increasing the therapy's success or on drastically altering the therapy's nature, identity, form and shape. On the other hand, if the common element is substantial, and substantially new to the psychotherapy, proponents can be faced with a serious choice of heightening the effectiveness of the therapy at the cost of drastically altering the nature, identity, form and shape of the psychotherapy. The serious question is whether or not inclusion of a substantial new common element is an acceptable avenue for improving and advancing a given psychotherapy. How much change can occur in psychoanalytic or cognitive therapy so that it no longer qualifies as psychoanalytic or cognitive psychotherapy?

3. The search for common elements is inclined to be fuelled by a mindset in which component elements are understood as having an additive relationship to one another in totalling the whole event, e.g. relationship elements plus intervention elements plus other elements add up to the whole event. On the other hand, the search for common elements can essentially lose its meaning in an alternative mind-set in which events are open to full and complete descriptions from alternative descriptive systems. Accordingly, the serious problem may be framed as follows: 'To what extent does the search for common elements become essentially meaningful or meaningless, depending on whether the researcher's mind-set is one of the whole being the sum of its parts or the whole being open to alternative systems of description?'

4. In a continuing theme, this reason for doing psychotherapy research seems to contribute little or nothing to learning more and more of what psychotherapy can accomplish, and to learning better and better ways of accomplishing what psychotherapy can accomplish.

CHAPTER 7

Is this theory of psychotherapy good?

This kind of research is aimed at showing that this particular theory of psychotherapy is good, sound, tight, scientific, worthwhile, and meets criteria of a good theory in general and a good theory of psychotherapy in particular.

This chapter concludes with a number of serious problems that are relatively unique to this reason for doing research on psychotherapy. One of these is a specific form of a more general problem that has shown itself before, namely that proponents of some favorite thing, in this case theory, can be reluctant to identify whatever grounds they would accept as sufficient to let go of the favorite thing. This is emerging as quite a serious problem, in different specific forms in different reasons for doing research on psychotherapy.

The nature of the serious problems associated with this reason for doing research indicates a call for serious and careful thinking, rather than research.

Is questioning the goodness of one's theory dangerous to the researcher's health?

It can be risky for a researcher to dare to do research for this reason. The more neutral, objective, removed, scientific the researcher is, the more dangerous the researcher can be, and the riskier it can be to the researcher's health, publication track record, stature and reputation, at least in the researcher's theoretical family. Things may come out all right if the findings show that the theory is good, but even daring to see if the theory is good raises the specter of risky findings. Suppose that the researcher finds that the theory is not so good or is even bad. Can such a possibility be allowed? How can the researcher have the effrontery to raise the possibility that the theory is not good? How dare the researcher set out to do this kind of research?

Researchers often proclaim that they are trained to be skeptical, and to question and challenge much of what is generally taken for granted as true, to check out and put to the test what has not yet been properly checked out and put to the test. However, it can be understandable that many researchers exercise reasonable judgment, prudence and caution in what they choose as the actual target of their skepticism. Precisely what to be skeptical about is often a matter of judicious selection. Researchers do not typically challenge their own deeper beliefs about research or the foundational beliefs of their theoretical system (Mahrer, 2000a).

Psychoanalytic investigators who dared to question psychoanalytic theory, or even to suggest substantive modifications to the theory, can point to a history of getting into big trouble with their psychoanalytic communities (Moras, 1994). Nor is this limited to psychoanalytic communities. Both the elders and the true believers in almost any theoretical community make it almost foolhardy to have the gall to question hallowed truths. If you must do research, do it to show that the theory is indeed good, right and true, but do not cross the line into daring to check out, take a careful look at, actually question the theory. That can be dangerous to the researcher's health.

What are the rights of the accused if you dare to question the goodness of someone else's theory?

Picture three graduate student friends who do studies that are critical of three theories: one attacks psychoanalytic theory, one attacks cognitive social learning theory and the third sees whether personal construct theory measures up. Suppose that each graduate student researcher believes that she or he found enough problems and holes to suggest that there may be grounds for considering lots of serious repair work on the theory, or perhaps even considering each theory seriously inadequate, maybe in need of replacement. If enough of these studies were published, sooner or later someone would come along, review the body of studies, and draw some rather negative conclusions about the three theories.

Is this fair? Should Sigmund Freud, Albert Bandura and George Kelly accept their respective theories as seriously flawed, in big trouble, because of a stacking up of such studies? Should colleagues and consumers and other researchers be influenced by the findings and discussion and conclusions of such studies? I would say no. If I were part of the public, I would want to know at least two things. First, I would like to know who hired the graduate students and whose side the researchers are on. It would be important to me if the research attack on psychoanalytic theory came from a researcher who is far from a proponent of psychoanalysis, and might even be honestly antagonistic or critical of psychoanalytic theory, or of whichever theory the researcher attacked. Researchers who set out to attack a theory will usually succeed in having findings that allow the researcher to say unfriendly things about that theory.

Second, I should like to hear what Sigmund Freud or Albert Bandura or George Kelly, or proponents of their theories, have to say in their own defense, if they choose to defend themselves. Before I draw a conclusion from evidence presented by the prosecuting researchers, I should like to hear from the accused. Unfortunately, those who draw conclusions from a body of studies rarely make an explicit effort to make room for what the accused have to say for themselves, or even for the accused to present their own studies on the matter. To be fair, evidence from the prosecution should be balanced by statements and studies from the defense.

Do our theories have a distinguished track record of important discoveries and breakthroughs on long-standing problems?

Some sciences, especially technological sciences, can make a case that they have only been around for much less than a century, yet they can point to a showcase of respected achievements. But we are talking about theories, not sciences, and especially not fashionable high-technology sciences.

For a respectable theory to show it is good, one way is to be able to point to a track record of producing a whole series of big discoveries and impressive advancements stretching over a solid period of time, and of providing a parallel series of breakthroughs on long-standing big problems, especially if the theory can do all of this in a number of fields, not just one. Historians in the philosophy of science (e.g. Kuhn, 1959, 1970, 1973; Lakatos, 1963, 1970, 1974) have shown how some theories that have been around for a while, e.g. physics, have had enough time to meet and pass this test. However, most theories of psychotherapy are simply too young. They have been in action usually for less than 100 years. That is simply not long enough to use this way of showing that a theory is good.

It seems that researchers might have to be patient enough to wait for more than 20–40 years or so, perhaps closer to at least a century, to allow a theory to be judged by history as good because it led to an impressive series of discoveries, advances, breakthroughs and problem resolutions, and maybe in a few fields other than just psychotherapy.

How can research judge a theory's description of reality when there is no independent description of what that reality is really like?

It would be nice to say that this theory is good because it provides a good picture of reality, it comes very close to describing reality, it offers a fine approximation of the real world. It would be nice if research could assess this quality or characteristic or ability of a theory.

Here is a theory of cognitions. How can we do research to show that this theory provides a fine picture of what cognitions are really like if we have no description of what they are really like, independent of some theory? Here is a theory of the intrapsychic processes in a borderline condition. It is very hard to see if this theory provides a very close approximation of what the intrapsychic processes are like when we have no independent criterion or picture to compare it against, some criterion or picture of what these processes really are in a borderline condition. Here is a theory of infant and child development. How can we tell if this theory comes close to what the reality is of infant and child development when there is no way of knowing the reality of this development quite independent of that, or some other, theory?

A strong case can be made that we cannot. Most of the so-called realities that our theories try to describe cannot be judged against some independent knowing of that so-called reality. We simply have no independent descriptions of what cognitions are really like, of what the true reality is of the intrapsychic processes in a borderline condition, of what really occurs in what we call infant and child development. We are simply unable to do research to judge our theories 'from the point of view of the extent to which they describe the world as it really is, simply because we do not have access to the world independently of our theories in a way that would enable us to assess the adequacy of those descriptions' (Chalmers, 1982, p. 163; compare Held, 1995; Mahrer, 2004).

It would be nice to do research to show that this theory is good because it comes impressively close to describing reality, the way the world really is, to psychotherapeutic reality. The truth is that we lack an independent measure of our psychotherapeutic realities to measure our theories against.

The findings: do they tell us about the session or about two people talking about the session?

The researcher may want to study what happens in sessions of psychotherapy, and may want the findings to say something about the sessions. On the other hand, the researcher may be interested in studying two people who talk together about what happened in the psychotherapy sessions. In this case, the object of study and the findings mainly have to do with the two people talking about the sessions.

If the researcher wants to study what happens in a session, and wants the findings to be about the session, it probably makes sense to study the sessions direct. Studying two people talking about the sessions will tell the researcher about two people talking about sessions, but it tells little or nothing about what happens in the sessions themselves.

Yet many studies focus on an interviewer talking with a client about the session, or a tester and a testee who takes the tests. These studies are sensible if the researcher is interested in studying these interactions, but they make little or no sense if the researcher is truly interested in studying what happens in the sessions themselves, e.g. suppose that the researcher is interested in showing that narrative theory is a good way of making sense of psychotherapy, that 'psychotherapy is an opportunity for the client to tell and "re-author" the story of their life . . . [that] therapy represents an opportunity for the client to tell and explore troublesome aspects of their life narrative' (Grafinaki and McLeod, 1999, pp. 289–290). The clients had 12 sessions, were interviewed for 60–150 minutes after sessions 1, 6 and 12, and the interviewer and interviewee talked about the sessions. The data that were studied consisted of their dialogue with each other.

However, the findings were used to inform about the sessions themselves, rather than the interviews about the sessions. The findings were used to inform about 'narrative processes in the construction of helpful and hindering events . . .' (Grafinaki and McLeod, 1999, p. 289), e.g. 'When therapy is viewed as a process of storytelling, it would appear that it is possible to see that clients and therapists frequently generate possible new story lines' (Grafinaki and McCleod, 1999, p. 299). It can be a serious error to presume that studying post-session interviews provides findings about the session itself rather than merely about the two people who talk about the session outside and after the session.

Are our theories too fuzzy, vague and loose for research to show that a theory is confirmed or disconfirmed, good or not so good?

Picture a researcher as the featured speaker at a convention of thousands of psychotherapists, and the researcher simply asks for one psychotherapy for the researcher to test, to see if the theory can be confirmed or disconfirmed. 'Just let me study one authoritative, clear enunciation of a theory, any one at all.' The first brush the researcher would probably have with the problem of fuzziness, vagueness and looseness is that the poor researcher would be swamped with thousands of different publications without being able to say that here is a particular theory and here is the authoritative, clear statement of that theory.

The researcher might get the impression that there is something called cognitive theory, but where is the authoritative clear enunciation of cognitive theory? The researcher might get the idea that there is something called behavior theory, psychodynamic theory, gestalt theory, Jungian theory, integrative/eclectic theory, psychoanalytic theory. However, the poor researcher could not even get started seeing if the theory can be confirmed or disconfirmed because she or he would be looking in vain for the authoritative clear exposition of the theory that might be examined. I may hand the researcher what I think of as the authoritative clear version of my experiential 'theory' (Mahrer, 1989a), but the poor researcher is entitled to become so confused when she or he is also swamped with at least two to four dozen other authoritative experiential theories (Mahrer and Fairweather, 1993).

Even if the researcher reads some theory as the supposedly authoritative version of that theory, it is almost assured that the researcher would soon be lost in a sea of fuzzy, vague, loose confusion. What passes as theory is often much ado about nothing, and the poor researcher is faced with the almost impossible task of having to distil cloudy nothingness into meaningful theoretical propositions (compare Medawar, 1969; Popper, 1972a, 1972b, 1980).

Almost without exception, our so-called theories are simply too fuzzy, vague and loose to be subjected to confirmation, and especially to disconfirmation. Popper (1974) selected out psychoanalytic theory as impossible to test because it was so able to provide equally good explanations for when its predictions were verified or when they were not. 'This was a serious challenge that was mounted on philosophical grounds. For if psychoanalysis could not be refuted "come what may", then any attempt by a psychologist to test psychoanalysis empirically was misconceived' (O'Donohue and Kitchener, 1996, p. 280). Although psychoanalytic theory is an easy culprit, almost all of our theories would seem to fail this test and cannot be confirmed or especially disconfirmed, refuted, shown to be wrong. Doing research for this reason is essentially defeated before it begins, and fruitless, mainly because our theories are almost uniformly far too fuzzy, vague and loose. The net result seems to be that these kinds of studies 'are attempts either to validate one or more "vague preconceived ideas" that can never be disconfirmed, or to provide evidence in support of "grandiose and comforting generalizations"' (Spence, 1994, p. 19). Here is another reason why our theories are not ready for research to show that some particular theory is a good theory.

Are most theoretical descriptions and accounts cheap, easy, unfalsifiable and just outside the researcher's reach?

One of the main jobs of a theory is to be a reliable resource of ever-ready descriptions and accounts. If a theory survives, one reason is that it provides practitioners with a reassuring sense that this thing, indeed just about any psychotherapeutic thing, can be described and accounted for. This woman is starting to come late for work and to keep more to herself. This man is scared of small furry animals. Theories that have been around for a while can cheaply and easily provide adequate descriptions and accounts, adequate at least for the consumers of the theories. If Jungian theory or biosocial theory were unable to provide practitioners with a comforting continuing sense of being able to describe and account for things, neither of these theories would survive for long.

This means that virtually every theory with a substantial history in the field of psychotherapy is almost certainly able to provide a working description and account of almost everything that the practitioner finds in the field of psychotherapy. Most theories are all-purpose and quite comprehensive. A biosocial or a learning theory or an information-processing theory can provide a description and account of a woman starting to come late for work and keeping more to herself, and also of a man being scared of small furry animals, and a broad sweep of things that the practitioner faces in the course of therapeutic work. If a theory were asked what kinds of psychotherapeutic happenings it was unable to describe and account for, most theories would probably first pause, then search for some limited or esoteric class of phenomena acceptably outside its ability to describe and account for them.

One of the reasons why so many theories can so easily and cheaply spin out descriptions and accounts, why so many theories have such long and comprehensive appeal, is that the descriptions and accounts are cleverly kept just outside the reach of researchers. The descriptions and accounts are typically worded well enough and carefully enough that they almost defy disproof, disconfirmation, falsification. They cannot be shown to be wrong. The poor researcher could easily just give up because the description and account are forever just out of reach, cannot quite be grasped. Remember, these are mere descriptions and accounts, and not causal explanations that might be open to being shown to be verified or not verified or even wrong.

Once a theory offers its description or account of the woman starting to be late for work and staying more to herself, or of the man being scared of small furry animals, if the theory has been around for a while and has a substantial constituency, the chances are very good that the theory is safe.

The moral is that, if you look at therapy from a given theoretical perspective, you will almost be ensured success in showing that therapy can be seen from that theoretical perspective, e.g. if you think of therapy from a theoretical perspective that emphasizes values, you can show that what is found to be the good moments, the important in-session events, the significant changes, will indeed be understood in terms of a system of values (Walsh, Perrucci and Severns, 1999). Your findings will indicate, for example, that these good moments will include such valued changes as a shift from argument to collaborative discussion, the client's acknowledgment of previously undisclosed fears, the therapist's facilitation of client self-disclosure and the therapist's reframing of the client's experience. Most researchers are able to design studies to show that their theoretical perspective can make sense of selected parts of what happens in psychotherapy. The study is virtually ensured of being successful once the design and methodology are put in place.

Instead of making sense of, accounting for, explaining significant in-session change events in terms of a theoretical perspective emphasizing values, suppose that you wanted to show that some other theoretical perspective can make fine sense of those events. Your theory may be psychoanalytic, social learning, communication theory, interpersonal theory, sociological role theory. Suppose yours is a narrative theory, based on the work of Sarbin (1986), Polkinghorne (1988), Bruner (1990), White and Epston (1990), and others. Can a researcher show that such a perspective can do the job? Can it make sense of significant in-session events? The answer is almost certainly yes, even before the researcher designs the design and gets findings.

Going back to the study mentioned earlier, it aims at showing that narrative theory, telling one's story, what is called 'narrative processes' or 'narrative reconstruction' can provide a framework for understanding, making sense of, accounting for and explaining in-session significant change events (Grafinaki and McLeod, 1999). Clients are given 12 sessions of therapy, interviewed after sessions 1, 6 and 12, and the interviews are studied to see if narrative theory can make sense of and account for those significant in-session change events. Even before the findings are in and the conclusions drawn, it is a reasonably safe bet that the theory can be shown to be able to make sense of and explain these significant in-session change events. It is probable that so also can a theory of values, psychoanalytic theory, communication theory, social learning theory, interpersonal theory, sociological role theory, and almost any reasonably respectable theory. If a researcher sets out to show that one's theory is good, the study can probably end up showing that one's theory is indeed good.

Suppose that the researcher sets out to see if the researcher's notion of how change occurs is confirmed by the findings. The researcher's theory is that the client's problem will go through a predetermined series of stages or phases in a psychotherapy that is judged as meeting the theory's meaning of a successful outcome. Using a design that has reasonably high goodness of fit with the theory, the results confirm that the problem proceeds through thematic changes over the predetermined series of stages or phases (Meier and Boivin, 2000). A theory that the researcher believes in can be shown to be one that the researcher is justified in believing in.

In general, researchers are probably safe in setting out to show that their theoretical descriptions and accounts are good ones. With a little research carefulness, such studies are almost doomed to success.

Is some desirable change, consequence or outcome weak evidence that a theory is true or good?

It is quite common that practitioners have confidence in their theories because they can point to some desirable clinical changes in their clients. Researchers often think in much the same way. If their studies can point to some desirable changes, consequences or outcomes, here is evidence that the theory is probably true or good. Cognitive theory or psychodynamic theory must be true and good because researchers point to such impressive clinical changes, consequences, outcomes. The trouble is that such thinking is not especially justified.

Is it weak evidence if rival theories provide similar predictions?

A group of psychoanalytic theorists may pride themselves that psychoanalytic theory is really good because its predictions of outcome are verified. 'Oh!,' say 30 or 50 other theories, 'for example, what kinds of predictions?' The psychoanalytic theorists try to think. Then they come up with two. One prediction is that therapeutic outcome will be successful if the patient has sessions each week for a few years. The second is that psychotic patients will be less successful than non-psychotic patients.

Almost all the other theories cock their heads. 'Then we must have equally good theories because we would make the same predictions.' A theory's verified prediction of desirable changes/outcomes is relatively weak evidence of the truth of a theory if rival theories provide similar predictions, especially if the rival theory is an incompatible one: 'Research in the natural sciences often tempts us to believe that a theory is true because some consequence of the theory has been verified. Nevertheless, an identical consequence may be drawn from an alternative and incompatible theory. We cannot, therefore, validly affirm either theory' (Cohen and Nagel, 1953, p. 138). Verification of a theory's predicted outcomes is not necessarily impressive evidence.

Does this account for the desirable change/outcome?

Just pointing to some desirable change or outcome is probably not enough to be confident that a theory is a good one. It helps to be able to identify something that is trusted as helping to account for the desirable change/outcome. A theory that God's will determines whether or not she becomes pregnant may be helped along a little if the fellow has a condom: 'the practical success or failure of a scientific theory is no objective index of its truth value . . . it is possible to improve the conditions of neurotics by means of shamanism, psychoanalysis, and other practices as long as effective means, such as suggestion, conditioning, tranquillizers, and above all, time, are combined with them' (Bunge, 1972, p. 65). But this alone is not usually enough to allow the theory to feel self-confident.

Does this theory lead to whatever accounts for the desirable changes/outcomes?

First you have to be able to say that these particular in-session things accounted for the desirable changes/outcomes. Then you almost have to show that it was this theory that led to those particular in-session things that accounted for the desirable changes/outcomes. The desirable change or outcome may be that the ulcer went away after the person had a session and carried out his homework over and over again in his post-session world. Research may strongly suggest that what accounted for the ulcer going away was the person's starting with a scene of painful feelings involving the ulcer, discovering a particular deeper quality, fully being this deeper quality, and actually being this new way wholesomely in the post-session actual world. But it must be shown that the theory connected with, led to and produced this stepwise sequence. When the theory can legitimately claim credit for producing what accounted for the desirable changes/outcomes, here is some evidence that the theory may be true and good. Just pointing to some desirable change, consequence or outcome is usually inadequate evidence that a theory is true or good.

Does research to test if a theory is good help to improve the theory?

Doing research to test the theory, to see if the theory is any good, is rarely intended to make the theory better. If the findings are used to conclude that the theory is good or not so good, that is pretty much the end of the matter. It would require a whole new and different intent to use the findings to try to make the theory better, to improve the theory.

Even if the researcher wanted to use the findings to improve the theory, there are grounds for saying that the findings are simply not helpful for improving the theory. If the findings are negative, if the theory is found to be not so good, the problem is that the findings do not tell us what part of the theory needs fixing, which proposition or premise or principle or variable is the culprit. About the best that may be concluded 'is that among the propositions used to predict the phenomenon there is at least one error; but where this error lies is just what it does not tell us' (Duhem, 1953, p. 239).

If the findings are friendly, again there is virtually no way of improving or even giving credit to particular bits and pieces of the theory, particular propositions or principles that help make up the theory. 'When these consequences . . . are confirmed by observation . . . the whole theory is said to be confirmed; but none of the propositions which go to make up the theory has been or can be tested directly' (Kneale, 1953, p. 359). It seems that doing research to test if a theory is good rarely helps to improve the theory.

Does research showing that a theory is good make much difference for the practitioner?

There can be a fine body of research showing that some theory is good. This is good news for attachment theory or arousal theory, self-regulation theory, identity process theory, bioenergetic theory, cognitive theory, object-relations theory, any theory that is supported by the research.

The problem is that all this fine research may have little or nothing to do for the practitioner. One reason is that the practitioner is a proponent of some other theory. Do all the research you want on attachment theory. I am behaviorist. I follow behavior theory. Whether attachment theory is weakened or strengthened by research makes little or no difference to me.

Another reason why this research makes little or no difference to the practitioner is the long way from the theory to what the working practitioner does. Someone would have to start from the theory and proceed step by step, over many steps, to arrive at the actual level of the working practitioner. The implication or application has usually lost its steam, dissipated away, by the time the level of actual practice is reached. Typically, the researcher may beat the drums for the theory, and the practitioner simply walks away to carry out much the same work as before, watching the researcher's performance. The leap from the theory to actual in-session work is anything but a careful, precise, direct, single little step. It is often more of a flailing leap into the unknown.

Difficulties of producing a hypothesis to confirm or disconfirm a theory by reasoning from it

Some researchers either act as theorists or depend on theorists to provide hypotheses that are then tested, on the understanding that the findings can either confirm or disconfirm the theory. However, there can be some serious problems at each step in this work:

1. An initial problem is how to select an official version of that theory. How does the researcher ever know that this is the official, acknowledged, authoritative version of social learning theory, or of psychodynamic theory, or of cognitive theory? When I read that some studies had tested my experiential 'theory', I was suspicious until I read the studies and found out that they examined hypotheses that seemed to come from a rather loose amalgamation of client-centered theory, gestalt theory and a brand of cognitive theory. It is very hard to start from some official version of what the proponents would agree is the formal statement of their theory. What those studies studied was not even close to my experiential conceptual system.

2. To arrive at a logically deduced hypothesis, the theory ought to have basic postulates, premises, starting points, axioms, fundamental propositions that allow for a process of logical deduction. In sciences, such as mathematics and physics, there are such basic propositions. From these fundamental starting points, it can be possible to engage in rigorous reasoning to arrive at some hypothesis. Do we have such fundamental propositions in the field of psychology? Whitehead (Mays, 1977) says no. I tend to agree. Before we even try to arrive at deduced hypotheses, there is plenty of work to be done in making our fundamental premises and starting points much more carefully rigorous (Mahrer, 2003).

3. Once we have acceptably rigorous basic premises and fundamental propositions, our theories have to be rigorous enough to allow for a lattice of deductive reasoning, ending with a hypothesis. This rarely if ever occurs. What usually happens is that a researcher provides a loose package of notions and ideas, and states some hypothesis as somehow coming from that loose package. What is missing is a demonstrated lattice of careful, rigorous, deductive reasoning, culminating in a logically derived hypothesis. For this job, almost all our theories may be judged as 'scientifically unimpressive and technologically worthless' (Meehl, 1978, p. 806). Our theories would be more acceptable, and the

researcher would meet this test, if the researcher could first show that the hypothesis was indeed arrived at by the principles of formal deductive reasoning (Hempel, 1953). Unfortunately very few studies of psychotherapy meet this test.

4. The hypothesis has to be more than merely testable. First, the hypothesis must be connected to a specifically identified proposition so that the fate of that specific proposition is, at least in large measure, tied to the findings. The benefactor or culprit of the findings is some identified proposition rather than the theory as a whole. Has this typically been done before the study is carried out? Rarely.

   Second, the hypothesis should be in such a form that the findings are able to lend strength to, verify, confirm the hypothesis, and the findings are able to disconfirm, refute, falsify, show that the hypothesis is wrong. Again, that is rarely a characteristic of most hypotheses.

5. Even before the study is carried out, the research design should be shown as passing a test. The test is whether or not negative or unfriendly findings can easily be blamed on the research design. Usually, once the findings are seen to be negative or disappointing or downright unfriendly, the researcher finds all sorts of weaknesses and flaws in the research design to take the blame. The research design should be examined before the study is launched so that the research design is not an easy target for blame.

6. Once the findings are in, you ordinarily have to arrive at some conclusion, which usually means traveling back up the logical lattice that led to the hypothesis in the first place. Suppose that the findings confirm the hypothesis. Does that mean the theory is confirmed? Not really. Because logical deductive reasoning can arrive at a testable prediction does not necessarily mean that confirmation of the testable prediction lends even moderate support to the theory (Erwin and Siegel, 1989). It usually entails another process of careful reasoning to see just what conclusions are warranted by the findings, even or especially if they are friendly to the hypothesis.

What does all this mean? It means it is very hard to test our theories in an acceptably reasonable, rigorous, and systematic way (compare Feyerabend, 1962, 1971; Lakatos, 1970, 1974; Meehl, 1978).

What research findings would you accept as sufficient for you to give up your theory?

Proponents of just about any theory usually radiate a sense of pleasure when they pronounce that their theory is upheld, confirmed, given the seal of approval by research. What is the worst damage that research might do to proponents of a theory? The answer is: almost none at all. Proponents can continue clinging to their chosen theory virtually safe from whatever findings researchers find. About the worst damage that researchers can realistically do is to provide weak support, or maybe little or no support, to the proponents of the theory. But that is almost never enough for proponents to take the dramatic step of giving up their theory. No matter what the research finds, the proponents are usually safe.

Picture a scene in which I ask the proponents of just about any theory: 'What research findings would you accept as reasonably sufficient for you to give up your theory?' 'Would you please name what these findings might be?' If the proponents do not name what these findings might be, a case can be made that it is futile to do research to see if a theory is really good because proponents will continue to hold the theory no matter what the findings are (Mahrer, 1995).

Popper (1972a, 1972b, 1980) thundered against this hard-to-believe state of affairs, and carefully showed how to design studies that can put a theory to the stringent test of risking being shown to be wrong, refuted, falsified. 'The question is not, Is my belief confirmed? But rather, Is there evidence that can be gathered which falsifies this belief? . . .' (O'Donohue and Vass, 1996, p. 314). But it is not enough for philosophers of science to hold forth this question. What is required is for proponents of the theory to have the courage to step forward and actually name the research findings they would deem acceptable, reasonable and sufficient for them to give up their theory.

Philosophers of science go even further. Whereas many proponents of a theory and many researchers believe that research can provide degrees of confirmation of a theory, and most proponents have a rigid mind-set that no research findings can ever be sufficient for them to give up their theory, some philosophers of science simply reverse this way of thinking. They assert that research is essentially unable to show that a theory is true, but research can show that a theory is wrong, false, refuted. 'Theories can be conclusively falsified in the light of suitable evidence, whereas they can never be established as true or even probably true whatever the evidence. Theory acceptance is always tentative. Theory rejection can be decisive. This is the factor that earns falsificationists their title' (Chalmers, 1982, p. 60).

There are at least two practical tests of whether or not any research findings can ever be deemed sufficient for proponents of any theory to abandon that theory. One practical test is to locate a convincing number of instances where proponents of a given theory have indeed named the reasonable kinds of research findings that they would deem sufficient for them to give up their theory as wrong, refuted, falsified.

If few or, as I believe, no such instances can be produced, why go ahead and do research? If the proponents remove the possibility of accepting their theory as wrong, false, refuted, and as warranting their taking the scientifically honorable step of abandoning their theory, the theory can rest safe even before the researcher makes plans for doing the research.

A second practical test is to find several actual times when a theory has been given up when proponents did spell out the kinds of research findings that would be sufficient to drop the theory, the research findings were found, and the proponents dutifully went ahead and gave up the theory. I am not picturing that the proponents walked aimlessly around with no theory. I am picturing that the proponents did the honorable thing and let go of their theory. Nor am I picturing that the proponents exchanged their theory for a dramatic leap over to the other side of the street. Instead, the proponents might well exchange their theory for a related one that is not especially vulnerable to the same research findings that led them to give up the original theory. 'For example, a behavioral researcher initially committed to understanding phobias as being classically conditioned might, given many prediction failures, try to understand phobias using an operant analysis. It would be much more unlikely for the researcher to begin to investigate hypotheses involving anxiety over surfacing id impulses' (O'Donohue, 1989, p. 1466).

It is certainly not the rule that the field of psychotherapy has passed both practical tests, i.e. it is not especially common that proponents of some theory have named the formal, reasonable research grounds they would deem sufficient for them to give up their theory. Nor can many instances be found where proponents have gone ahead and respected a body of research findings so that they then did the honorable thing and gave up their theory.

We are faced with the same question: 'Why should researchers even bother to do research to see if a theory is any good if it is virtually impossible for proponents to name the research findings that they would deem sufficient to abandon their theory?' The picture of proponents naming the sufficient grounds and actually giving up their theory if these grounds occur is probably an illusion, a noble myth that almost never happens in the real world (Fuller, 1996; compare Howard, 1985). The more realistic, clever and safer practice is to use research to muster support for your theory, to play down submitting your theory to a test of its truthfulness, and to absolutely avoid the risk of seeing if it is wrong, refuted, false. 'The predicate in terms of which theory is valued is not truth, as the earlier account had it to be. We speak of a theory being "well-supported," "rationally acceptable," or the like. To speak of it as *true* would suggest that a later anomaly would force a revision or even abandonment of the theory can in principle be excluded' (McMullin, 1983, p. 7). It seems that a great deal of embarrassing studies would never have to be done if researchers dared to ask proponents of a theory what kinds of research findings would be deemed reasonably sufficient for the proponents to actually accept that their theory is sufficiently poor, inadequate, wrong, to be abandoned.

Verification of predictions versus laying out sufficient conditions to give up the theory

Most research is aimed toward verifying a theory's predictions, and the logic is that if the theory's predictions hold up then the theory is good. An alternative strategy is that mere verification of a theory's prediction is exceedingly weak support for the theory (Adams, 1937; Rychlak, 1981; Slife and Williams, 1995). A theory of the power of God's will to account for things can be confirmed by pointing to the leaf falling off the tree or the sun's rising or biblical predictions coming to pass. This is weak evidence of the power of God's will.

Stronger evidence is when proponents of the power of God's will actually lay out the reasonable conditions they would accept as sufficient to abandon the theory of the power of God's will. Few theologians have stated these conditions. Few proponents of psychotherapeutic theories have stated these conditions. Mere verification of predictions is weak evidence of the strength and goodness of the theory.

Immunity of theories from unfriendly studies

Are most studies too weak to cause any real damage?

Almost without exception most studies are designed and built to allow for a modest small increase or decrease in the confidence with which a theory is retained. These studies are relatively harmless because, if they suggest having somewhat less confidence, the studies can be ignored, and it is almost certain that there is no penalty.

A tough design actually has its sights on being able to show that a theory is just plain wrong, false, refuted, and these aims are far more serious than politely questioning the confidence with which a theory ought to be held. What proportion of studies on psychotherapy has raised the stakes beyond merely asking if a theory is confirmed by the higher stakes of seeing if the theory can pass the test of whether or not it can be shown to be wrong, false, refuted? Unfortunately, the low proportion ought to be embarrassing to the field of psychotherapy, but the field manages not to be too embarrassed that there is so little concern with the low proportion.

Goldman (1996) says that this tough kind of research design has already had a three-decade history in experimental psychology. Meanwhile, research on psychotherapy continues to allow theories to rest assured and to be safely immune from the weak designs that barely ruffle the various theories. This is too bad.

Are there plenty of other things to be blamed for unfriendly findings?

Suppose that a threatening body of studies shares findings that seem to be ominously targeted on the theory. Is the theory in trouble? Should it seek the protection of a clever lawyer? The answer seems to be no, not as long as the theory is clever and tough enough to put the blame on some other culprit. Of the many other things that are qualified at taking the blame, here are three good ones.

One is to attack the findings. Getting scared by the supposed findings thereby endorses the findings as scary. Start with the findings themselves, and object. If there is a clash between the theory and the findings, or what is called the observations, blame the observations. If 'a theory or part of a theory clashed with some observation statement, it may be the observation statement that is at fault. Nothing in the logic of the situation requires that it should always be the theory that is rejected on the occasion of a clash with observation. . . . Consequently, straightforward, conclusive falsifications of theories are not achievable' (Chalmers, 1982, p. 61; compare Quine, 1961; Duhem, 1962; Lakatos, 1970). Preserve the theory by attacking the findings.

Second, you can almost always attack the research design. Just about any good research designer and methodologist can find plenty of problems, holes, weaknesses and flaws to pronounce the design at fault. Of course a theory is not to be endangered by such a poor research design. The researcher used the wrong design, used the right design in the wrong way, did not use the design according to the instructions, and on and on. Any researcher can keep a theory safely immune by having plenty of time to study a rival's research design to find plenty of reason to blame the research design, leaving the innocent theory safe and sound and immune.

A third way of protecting a theory is to sacrifice any of the many principles, propositions, auxiliary notions, intervening corollaries, working statements that fill all the space between the actual theory and the fatal findings. The king has a court, the business has a bureaucracy, the general has officers, and just about every theory has a whole staff of auxiliary and secondary principles and propositions that are fair game for taking the hit from truly unfriendly findings. Most theories never have to endure such sacrifices, but, if such sacrifices have to be made, theories can almost certainly survive.

Theories have rarely been damaged by unfriendly findings. It is almost unthinkable that theories have been mortally wounded by unfriendly studies. It is far more likely that theories enjoy safe immunity behind plenty of other things that can be blamed or sacrificed to protect the theory.

How do we show that a theory or a model is good?: truth versus usefulness

In the field of psychotherapy, almost all bodies of thought or systems of ideas, concepts, constructs, are made of bits and pieces that are supposed to be real and true. If the body of ideas and concepts includes cognitions or an ego or extraversion or conditioned responses or an unconscious, these things are to refer to things that are real and true. A theory is made up of bits and pieces that are presumably real and true.

One way to do research to see whether a theory is any good is to do it to show that there really is something called a cognition or a cognitive structure or an ego or extraversion or a conditioned response or an unconscious. If research shows that there really and truly is something called an unconscious, that kind of research helps to show that the theory is good.

Most theories also presume that there is a single grand truth out there, and the theory is good if it is able to come impressively close to approximating that truth, if it can provide predictions of what things are really like out there. The theory predicts that people with this mental disorder will have these kinds of ego defects, or that people with this degree of effectance will show this kind of chemical profile in their blood or that men and women will differ in this particular part of the structure of the brain.

Research can then show that the theory is good by testing out and confirming its predictions of truth, of what things really are like. If the findings confirm the predictions, the research tends to show that the theory is probably pretty good.

If psychoanalytic theory is good, research can be done to show that its bits and pieces are really true, that there is confirmation of concepts such as the unconscious and anal stage of development and ego. In addition, research can show that theoretical predictions actually predict things that are real and true. Men and women do indeed have different kinds of ego structures and intrapsychic pathologies. People with this mental illness are fixated at this psychoanalytic stage of development. If Freudian theory is good, research can confirm its predictions. 'Freud, for example, despite his respect for the scientific method and his general naturalistic outlook, was not interested in the experimental confirmation of his doctrines. But . . . it seems imperative at least to formulate them in such a way that an experimental confirmation or disconfirmation becomes possible' (Feigl, 1959, p. 118). Research can see if a theory is good by testing its component parts and by checking out its predictions of what is real and true.

However, this kind of research is fruitless, has nowhere to go, if the conceptual system is a model of usefulness rather than a theory of truth (Mahrer, 1989a, 1996/2004, 2004). There are two main ways in which models are different from theories of truth, and both ways suggest that the kinds of research designed to show that a theory is good have little or no relevance to seeing if a model is any good.

For one thing, both the models as a whole and their component parts, notions, ideas, concepts, are thought of as conveniently useful fictions, as hypothetical constructs (Whitehead, 1929; MacCorquodale and Meehl, 1948; Rotgers, 1988; Mahrer, 2004), rather than as truths. 'They are not . . . to be proved or disproved, but are convenient representations of things' (Skinner, 1938, p. 44). Models are treated as pictorialized metaphors, helpful pictures and guides (Chalmers, 1982), as 'free creations of the human mind' (Einstein, 1923, p. 29), as convenient fictions. In the experiential model (Mahrer, 1996/2004), there are deeper potentials for experiencing, relationships between potentials for experiencing, and other pieces and parts. But these are understood as conveniently useful fictions, not things that are real and true. Research dedicated toward finding deeper potentials for experiencing in the brain or bloodstream is little more than a ridiculous pursuit of a non-existent will-o'-the-wisp. There are no real and true deeper potentials for experiencing. Research is not done to show that the experiential model or any of its pieces and parts is real and true. They are not supposed to be in the first place.

The second main way that a model is different from a theory is that the test of a good model is that it works. It accomplishes impressive changes in just about every session or helps a practitioner to sense and feel what the person is sensing and feeling. A theory is good if its predictions and hypotheses about the world of reality and truth are confirmed and verified. Research is to see whether the theory's predictions and hypotheses about the world of reality and truth are confirmed and verified. When a researcher works from a model, the researcher seeks better and better ways of accomplishing some end, goal, particular job, designated use, and not to see if a theory's predictions and hypotheses about the world of reality and truth are confirmed and verified.

Research aimed at showing that a theory is good is mainly geared toward showing that the theory's component parts are real and true, and that its predictions and hypotheses about the world of reality and truth are confirmed and verified. Research aimed at seeing if a model is useful is mainly geared to seeing whether the model is useful in helping to accomplish some job, end or goal, use.

How can we show that one theory is good without comparing it with rival theories?

It may be possible to show that a particular therapy or treatment is good if there is some generally accepted seal of approval with criteria for what qualifies as a good therapy or treatment, e.g. if a treatment is to reduce excess bodily weight, it may be awarded a seal of approval if the criteria are: (1) the treatment enables patients to shed at least 50 per cent of designated excess bodily weight, (2) within this designated period and if (3) a designated proportion of patients keep that weight loss for some designated period after the treatment. You do not necessarily have to compare this therapy or treatment against rival therapies or treatments.

However, it is almost impossible for research to show that one theory is good without comparing it with rival theories. There are almost no ways of showing that this theory meets a set of criteria of a formal theory with a structure that wins the gold medal. Even if some such criteria exist, which they don't, it is almost impossible to award a gold medal to one theory without implicitly or explicitly saying that this theory is therefore better than its rivals. But such criteria can hardly be found, even to apply to one theory. Should we say that this theory has a good formal structure because it has parsimony of constructs, because its auxiliary propositions provide a deductive ladder? How many people know what that means? And how could research test these criteria?

Can research show that one theory, all by itself, is good because of something it can do, accomplish, provide – such as it can wiggle its ears, or play a cello, or make a gourmet meal? Even if there were such criteria, saying that one theory is good because it can do these things gives a powerful impression that most other theories can't.

The conclusion seems to be that almost any way that bestows a seal of approval or goodness on one theory is virtually saying that it is better than most of its rivals. It seems inevitable that research trying to show that this theory is good will fail because a much more preferable strategy is to go ahead and compare a theory with its rivals (compare Erwin, 1997; Erwin and Siegel, 1989; Fine and Forbes, 1986; Grunbaum, 1984).

Does a theory provide a better solution to a particular problem?: comparison with rival theories

Suppose that we are determined to try to solve two problems. One is to develop a machine, a device that can televise or record a dream while the person is sleeping. A second is to find a way in which a person can become a whole new person, qualitatively different and much happier, all in a single session of psychotherapy.

We take a step toward solving these problems by asking likely sources for their suggested solutions, but we do not ask the particular theory in question. Suppose that we get 10 or 20 suggested answers and solutions from 10–20 sources. Then we ask the theory if it can provide a good solution to our problems. If the theory modestly declines, we can conclude that this theory is not very good at providing solutions to these particular problems. If the theory does provide a solution, we can compare this solution against the other solutions, and we can see if this theory seems to provide a better solution than the other sources.

So far, research has not played much of a part. However, research does come into play when we go ahead and see if the solution that the theory provided actually seems to work out better than the other proposed solutions, and actually seems to solve the problem.

A theory is good if it provides a better solution to a particular problem than other sources provide, whether or not those other sources are theories, and if research suggests that the solution is better than the others and that the solution does a good job in solving the problem. However, whether straightforwardly or in a roundabout way, this kind of research almost certainly involves comparison with other theories.

Conclusions, serious problems and suggestions

For proponents of a given theory, it can seem appealing to welcome research that lends support to the goodness and worth of the theory. However, a case is presented that doing research for this reason is accompanied by a relatively unique set of problems that are sufficiently serious to effectively block doing research for this reason.

Accordingly, this suggestion is for interested researchers to take time out from doing further research for this reason, and for these researchers, and interested others, to put their attention to solving these serious problems (1) to remove these frustratingly effective road blocks, and (2) to take baby steps in the direction of nudging the field of psychotherapy toward a revolutionary shift forward. Here is a summary of some of these serious problems:

1. The serious problem can be stated in its larger and more general form: 'How can a theory of psychotherapy be improved and advanced?' Stated in this form, the serious problem sits there, waiting for and inviting study and solution.

The serious problem can also be stated in its more moderately sized form: 'How can research help to improve and advance a theory of psychotherapy?' In this form, other avenues are declined in favor of focusing on research. Nevertheless, the serious problem also sits there, a smaller but perhaps equally serious problem.

The serious problem can also be stated in an even smaller form, yet the problem remains serious: 'How can a theory be improved or advanced by daring to refute and falsify the theory?' This is a serious problem because such attempts are almost uniformly counter-attacked as aggressive attacks on the theory, somewhat understandable when attempts to refute and falsify the theory are mounted by researchers in rival camps, and treasonable when attempts are carried out by one's own researchers. This is also a serious problem because very few psychotherapy researchers or theoreticians have either the intent or the proficient means of improving and advancing a theory by refutation and falsification of the theory.

2. A serious general problem becomes a relatively unique specific problem when proponents of a given theory are rarely ready and willing to state the reasonable grounds that they would accept as sufficient to abandon their theory or important parts of their theory. Until this problem is resolved, proponents of theories can become increasingly proficient at discounting and counteracting unfriendly research findings, and researchers can continue attacking, challenging, testing theories, the proponents of which are unwilling to accept any reasonable grounds for abandoning their theories or important parts of their theories. Until this serious problem is solved, doing research for this reason may be considered either essentially fruitless and infeasible, or a kind of Alice in Wonderland game where nothing is to change when the winners win and the losers lose.

Even if proponents of a theory are willing to acknowledge unfriendly findings, typically there are plenty of ways for proponents to shield their theories protectively, to discount and undermine the unfriendly studies, to reluctantly sacrifice a few unessential auxiliary notions, and thereby to refuse to allow their precious theories to be dumped on the trash pile. Proponents can and do find ways of clinging to their precious theories in spite of what the unfriendly researchers say, and this unbudgeable reluctance can be a serious problem.

3. A serious problem may consist of a serious difficulty in being able to answer this question: 'What constitutes strong evidence for the goodness and worth of a theory of psychotherapy?' A case was presented that the following qualify as relatively weak evidence: (a) a theory's ability to provide explanations of therapeutic phenomena is weak

because most theories can easily provide explanations. (b) Research evidence for the effectiveness of a therapy does not necessarily constitute strong evidence of the goodness and worth of that therapy's theory. (c) Until there are generally accepted, independent criteria of what the real world is like, it can be difficult to demonstrate convincingly that a given theory provides an impressive approximation of the nature, content and structure of the real world of therapeutic phenomena. (d) For a theory to be declared good, of worth, a theory usually has to achieve a sufficient degree of rigor, stringency, structure and logical organization to warrant systematic analysis, inquiry and testing of its basic propositions. Few of our theories can be convincingly shown to have achieved this status. (e) In some other fields, strong evidence for the goodness and worth of a theory can consist of the theory's historical track record of achievements, accomplishments, discoveries. In the field of psychotherapy, few theories can be shown to be able to point to such a convincing track record, partly because few of our theories have been around long enough to have a long history of their achievements, accomplishments and discoveries.

4. The field of psychotherapy is filled with theories that accept the truth of their personality parts and their subject matter, from egos to cognitive schemata, from basic needs to paranoia, from stages of child development to depressive disorders. Showing that the theory is good consists mainly of confirming the truth of what the theory theorizes. What is essentially missing are models of usefulness, conceptual systems made up of 'convenient fictions' that can be evaluated in terms of their usefulness for given ends, goals, tasks, jobs. The two-sided serious problem may be stated as follows: (a) how can the field of psychotherapy complement its virtually exclusive reliance on theories of truth with a provision of some room for models of usefulness? (b) How are the criteria for assessing the worth of models of usefulness similar to and different from the criteria for assessing the worth of theories of truth?

5. A fifth serious problem may be stated as follows: 'By whose criteria is this theory to be judged as good or not good?' There are at least three sides to this problem. (a) If the criteria belong to the proponents of the theory, each theory can be entitled, if it is so inclined, to judge itself as worthwhile by its own criteria. (b) If the criteria belong to proponents of a rival theory, the judged theory can have grounds for declining the criteria as unfair. (c) If the criteria are accepted by a number of theories, judging the goodness and worth of a single theory are inferior to judging the goodness and worth of a number of theories relative to each other.

6. It seems, once again, relatively clear that doing research for this reason can be seen as exceedingly weak in learning more and more of what psychotherapy can accomplish, and in learning better and better ways of helping to accomplish what psychotherapy can accomplish.

Chapter 8

Is this theory of psychotherapy better than that theory?

This kind of research is done mainly to compare several theories of psychotherapy, and to show that one is best, superior, better than its rival(s). Perhaps the title of the chapter would be better if it were worded as follows: is this theory of psychotherapy better than that theory or those theories?

Should this reason for doing research on psychotherapy be combined with the previous reason into a single chapter that covers both doing research to show that this theory is good (see Chapter 7) and is better than its rival theories (this chapter)? After all, both chapters seem to deal with much the same topic, namely theories of psychotherapy, and much the same aim, namely showing that this theory is good, whether by itself or in relation to its rivals. Here is a case for combining the two chapters.

But there is also a case for treating these two reasons as sufficiently different to warrant two separate chapters. They are different in regard to their underlying serious problems. Take a look at the serious problems summarized at the end of this chapter, and compare them with the serious problems summarized at the end of Chapter 7. Somewhat surprisingly, there is little or no substantial overlap among the five serious problems distinctive to doing research to show that a theory is good (see Chapter 7) and the four serious problems distinctive to doing research to show that a theory is better than its rivals (this chapter).

If the serious problems had been relatively similar, the two chapters might well be merged into one. As they seem so substantially different, the case is that there are substantially different serious problems underlying each of these two reasons for doing research. Hence there are two chapters, but they are back to back.

How common is it for the theories to agree explicitly on the explicit game in which they are to compete?

It would be hard to stage a competition between a theory of friction and a theory of pupillary dilation, or between a theory of crop rotation and a theory of the development of soccer skills. There ought to be an explicit agreement on just what the theories are theories of. A competition might take place if all the contestants claim that they are theories of simple phobia. A behavioral theory and a cognitive theory can have a game to see which is better if they both agree beforehand that they both provide a good theory of the acquisition and use of language in children (e.g. Chomsky, 1957; Skinner, 1957).

When theories have trouble agreeing on what the game is to be, on what they are good at offering theories of, Feyerabend (1977, 1978) termed this 'incommensurability', and shows how such incommensurability prevents a real contest between classic mechanics and relativity theory.

Many theories would decline to enter a competition on the understandable grounds that they do not play that particular game. I doubt if classic mechanics or relativity theory would be eager to enter a contest to see which theory is best at providing a theory of the development of soccer skills. The experiential system of thought would not compete to see if it can be the best theory of simple phobia, if only because the phrase 'simple phobia' has little or no meaning in that system of thought.

It seems to be rather uncommon for researchers to get the owners of the theories to agree explicitly on the explicit game in which they are to compete. For such a competition to be held, the burden of proof is on the researcher to get these written signatures on the contract for the game.

Do the contestants explicitly agree on the rules of the game and how to determine who wins?

To do research to show that one theory is better than its rivals, someone has to get the competing theories to agree explicitly that these are the rules of the game and these are the rules for being able to say that one theory wins. In other words, the competing theories really ought to agree on how to do this research. That is a relatively rare achievement, probably because it is so hard to achieve explicit agreement from the competing theories.

Picture the respective owners of behavior theory, social learning theory, psychoanalytic theory and experiential theory negotiating with the promoter of the contest to agree on the exact rules whereby the research will be conducted and one declared the winner. The negotiations would call for a most unusual mediator: 'proponents of rival paradigms will subscribe to different sets of standards, metaphysical principles, etc. Judged by its own standards, paradigm A may be judged superior to paradigm B, while if the standards of paradigm B are used as premises, the judgement may be reversed. . . . Supporters of rival paradigms will not accept each other's premises and so will not necessarily be convinced by each other's arguments' (Chalmers, 1982, pp. 96–97; compare Kuhn, 1970, 1977).

One strategy used by some proponents of some theories is to try to convince everyone that their way of doing research happens to be the only way to do research, the scientific way. 'There is only one scientific way to do research and it is mine! Everyone therefore ought to abide by my game rules.' Such a negotiating strategy can be successful when negotiating with inexperienced rivals. It falls apart when rival negotiators easily spot that as pressure to accept the opponent's game rules, and when rival negotiators can just as easily call on their own scientific experts to present counter-arguments on behalf of the rival negotiator's preferred rules of the research game. It is not all that hard to call on science in the process of negotiating which contest rules shall be used and in determining who is to be crowned the winner.

Is a contest with directly competing rival theories superior to single-contestant contests?

In the field of psychotherapy, a rather large proportion of contests are held with only one contestant present, with its rivals as mere shadow contestants or implied contestants. These studies conclude that this theory is a good one, and the implication is that it must be better than its rivals even though its rivals never actually competed in the contest.

Proponents of one theory hold that dreams are meaningless neurophysiological noise. A rival theory holds that dreams are symbolic expressions of psychoanalytic unconscious impulses. Proponents of the former theory carry out an extensive program of research, the findings confirm that dreams are meaningless neurophysiological noise, and the conclusion is that the former theory wins the contest. Not only has the psychoanalytic theory been left out of the contest, but the psychoanalytic theory has been declared the loser by the researchers, even though the psychoanalytic theory has never gone head to head in direct competition. It lost the contest without ever directly competing.

One-contestant contests may make some sense when the researcher believes that (1) if one theory can be shown to be good, its rival theories must therefore be not as good, and (2) in a contest between rival theories, there can be only one winner. If the contest is to see which theory can provide the best theory of why these two people got married, this line of thinking is that, if one particular sociological theory can be shown to be good, (1) all other sociological theories, cultural theories, psychological and genetic and historical theories must not be very good, and (2) no other theory could provide an equally good theory of why these two people got married.

I am inclined to reject both beliefs. Instead, I am inclined to believe that (1) if one theory is shown to be good, that tells us very little about the worth of rival theories, and (2) when it comes to comparing the goodness of theories, it is often the case that more than just one theory can have grounds for declaring itself one of the winners. It is hard enough to do research to see which theory is best (e.g. Hansen, 1958; McMullin, 1983; Howard, 1985). Whatever the case, it seems to make more sense for the rivals actually to be present and to compete with one another at the same contest.

Does determination of which theory is better help to make the competing theories better?

Suppose that there is a contest or series of contests, and one theory is declared the winner. The winning theory can use the trophy to provide its proponents with more confidence, to gain more proponents or to enter more contests. If the contest were between rival football teams or boxers, the contestants might use the contest to improve their game, get better, study their strengths and weaknesses to improve.

However, it is exceedingly rare that competing theories actually use the findings to help themselves to improve, get better, become better theories. Indeed, the spirit behind doing this kind of research has little if anything to do with enabling the competing theories to get better. This kind of research is almost solely aimed at showing that this particular theory is better than rival theories.

What research grounds would be sufficient for you to give up your theory in favor of the winning theory?

In several of the previous chapters, serious problems were evolved from a general idea that it seems to be exceedingly uncommon for proponents to identify the sufficient grounds for them to be willing to give up something of value. As applied to the present reason for doing research, the general idea evolves into a rather distinctive, specific and serious problem, namely that the proponents not only would abandon their prized theory, but in addition would take the further step of adopting the rival winning theory!

Picture a large body of studies showing that one theory was better than some other theory. Then what? What are we supposed to do differently? Would proponents of the winning theory expect proponents of the losing theory to concede the loss, to concede that the winning theory is indeed better, and that their own theory is defeated, the loser, not as good? Even if that is possible, which I doubt, what is the defeated proponent to do any differently than before? The answer, or at least one, is for the losing proponents to declare allegiance to the winner, to give up their losing theory in favor of the winner.

Even before the studies are run, imagine the researchers asking proponents of cognitive theory, Jungian theory and social learning theory to specify the research grounds they would accept as sufficient for them (1) to declare their theory as the loser and, therefore, (2) to give up their theory in favor of the winning theory. I believe the whole picture is so preposterous and fanciful that it qualifies as a whimsical myth (Mahrer, 1995).

How many bodies of studies can you find where each of the contesting theories laid out the sufficient research grounds before the studies were undertaken? I doubt if there were many. Can you find three?

How many instances can you find where rival theories actually declared the sufficient grounds and, after the studies were all done, publically declared that (1) their theory lost, was defeated by the winning theory, as evidenced by the research grounds that were agreed on, and (2) proceeded to give up their theory in favor of the winning theory? Has this happened often? Occasionally? Would you be impressed if you might find where it happened even once? My impression is that it has never occurred, with the exception of one instance or so of which I am unaware.

When it comes to comparing theories of psychotherapy, I believe that it is virtually impossible for proponents of competing theories to state the research grounds they would deem sufficient for them to give up their theory in favor of the winner. If no such grounds can be stated, it almost seems that, no matter which theory the researchers favor, the findings will almost certainly not be sufficient for proponents of the losing theory or theories to give up their theory in favor of whomever the researchers declare as the winning theory. And this raises a question: Why do the research in the first place?

Which theory a psychotherapist adopts: does research have a role?

Many researchers do research to show that one theory is better than rival theories on the understanding that research findings do, or at least ought to, play a significant role in determining which theory a psychotherapist adopts. If a body of studies compares social learning theory, humanistic theory and psychodynamic theory, the researcher usually believes that psychotherapists would or should adopt the winning theory. The picture is of psychotherapists accepting the research findings in deciding which theory to adopt. Beginning trainees should choose their theory on the basis of solid research. Practitioners should adopt whatever theory emerges as the research-declared winner.

I doubt if there is overwhelming research evidence that psychotherapists adopt their chosen theory largely on the basis of research declarations of which theory wins a competition, or even that such research contests play a significant role. I am not sure how or why most psychotherapists adopt whatever theory they adopt, but here are a few guesses.

One is that many psychotherapists adopt whatever theory they do partly because it offers a rather high goodness of fit with the way they already think, with their deep-seated notions and ideas about the way people are, the structure of personality, how a person got to be the way the person seems to be, how and why people feel good or bad, how and why people change. Many psychotherapists come equipped with such notions and ideas before they are in psychotherapeutic training, and before they adopt some formal theory or other.

A second is that psychotherapists adopt whatever theory they do on the basis of much the same considerations that might account for the professions they choose, their political choice, the person they live with and the way they choose to dress. Some may adopt existential theory because it is the departmental choice, outside the departmental offerings, aligns them with powerful philosophical thinkers, and they can be the local authority because few colleagues or anyone else is really an expert in existential theory. Choosing a theory as one's own can be understood by whatever principles you use to explain many other choices, few of which are explained by the findings of researchers.

Here are two reasons why a psychotherapist may end up having a psychoanalytic theory, an existential theory or some other kind of theory. Neither of these reasons has much to do with a psychotherapist studying research aimed at seeing which theory is best, weighing the findings and arriving at a rational judgement that here is the theory that is best supported by comparative studies and, therefore, it is the psychotherapist's choice.

If research does seem to play a virtually insignificant role in determining which theory a psychotherapist adopts, just why do researchers try to do research aimed at showing that one theory is better than this other theory or these other theories? Perhaps the researcher might find some other reason to do research on psychotherapy.

Can research show that one of several rival theories has a better explanation of research findings and facts?

One way of showing that a theory is better than its rivals is for a researcher to show that one theory is better than its rivals in providing an explanation for particular research findings and facts. This research starts by citing some phenomena, findings or facts that have been supported and confirmed by research. Here are some possibilities:

1. For most psychiatric/psychological problems and mental illnesses/disorders, short-term treatment is just as effective as long-term treatment.
2. The therapist–client relationship is an important determinant of successful outcome.
3. In long-term, intensive psychotherapy, there is frequently a reoccurrence of initial symptoms during the termination phase.
4. Success rates are higher when female patients are seen by female therapists rather than by male therapists.

The job is to see if one theory can be shown by researchers to be better than its rivals at providing a better explanation of any or all of these research findings and facts. Can this be done? Here are four reasons why research would have an exceedingly difficult time doing this:

1. One reason depends on whether you believe that there can be only one best, superior, explanation or that there can be several equally fine, worthwhile, sound explanations. Believing that there can be only one solid explanation of how and why the way the therapist and client are with each other seems to be closely related to what is called a successful outcome. I hold to a philosophy of science position in which there might well be a fine Jungian explanation, a well-done behavioral explanation, a solid explanation in terms of role theory, another excellent explanation in terms of sociological theory, and so on. If my theory can provide a fine explanation, and if I believe that your theory is also capable of providing an equally fine, but different, explanation, there is little basis for a researcher to set out to see which one theory can provide the one best explanation, as if there were just one best explanation.

2. Second, some researchers may firmly believe in a cluster of theories over here, and a cluster of research findings and facts over there. In this picture, the cluster of research findings and facts is unblemished by theories, it is neutral and free, objective and beyond arm's length from the theories. In this picture, the question stands with a sense of purity: which of these theories can provide the best explanation of those research findings and facts? However, there is another way of organizing this picture. Those research findings and so-called facts are produced by particular theories, are the products of particular theories, and are theory-driven, theory generated, theory produced. Very particular theories have special meaning for 'termination phase' and looking for a reoccurrence of 'symptoms'. Only particular theories give rise to and are devout proponents of 'mental illnesses' and the softer version: 'mental disorders'. Doing research to see which theory provides the best explanation loses much of its appeal when the question becomes 'Can rival theories offer a better explanation of research findings and facts that come from a particular theory, are sensible and meaningful mainly from and in that theory, and are factual mainly from within that particular theory?' I am inclined to answer no.

3. A third reason why there is little or no basis for doing research to see which of several rival theories can provide the best explanation is that some theories simply provide explanations with all the ease of a popcorn popper. Seeing whether a theory can provide the best explanation can easily mean that you are merely seeing whether some theory can spew out nice ample explanations. I have often turned to Jungian and psychoanalytic explanations, not because they are the best, but because they are so all purpose, and because they seem so rich, so full of a whole world of intrapsychic convolutions and intrigues. I have often turned to cognitive and behavioral explanations because they too are so all purpose, and seem so simple yet so rigorous and scientific sounding. Yet such theories are probably inadequate, not good, precisely because they produce such fine explanations on demand. 'Theories that can assimilate any state of affairs are inadequate precisely because they can do so' (O'Donohue, 1989, p. 1462). Doing research for this reason may not have much of a solid base.

4. A fourth reason is that researchers have yet to figure out a good way to do research to show that one of several rival theories has a better explanation of research findings and facts. Look at those research findings and facts, or put some others on the table. Then devise a rigorous study that can do a careful job of seeing and showing that one theory provides the best explanation. It may be more a problem for logicians and philosophers of science. Try to find a dozen studies that soundly and convincingly showed that one of several rival theories has a significantly

better explanation of research findings and facts that the researchers and the theories agreed are to be explained.

It seems to me that a strong case can be made that research cannot demonstrably be carried out to show that one of several theories has a better explanation of so-called research findings and facts.

Conclusions, serious problems and suggestions

A case has been presented that doing research to show that one theory is better than rival theories can be accompanied by a relatively unique set of problems that may well be sufficiently serious to effectively block or derail efforts to do research for this reason. The main conclusion consists of this case.

For researchers and others who can accept such a case, the suggestion is to take some time out in order to solve these serious problems for at least two purposes. One is to enable interested researchers to get on with doing research for this reason, provided that these serious problems can be solved, and these serious road blocks removed. A second reason is that solving these serious problems can help nudge the field of psychotherapy in the direction of a revolutionary shift forward. Here is a summary of some of these serious problems:

1. A serious problem occurs when theories are compared with each other, and the findings are generalized and extended to apply to theories that did not participate in the contest, or that were given little or no opportunity to participate in laying down the rules of the contest. The serious problem is how to arrange the contest and to apply its findings to theories that were bona fide contestants in the research.
2. It is somewhat common that research consists of a competition among several theories' ability to provide an explanation or conceptualization of a particular psychotherapeutic phenomenon. Under these conditions, a serious problem is that the field of psychotherapy has yet to devise rigorous and generally accepted criteria to determine that one theory's explanation or conceptualization is soundly, objectively, stringently and convincingly superior to the explanations and conceptualization of competing theories.
3. The roots of a serious problem lie in a case for a gaping hiatus between whatever theory a practitioner publicly proclaims and, on the other hand, the actual, working, theoretical principles that determine the practitioner's actual in-session operations. If this case holds, a serious problem is whether or not research findings can be sufficiently sound and robust to make a significant change in the actual, working,

theoretical principles that guide and determine the practitioner's actual, working, in-session operations.

4. There can be a package of serious problems in designing research to show that this theory is better than that theory or those rival theories. Here are some of these serious problems: (a) What are the acceptable research grounds for concluding that one theory is better than its rival or rivals? (b) How can research, comparing several theories with one another, be designed so that the findings can enable the competing theories to improve and advance? (c) To what extent are proponents of the rival theories ready and willing to identify and abide by the reasonable grounds they would accept as sufficient to abandon their theory, and to accept the superiority of the winning theory? (d) Does research play a relatively substantial or a minimal role in determining which theory a practitioner adopts?

5. What seems to be occurring as a common theme is that doing research for this reason is neither designed for nor especially able to help learn more and more of what psychotherapy can accomplish, or to learn better and better ways of helping to accomplish what psychotherapy can be found to accomplish.

CHAPTER 9

Does the research contribute to the cumulative body of psychotherapeutic knowledge?

This is perhaps the highest, most noble and most fundamental mission of research on psychotherapy. Major conferences 'documented that the basic aim of psychotherapy research was the advancement of knowledge' (Strupp, 1986a, p. 127; compare Rubenstein and Parloff, 1959; Strupp and Luborsky, 1962; Shlien et al., 1968). To appreciate this kind of research, the picture includes a presumed body of psychotherapeutic knowledge. There almost has to be a cumulative body of psychotherapeutic knowledge in order for research to contribute to it.

What are the pieces of knowledge in the cumulative body of psychotherapeutic knowledge?

It would be nice if there were an authoritative list of the pieces of knowledge in the cumulative body of psychotherapeutic knowledge. It would be nice if there were a place where we could read the pieces of knowledge that have been put into a body of knowledge about psychotherapy. We sometimes act as if there were indeed a body of research-approved psychotherapeutic knowledge. But I do not know where it is, and I have a strong suspicion that it does not really exist, although it is commonly cited that there is one somewhere.

Therefore, I have read a fair number of books and articles, searching for some actual pieces of knowledge in our cumulative body of knowledge. I have read the works of researchers, theoreticians, practitioners and educators/trainers, from a rather wide variety of perspectives and approaches. I have marked down whatever was presented as basic and fundamental pieces of accepted knowledge in the field of psychotherapy.

Below are some of these pieces of knowledge in the field of psychotherapy. They are in no special order. They range over various levels

133

of abstraction and generality, and they may be tightly consistent with each other or embarrassingly inconsistent or even contradictory.

Instead of looking for some way of questioning whether each piece of knowledge really belonged in the list, I just accepted when some authority said that this piece of knowledge is part of the cumulative body of knowledge in the field of psychotherapy. Some deal with practice, some with theory or research or education/training. Some may not even seem to deal with psychotherapy, but may appear more general, more basic or more from larger fields related to psychotherapy, yet they were presented by authorities as part of the cumulative body of knowledge in psychotherapy, so they are included.

How many of these specific pieces of cumulative knowledge would probably be sufficient to show what they are, that they are found in virtually every part of the field of psychotherapy, and that they are so dense and numerous that they almost blanket the entire field of psychotherapy? I doubt if a handful or so would be sufficient. The absence of any authoritative lists of the specific contents of the cumulative body of psychotherapeutic knowledge may well indicate the strength, breadth and depth of reluctance to know what the contents are, how numerous and how extensive.

Accordingly, what follows is a list of 75 items, taken almost verbatim from a large number of authoritative sources, representative of a broad spectrum of approaches, and covering psychotherapeutic theory, research, personality, psychopathology, psychotherapy, education and training (Mahrer, 2000a, 2003, 2004). Each item constitutes a statement of what an authority offered as a part of the cumulative body of psychotherapeutic knowledge.

Theory and research

1. There is a cumulative body of psychotherapeutic knowledge; research is a primary gatekeeper for what is admitted into or withdrawn from the cumulative body of psychotherapeutic knowledge.
2. Research is superior to theoretical or philosophical analysis in arriving at, extending or revising the cumulative body of psychotherapeutic knowledge.
3. The cumulative body of psychotherapeutic knowledge is relevant and applicable across virtually all psychotherapeutic theories and approaches.
4. Conceptual systems of psychotherapy are to include common foundations comprising fundamental truths, postulates and axioms.
5. There are generally accepted, rigorous criteria for judging the goodness, soundness and worth of theories of psychotherapy.

6. Once a theory of psychotherapy is conceived, it is subjected to research inquiry, examination and testing.
7. Prediction and explanation of empirically validated facts are important criteria for judging the worth of theories of psychotherapy.
8. Theories of psychotherapy are judged, examined and tested by deriving hypotheses that are subjected to scientific verification, confirmation, disconfirmation. refutation and falsification.
9. Exploratory searching and preliminary trying out are significant components of an initial research phase aimed at yielding hypotheses, which can be examined and tested scientifically.
10. Research is to confirm, verify, disconfirm, refute and falsify the tested hypothesis.
11. Controlled empirical research is superior to research that is not controlled empirical research.
12. Psychotherapy researchers are to be essentially unbiased, objective, free of theory-driven expectations, observations, pre-judgments.
13. The existence of a scientifically acceptable measure is evidence for the existence of the measured concept, construct or dimension.
14. Psychotherapy is usefully organized into psychotherapy process, post-treatment outcomes and the relationships between them.
15. The outcomes of psychotherapy can be rigorously assessed as successful, effective, beneficial, or not so, essentially apart from philosophical value systems.
16. New and improved psychotherapeutic methods and techniques are largely the products of research.
17. Meta-analysis is a powerful tool for analyzing the findings of a pool of psychotherapeutic studies.
18. Psychotherapeutic theories, orientations and approaches acquire, maintain or lose acceptability largely on the basis of careful evaluation of their conceptual soundness and clinical efficacy.
19. The ethical principles and code of conduct of psychologists are based on underlying premises that are essentially valid, sound, consistent, and have an evidential underpinning.
20. Biological, neurological, physiological and chemical events and variables are basic to psychological events and variables.
21. Bodily events and phenomena are to be described and understood in terms of the concepts and constructs of systems such as biology, neurology, physiology and chemistry.
22. Behavioral and neurophysiological data are generally harder, more observable, more objective and preferable to mentalistic data.
23. The brain is a basic determinant of human behavior.
24. Input from the past is stored in the brain and used in the form of concepts to process present input.

25. Human beings are essentially information-processing biological organisms.
26. Human beings have inborn, intrinsic, biological and psychological needs, drives, instincts and motivations; these include needs and drives for survival, sex, aggression, object seeking, contact/comfort.
27. There are biopsychological stages of human growth and development.
28. Behavior is a conjoint function of predominantly genetic endowment and environmental circumstances.
29. The person and the external world are integral independent entities that interact and affect each other.
30. Behavior and meaning are grasped through careful observation and measurement of the empirically determined relationships between the person and the external world.
31. Pain is aversive; behavior tends to reduce, avoid or eliminate pain.
32. Responses followed by satisfying consequences tend to be strengthened; those followed by unsatisfying consequences tend to be weakened.
33. The goal of psychological science is understanding, prediction and control of human behavior.
34. Causal determinants of human behavior generally lie in antecedent events.
35. Causal determinants of psychological problems generally lie in antecedent events, predominantly occurring in childhood.

Problems and psychopathology

36. There are mental illnesses, diseases and disorders.
37. The causal determinants of mental illnesses, diseases and disorders are predominantly genetic and environmental.
38. Interpersonal relationships, largely during infancy and childhood, are significant causal determinants of current interpersonal problems.
39. Interruption of physical–psychological contact between infant and mother is a significant causal determinant of abnormal development.
40. When there are multiple causal descriptions or explanations of a psychotherapeutic event: (a) only one is superior as more true, accurate, correct, and (b) an approach that incorporates multiple causal descriptions or explanations is superior to one that does not.
41. Clients seek psychotherapy for, and psychotherapy is, treatment of psychological–psychiatric problems, distress, mental disorders, personal difficulties and problems in living.
42. Deviant or aberrant behavior is caused by mental pathology, and it is the task of the mental health profession to identify and treat such mental disorders.

Psychotherapeutic practice

43. Psychotherapy is an interpersonal relationship that provides a corrective experience for problematic interpersonal relationships.
44. There is an intrinsic drive toward healthy normal functioning; psychotherapy removes blocks to intrinsic healing and growth.
45. The practitioner initially assesses and diagnoses the problem or mental disorder, and then selects and applies the appropriate treatment.
46. Psychotherapeutic change occurs predominantly by means of effective changes in clients' ways of understanding, making sense and meaning of and construing/constructing, their selves, lives, relationships and worlds.
47. The therapist–client relationship is a prerequisite to successful psychotherapy.
48. Therapists and clients attending to and talking to one another are a prerequisite to successful psychotherapy.
49. Empathic listening and responding are a prerequisite to successful psychotherapy.
50. Client expressiveness is an important factor in client productivity and involvement in successful psychotherapy.
51. Insight and understanding are a prerequisite to successful psychotherapy.
52. Interpretation is an effective intervention for enabling clients to know, become conscious and aware of deeper, unconscious, psychic material outside clients' awareness and consciousness.
53. Effective interpretations are parsimonious and close to the client's current understanding and affective experience.
54. There are common factors across successful and effective psychotherapies, and it is beneficial for research to identify them and for psychotherapies to incorporate them.
55. There is a relatively close, direct, logical relationship between the practitioner's theoretical approach to psychotherapy and the practitioner's actual, in-session operations, methods and working strategies.
56. There are differential treatments of choice for differential psychological problems and mental disorders.
57. Most psychotherapies yield generally equivalent outcomes.
58. Most psychotherapeutic theories and approaches may be rigorously identified and differentiated from one another.
59. Single approaches may be combined or integrated into a larger framework that is superior to any component approach.
60. Psychoanalysis is the treatment of choice for deep-seated personality change.

61. Behavioral therapies are the treatment of choice for simple phobias.
62. Psychopaths do not do well in intensive psychotherapy.
63. Therapists should not criticize or diminish clients' precarious state of self-esteem.
64. Clients with low ego strength and inadequate defenses may be harmed by excessive stress in psychotherapy.
65. Therapists should ensure that clients guard and control the outbreak of basic impulses.
66. Therapists should be alert to signs and symptoms of psychosis.
67. Therapists should be vigilant for suicidal ideation in depressed clients.
68. There is typically a recrudescence of initial symptomatology in the termination phase of intensive, long-term psychotherapy.
69. Psychotherapy is an applied wing of more basic and comprehensive sciences and fields of knowledge.

Education and training

70. Psychotherapeutic education is to include provision of knowledge in the cumulative body of psychotherapeutic knowledge.
71. Graduates of professional education and training in psychotherapy have scholarly knowledge of the field of philosophy of science.
72. Psychotherapeutic education is to include training in the common core of basic psychotherapy skills and methods.
73. Psychotherapeutic education teaches theories and approaches that are significantly different and more elevated than those of people outside formal psychotherapeutic education.
74. In general, graduates of degree-granting programs in mental health are significantly more effective in psychotherapy than actors with a week of training in the role of psychotherapists.
75. In general, significantly more years of academic training yields significantly higher levels of competence in psychotherapy.

Is the cumulative body of psychotherapeutic knowledge almost exclusively composed of esteemed absolute truths?

If we take a close look at each piece of knowledge in the cumulative body of psychotherapeutic knowledge, and if we ask how it got admitted into this body, almost all of them were simply admitted without having to pass any test of worthiness, without being scrutinized by some committee.

They are there largely because they were already esteemed absolute truths that somehow were dutifully respected as belonging in our cumulative body of psychotherapeutic knowledge. Perhaps the name ought to be changed to the cumulative body of esteemed absolute truths.

Esteemed absolute truths

From supposedly foundational sciences

A large proportion of psychotherapists assume a respectfully submissive stance to sciences that are presumed to be foundational, basic and fundamental to the field of psychotherapy. These sciences include experimental psychology, biology, neurology, physiology, and others such as chemistry and physics. Whatever these basic fields accept as basic truths are generally bequeathed into the cumulative body of psychotherapeutic knowledge. Their absolute truths are our absolute truths without question, without examination. We are politely respectful of our elders, especially those we regard as the powerful ones, and many of the items on the list come from these supposedly foundational sciences.

We teach our students that psychological events and variables are best grasped and understood when they are reduced to the underlying events and variables of the basic sciences. We require our students to have knowledge of the basic truths in the basic sciences of experimental psychology, biology, neurology, physiology, chemistry, and others. These basic truths sit in most favored chairs in the cumulative body of psychotherapeutic knowledge.

Spilled over from fashionable intellectual movements outside psychotherapy

If we poke around in the previous list of items from the cumulative body of knowledge, a fair number of bits and pieces were admitted mainly as esteemed absolute truths from intellectual movements outside the field of psychotherapy. We welcome into our cumulative body of knowledge what we believe are the esteemed absolute truths from fashionable intellectual movements such as deconstructionism, operationalism, feminism, postmodernism, functionalism, Marxism, chaos theory, structuralism, relativism, pragmatism, logical positivism, isomorphism, phenomenology, network theory, empiricism, cognitivism, constructivism, hermeneutics, eclecticism, humanism, behaviorism, connectionism.

Once the absolute truths of whatever outside intellectual movement is fashionable come into the near vicinity of our cumulative body of knowledge, the doors swing open, and they are respectfully welcomed inside.

From the great thoughts of great thinkers in and near psychotherapy

Just as in most religions, the field of psychotherapy is inclined to elevate the great thoughts of great thinkers into esteemed absolute truths. When we trace the origins of some pieces of knowledge, in our cumulative body of knowledge, they are found to come from the great thoughts of great thinkers such as Freud, Titchener, Watson, Mahler, Fechner, Murray, Skinner, Pavlov, Jung, Fenichel, Mowrer, James, Hull, Piaget, Allport, Kohut, Kelly, Maslow, and many other conceptual giants.

Collective psychotherapists collectively believed them to be esteemed absolute truths

Many psychotherapists know that this particular statement is an esteemed absolute truth mainly because most of their colleagues consider it to be an esteemed absolute truth. Each of a group of psychotherapists may not be especially certain about that particular proposition, but if most of these psychotherapists believed that their colleagues regarded the proposition as an esteemed absolute truth, the proposition is likely to become an esteemed absolute truth.

Once collective psychotherapists believe in an esteemed absolute truth, it has a way of taking on the trappings of an esteemed absolute truth, and it thereby becomes easier for collective psychotherapists to know that it really is an absolute truth. It takes on a history so that the esteemed absolute truth has a long and distinguished tradition. It is stamped by authorities as an esteemed absolute truth. It is passed on to generations of students as an esteemed absolute truth. It spawns hundreds of papers and articles and research studies, but it itself is rarely if ever inquired into, questioned or studied because it is an esteemed absolute truth.

Everyone knows there are mental illnesses and diseases because everyone knows this esteemed absolute truth is absolutely true. Feigl (1959) referred to these as doctrines that are assumed to be true without question, mainly because they were already assumed to be true, and cited examples such as the eros–thanatos doctrine, the assumption of an indestructible soul and the pleasure–pain principle. Indeed many bits and pieces of the cumulative body of knowledge are assumed to be esteemed absolute truths, mainly because collective psychotherapists assume that their colleagues accept them as esteemed absolute truths.

Resulting from faulty reasoning

It is one example of faulty reasoning when a large proportion of individual psychotherapists believe that most of their colleagues accept some proposition as an esteemed absolute truth, and when that is the main reason for the proposition to be accepted as an esteemed absolute truth. But it is not the only example of something being dubbed an esteemed absolute truth by faulty reasoning. Kantor (1950, p. 26) gives some examples of how a kind of spurious and questionable generalization gives some propositions the halo of esteemed absolute truths:

> Because some psychological activities constitute conditioning, this is true of all psychological events. Because statistics is a necessary procedure in treating data, it constitutes the scientific method. Personal or private knowledge is subjective, hence mental. Logic deals with deductive systems, hence all systems are deductive. Because one theory is faulty, its opposite is correct.

An embarrassing number of bits and pieces of our cumulative body of knowledge may well be dubbed esteemed absolute truths mainly because of some kind of faulty reasoning.

In general, a rather impressive case can be made that the cumulative body of psychotherapeutic knowledge is almost exclusively composed of esteemed absolute truths, and that research had embarrassingly little or no part to play in justifying or questioning or testing that esteem.

Is the cumulative body of psychotherapeutic knowledge universal or are there are independent temples, each with its own bible of psychotherapeutic truths?

In the cumulative body of knowledge in the field of physics, there is something called mass; physical objects possess a property called mass and this mass works on the basis of a law of inertia. Mass and the law of inertia do not cavalierly come and go whenever you move from one theory to another. In much the same way, the directions for how to use the cumulative body of psychotherapeutic knowledge include instructions that the contents are for just about every theory and approach to psychotherapy. Our contents include empirical truths, basic knowledge, basic facts and laws that are more important than any particular theory, that are to be saluted by virtually every law-abiding theory and approach. The very idea of a body of knowledge is to mean that it is the body of knowledge for just about everyone, and that includes all those theories and approaches to psychotherapy.

Such a case is appealing to whatever theory or approach is on top, in power and therefore able to define the contents of the currently fashionable body of knowledge. Insisting that all theories and approaches must accept the body of knowledge as eternal and universal is a useful way of maintaining its dominant grip on power, especially because the contents are blessed by the dominant theory and approach.

But there is another case that holds that the very notion of a universal, theory-free body of knowledge is a myth. According to this case, the actual contents are theory driven, come from some approach. Theories and approaches define their own supposed truths, basic facts, foundational observations (Chalmers, 1982); 'our theory literally determines how we see the world; no sense can be given, therefore, to "observation without a theory" or "direct observation from all theory"' (Kitchener, 1996, p. 112; compare Hansen, 1958; Kuhn, 1970; Feyerabend, 1971).

The case holds that, instead of a single, universal, theory-free and approach-free cumulative body of knowledge, a more usefully realistic picture is of each theory and approach having its own worshipped body of knowledge. The picture is of independent temples of truth, each with its own bible of truths, each with its own cumulative body of psychotherapeutic knowledge.

If we go inside the behavioral temple, we may hear the priests and the congregation reciting in respectful unison: 'Undesirable behavior itself, rather than some presumed underlying cause, is the focus of change; undesirable behavior is learned through the same processes by which other behavior is learned; and undesirable behavior can be modified by using psychological principles, especially conditioning principles' (O'Donohue, 1989, p. 1466).

According to Eagle (1984, 1993), if we enter the object relations temple, we may hear the priest solemnly pronouncing these two truths from its bible of eternal knowledge:

1. Human beings have intrinsic inborn needs for object seeking and contact comfort with mother
2. Interruption of physical contact between mother and infant leads to abnormal development. Amen.

At the same time, the Jungian priest is quoting from the Jungian bible that archetypes are embedded in the collective unconscious, whereas the priests for each therapeutic temple are devotedly incanting their own hallowed truths from their own respective bibles of cumulative knowledge.

It seems to me that the case for a universal body of knowledge is rather weak, and that a stronger case can be made in favor of independent temples, each with their own bibles of psychotherapeutic truths, with their own priests who guard the eternal truth of their bibles, with their own congregations of followers who believe in their own bibles, and with their own cadre of researchers who believe that they are the upholders of the contents of their bibles of eternal and universal knowledge.

Can the cumulative body of knowledge serve as a waste bin for studies typically labeled 'basic'?

It is understandable that practitioners might find little or no relevance in studies outside the practitioners' particular theory or approach, or studies on methods and techniques that particular practitioners do not use in their work. However, an embarrassing proportion of studies seem to be judged as irrelevant because what they study, and what their findings find, make essentially no difference to what the practitioners do, or might do, in their actual work.

It is common that some of these studies are labeled as 'basic', which usually means that they are essentially of little relevance. It is common that in their introduction and their section on discussion, the studies do their best to make a case that what they are studying, and their findings, are indeed relevant, or ought to be accepted as relevant, or will be seen in the future as being relevant. In other words, the studies are labeled basic and as contributing to the cumulative body of psychotherapeutic knowledge. In this sense, the cumulative body of knowledge unfortunately serves as a waste bin for so many studies that are otherwise essentially irrelevant.

Is research being done to look for general truths or to help advance the practice of psychotherapy?

Researchers can use psychotherapy as a window into studying human nature. Psychotherapy can then serve as the researcher's laboratory for studying human beings in general, e.g. the researcher may be interested in studying cognitive structure, ego defenses or relationships between the body and the mind, and the researcher finds psychotherapy as an especially worthwhile arena for study of those topics and in coming up with general truths about cognitive structure, ego defenses or body–mind relationships.

Researchers can also be on a quest for general truths that apply to psychotherapy. Research done for this mission aims at coming up with general truths about, for example, the nature of the therapist–client relationship or the attitudes toward psychotherapy in varying cultures.

Researchers who set out to find general truths may start with much the same topics as researchers whose aim is to advance the actual practice of psychotherapy, but the two sets of researchers will probably walk by each other without noticing. They are on different missions, looking for different things, e.g. both may start with the emotional state of the client, but the researchers who are looking for general truths might be after general truths about the relationships between clients' emotional state and perceptions of the therapists' emotional state (e.g. Saunders, 1999), whereas researchers seeking to advance the practice of psychotherapy might be more interested in finding ways that the therapist can use the clients' emotional state to deepen and enhance the therapist–client relationship.

There seems to be a significant difference between doing research to find general truths for the cumulative body of knowledge, and doing research to advance the actual in-session practice of psychotherapy.

The significant difference can show itself even in setting forth the intent of the study. Many researchers do believe in a knowable order and logic to the way psychotherapy works. There are laws and principles, and it can be the duty of research to uncover these natural laws and principles. It is fitting that the intent of the study is framed in terms of such laws and natural principles, e.g. a study may set out to examine this psychotherapeutic truth: in successful short-term psychotherapy, the helping alliance conforms to a U-shaped curve, starting high, then a trough occurs, and then it resumes its initial height (e.g. Kivlighan and Shaunessy, 2000). The very statement of what the study studies looks and sounds like a natural law or principle of psychotherapeutic truth. This is the way things are. These are the truths.

The researcher with a different mind-set, who is geared to advance the in-session working trade, might more probably be inclined to see what the therapists and clients do to raise or lower the therapeutic alliance. Such rises and falls would be thought to result more from therapists and clients than from some kind of natural law of the universal nature of the therapeutic alliance. Looking for general truths is often a different mind-set from looking for how to advance the in-session, working practice of psychotherapy.

What role does research play in putting something into or taking it out from the cumulative body of knowledge?

The traditional litany is that what is put in and kept in our cumulative body of knowledge is research approved, research tested, research examined and research confirmed. Trust the researchers. They are the faithful and devoted gate-keepers to our cumulative body of knowledge. In ours, as in most sciences, the rule is along these lines: 'If a belief is to count as genuine knowledge, then it must be possible to justify the belief by showing it to be true, or perhaps probably true, by appeal to appropriate evidence' (Chalmers, 1982, p. 114). Failure to pass this test can and will 'lead to the abandonment of cherished beliefs for which no empirical corroboration can be found' (Strupp, 1989, p. 717). I believe that both sides of this notion are reassuring myths. The case will be made that, relative to other factors, research plays little or no role in putting something into or removing it from the cumulative body of psychotherapeutic knowledge.

Is research done on the presumption of the truth of believed truths, thereby indirectly confirming the truth of the untested believed truths?

A great deal of research is done not to test a believed truth, but on the presumption that the believed truth is quite true. The more research is done on the presumption that this belief is true, the more the belief is entrenched as true. This is a very clever ploy because we can then claim that a lot of research has been done on the belief when really almost no research directly examined the belief.

Here is how the clever ploy works. Do not do research to test whether the notion of schizophrenia belongs in or out of the cumulative body of knowledge. Instead, do research on whether schizophrenia is caused by these blood chemicals, these inherited factors, these environmental variables. Study how schizophrenogenic mothers facilitate schizophrenia in their children. Do research on which drugs help to cure schizophrenia. Do research on how people with schizophrenia score on loads of personality tests. Compare those with schizophrenia and others on short-term memory, ability to form lasting relationships, finger dexterity. The more you compile a body of studies on schizophrenia, the more you entrench its truth, and you have accumulated hundreds or thousands of studies without ever examining the truth of this thing called schizophrenia!

By using this ploy, we can invent personality disorders, and slide them into the cumulative body of knowledge without ever doing research to see if any of them are entitled to be in this esteemed body of knowledge. If we do enough studies comparing 'phrenophobia' and 'bipolar personality disorder' and 'schizothymic personality disorder', we can probably get all of them into the cumulative body of knowledge. And it can be justifiably proclaimed that there was a fair amount of research on all three. By the way, there is a fair amount of research comparing 'schizotypal personality disorder' and 'bipolar personality disorder' (e.g. Spitzer, Endicott and Gibson, 1979; Kernberg and Clarkin, 1994). Doing research on something without really doing research directly on it is a clever and effective ploy.

Using the very same ploy, you can entrench almost any piece of supposed knowledge in the cumulative body of knowledge without ever endangering its removal. Do research on the safe presumption that the therapist–patient relationship is a prerequisite to psychotherapeutic change, but make sure that you never test this belief directly. When you have hundreds or thousands of studies done on the safe presumption of the truth of the therapist–patient relationship, that belief is smugly entrenched in the cumulative body of knowledge and it has safely escaped direct examination!

It is a clever ploy to assert that there has been a great deal of research done on this particular piece of the cumulative body of knowledge. But if you are interested enough to take a next step of actually looking at all those studies, the picture becomes far more skeptical. Almost all of the studies were done as if it were true that the piece of knowledge were true. It almost seems as if the more honest statement is that research helps something get into the cumulative body of knowledge by producing a body of studies on the safe presumption that it is true, rather than directly examining the candidate itself.

Is the evidence for one belief typically another belief, rather than research?

Picture a number of proponents who are trying to get this candidate into the cumulative body of knowledge: therapeutic change is fostered by insight and understanding of early childhood relationships. Or picture proponents looking for ways of keeping this belief safely in the cumulative body of knowledge. How can these proponents achieve what they seek to achieve?

The proponents hold a meeting. How about doing research? Research would help, right? A seasoned and effective lobbyist has a better idea. Let's find a truth that is already a respected member of the cumulative body of knowledge. Citing that one should pave the way for our candidate. They find one: childhood experiences determine adult functioning. If childhood experiences determine adult functioning, it can be easy to accept that therapeutic change is fostered by insight and understanding of early childhood relationships. The proponents try out this ploy. It works. Who needs research?

The old boys' and girls' network confidently marches an extended family of beliefs right into the cumulative body of knowledge, and effectively keeps it there, quite safe from any threat of threatening inquiry. Each belief protects and is protected by its neighbors. Question any one, and protective fingers point toward a number of justifying others until the questioner is frozen and confused in the hall of mirrors. In this effective ploy, research emerges as irrelevant and ineffective (Mahrer, 2000a).

If someone dares to muck up the works by insisting on evidence, never fear. Simply accommodate the researcher into the infinite regress of the pursuit of evidence, and you will probably never hear anything further from the haplessly lost researcher.

> If some statement is to be justified, then this will be done by appeal to other statements which constitute the evidence for it. But this gives rise to the problem of how the statements constituting the evidence are themselves to be justified. If we justify them by further appeal to more evidential statements then the problem repeats itself and will continue to repeat itself unless a way can be found to halt the infinite regress that threatens.
>
> Chalmers (1982, p. 114)

The strategy is that evidence for one belief consists of one or more related neighboring beliefs. This strategy unfolds quite well without the distraction of research.

Is there a place for research on what is basically accepted as true by assumption, axiom or definition?

A large number of the bits and pieces of the cumulative body of knowledge are there mainly because they are simply accepted as true, assumed to be true or regarded as axiomatically true, or simply true by definition. Research had little or nothing to do with their being seen as true, put inside the cumulative body of knowledge, or with questioning whether or not they belong there.

In Euclidian geometry it is accepted that through two points in space there always passes one and only one straight line. Where did this come from? It is just a starting point, an assumption, an axiom, a definitional truth. It was not the culmination of a body of studies, nor is it very likely that studies can remove it from Euclidian geometry. If we shift over to the field of psychotherapy, here are two pieces from many lists of what is included in the cumulative body of knowledge:

1. Psychological events are reducible to more basic biophysiological events.
2. An individual is a part of a larger encompassing system.

It is highly unlikely that these truths became part of the cumulative body of knowledge because of research, nor that they will be removed because of the findings of research.

The field of mathematics includes a notion that $3 + 2 = 5$, and it is essentially fruitless to try to prove or disprove this by research. And this is so because the symbols "$3 + 2$" and "5" denote the same number: they are synonymous by virtue of the fact that the symbols "2," "3," "5," and "+" are *defined* (or tacitly understood) in such a way that the above identity holds as a consequence of the meaning attached to the concepts involved in it' (Hempel, 1953, p. 149).

In much the same way, a great deal of what is already included in the cumulative body of psychotherapeutic knowledge is true mainly because they are already accepted as true, and 'cannot be contraindicated by any experiment because they constitute in reality *definitions*' (Duhem, 1953, p. 247).

Take, for example, the definition of reinforcement in the law of effect, both of which are in the cumulative body of knowledge. If the definition of reinforcement includes that which, contingent on behavior, tends to increase the probability of that behavior, failure can be taken as evidence of the absence of reinforcement rather than disconfirmation of the law of effect (Erwin, 1997). What is defined as true is true by definition and is out of research bounds.

Syllogistic thinking starts with premises accepted as true because they are accepted as true:

All men are mortal; Socrates is a man; therefore, Socrates is mortal.

In the field of psychotherapy, we have hundreds of basic premises:

All people have inborn sexual drives; Socrates is a person; therefore Socrates has inborn sexual drives.

We start from hundreds of premises, assumptions, axioms and definitional truths, and generate hundreds more by syllogistic thinking, none of which is the product of research.

Research plays little or no role in putting something into or removing it from the cumulative body of knowledge when the knowledge is already accepted as true by assumption, axiom or definition.

If a researcher believes research is true, can the researcher find a way to show that it is true?

Many researchers have solid faith in the truth of their beliefs. They know that their truths are indeed true. What they know is true is already a part of the researchers' cumulative body of knowledge. What may be lacking is research confirmation of the truth of what they know to be true.

Researchers have plenty of options in doing the right kind of research to show that what they know belongs in the cumulative body of knowledge can be shown to be a part of the cumulative body of knowledge. Researchers are adept at searching through the literature to find friendly studies as background and support for their cumulative piece of knowledge. Researchers are clever in stating the right hypothesis in just the right way. There are plenty of different kinds of research designs and methodologies to choose from. Researchers can have little trouble searching through the many tests and questionnaires and instruments to find the ones that are friendly to what the researcher wants to show is true. There are plenty of statistics to choose from in order to use the right one to show the truth of what the researcher knows must be true.

A researcher with faith can be persistent in coming up with the right findings. It may take some careful tinkering with the raw data and the raw findings to find the findings that are friendly. It may take an emphasis on this part of the array of findings, the part that shows the truth of what the research sets out to show is true. It may take some clever wording to put the right spin on the findings. It may even take a further study, modified so as to show what the researcher is so inclined to show. Whatever it takes, the persistent and clever researcher can find the truth of what the researcher knows belongs in the cumulative body of knowledge.

Suppose that the researcher truly believes that (1) religious and spiritual issues have a role in psychotherapy and counseling or (2) there are psychological differences between women and men. It would not be difficult to devise study after study to uphold what the researcher is convinced belongs in the cumulative body of knowledge. The researcher could, for example, show that clients are quite ready and willing to discuss religious and spiritual issues with their therapists or counselors by asking clients if they would like to discuss these matters, and then conclude that clients are quite willing to discuss religious and spiritual matters with their therapists or counselors (e.g. Rose, Westefeld and Ansley, 2001). When sufficient research is done by enough recognized researchers, and the conclusions are politically well managed, it can almost be assured that the cumulative body of knowledge will include these two beliefs.

Suppose that two researchers are interested in studying the generally accepted truth that dreams are unique and special, and working with dreams adds something unique and special to psychotherapy. Each researcher meets their research team, and comes up with a design and methodology for carrying out their study. The first researcher truly believes that dreams are indeed special and unique. The first researcher is a classic psychoanalyst. The design and methodology ooze the truth that dreams are unique and special. The therapists are all classic psychoanalysts who value dream work. The patients are suitable for classic psychoanalysis. The design focuses on special sessions that reflect successful use of dream work. The entire research team is composed of classic psychoanalysts. It is highly likely that the findings will confirm that dreams add a unique and special element to therapeutic work.

But let us compare the design with one used by the second researcher who has a belief that what is unique and special in sheer dream work is the three-step procedure that the therapist uses in working with dreams. This second design and methodology do not ooze faith in the uniqueness and specialness of dreams. Instead, the design and methodology include therapists who are psychology students with approximately one practicum experience and 15 hours of training in the researcher's own three-step sequence of working with clients, including clients' dreams, and in which dreams are not used to get at the unique and special deep-seated material characteristic of psychoanalytic or Jungian dream analysis, and the research team is composed almost exclusively of psychology students (Hill et al., 2000).

The two researchers started from the same kind of supposed truth of the uniqueness and specialness of dreams. Yet the missions of the two researchers differed so much that their respective designs and methodologies oozed their different missions, even if their respective designs and methodologies were equally careful, rigorous and scientific.

What is almost rarely published is a study in which the devoutly believing researcher confesses that the devout belief was wrong, did not belong in the cumulative body of knowledge. It is rare that the researcher confesses that this study or series of studies shows that what the researcher truly knew belonged in the cumulative body of knowledge turns out to be wrong. Instead, it is almost always the case that, if the researcher truly believes it is true, the researcher can find some way to show that it is indeed true.

Can research remove anything from the cumulative body of knowledge when proponents are unwilling or unable to state the reasonable acceptable grounds?

Picture a researcher holding a meeting with 10–30 or more proponents, and representatives of a much larger number of proponents, of some hallowed piece of knowledge, some accepted truth, belief or factual assertion in the cumulative body of knowledge. The researcher wants to know what reasonable research grounds the proponents would accept as sufficient for removal from the cumulative body of knowledge. Do you believe the proponents would accept the researcher's offer? I doubt it. Do you believe the proponents would actually come up with grounds that the researcher could use? I doubt it. Then why should the researcher try to do the research in the first place (Mahrer, 1995)? Good question.

I have asked whole audiences of proponents of the therapist–client relationship or helping alliance being requisite for successful therapeutic change to state the reasonable research grounds they would accept as sufficient to give up that hallowed belief. Among the more polite responses were the following:

1. It is not a belief; it is true.
2. How dare you even question this truth!
3. What are you really after by even raising these ridiculous questions?

I tried a different tack. 'A prominent researcher wrote the following. Do you agree with this statement?' Then I read the following: 'Research has sharply etched the overriding significance of the interpersonal relationship between patient and therapist as the vehicle for therapeutic change' (Strupp, 1989, p. 723). Almost everyone agreed. Some wanted to replace the phrase 'the vehicle' with 'a vehicle'. Then I said: 'Another prominent researcher wrote the following. Do you agree with this statement?' I read the following, which I made up: 'Research has amply demonstrated that the interpersonal relationship between patient and therapist is not a vehicle for therapeutic change.' The audience's responses included things like: 'That's wrong! . . . How could that be?. . . Was that published in a good journal? . . . You made that up!' It is so gratifying to witness so many psychotherapists who are open to evidential grounds for maintaining or letting go of precious beliefs.

Picture a distinguished team of researchers asking classic psychoanalytic therapists what reasonable research grounds they would accept as sufficient to give up their hallowed role of the neutral removed analyst. The researchers could probably put aside their notebooks because the psychoanalysts are too clever to let themselves be ensnared in such a game. The distinguished team of Strupp, Fox and Lessler (1969) would have real trouble trying to convince their audience that they reviewed studies and concluded that there is no longer a justified place for the role of the neutral removed psychoanalyst. When an audience is unwilling or unable to state the reasonable research grounds they would regard as sufficient to give up a precious part of their body of knowledge, researchers would be wise to find something else to do, and stop trying to mess with a group's precious body of knowledge.

Tough-minded, hard-thinking, research-valuing behaviorists ought to be eager to state the reasonable research grounds they would accept as sufficient to give up their hallowed truths. Sorry. They seem to be equally vigilant and clever at avoiding such a game, at protecting, sheltering their central beliefs from sufficient grounds for being falsified, refuted, given up:

> The hard core of behavior therapy contains central beliefs that are not falsifiable. . . . For example, the hard core of behavior therapy contains sentences such as, 'Undesirable behavior itself, rather than some presumed underlying cause, is the focus of change'; 'Undesirable behavior is learned

through the same processes by which other behavior is learned'; and 'Undesirable behavior can be modified by using psychological principles, especially conditioning principles.' The statements in the hard core . . . are sheltered from refutation.

O'Donohue (1989, p. 1466)

If I asked these behavior therapists what reasonable research grounds they would accept as sufficient for them to give up any or all of these three propositions, these accepted truths, they would probably sound a lot like the psychoanalytic therapists, or almost anyone else whom I dared to ask for such reasonable grounds they would accept as sufficient to give up their preciously clung to bits and pieces of their body of knowledge. What a pity.

Many of my psychotherapy colleagues, theorists and researchers, practitioners and educators/trainers tell me that there are some patients who cling to their preciously held beliefs in spite of any evidence to the contrary, in spite of the therapists' best efforts to get the poor patients to see reality, to see that their absolute truths may not be so true. If these patients cling to these beliefs to such an extent that there are no reasonable grounds, no evidence at all, that would be sufficient for those patients to be willing to admit those beliefs are wrong, can be given up, my therapist colleagues assure me that these patients are out of touch with reality, psychotic, paranoid, demented, mentally ill, severely pathological, crazy. I know my colleagues are grateful to me when I carefully point out how such respected professional reasoning means that these colleagues are thereby equally out of touch with reality, psychotic, paranoid, demented, mentally ill, severely pathological, crazy.

If hard research plays little or no role in taking out bits and pieces from the cumulative body of knowledge, what accounts for their exit after 50 or 100 years or so? Our cumulative body of knowledge no longer includes truths about wandering wombs or masturbation leading to insanity. So what happened? Perhaps the gradual erosion occurs more by changes in what is fashionably believed to be true than from the efforts of hard-working researchers. Perhaps the contents seem to 'rise and decline, come and go, more as a function of baffled boredom than anything else; and the enterprise shows a disturbing absence of that cumulative character that is so impressive in disciplines like astronomy, molecular biology, and genetics' (Meehl, 1978, p. 807). This answer is echoed by others: 'The degree to which a given form of understanding prevails or is sustained across time is not fundamentally dependent on the empirical validity of the perspective in question, but on the vicissitudes of social processes' (Gergen, 1985, p. 268).

Can research remove anything from the cumulative body of knowledge when proponents can so easily find other things to blame?

Proponents of whatever is in the cumulative body of knowledge usually have an effective cadre of hired theoreticians, researchers and lawyers whose job it is to protect against dangerous findings and charges by putting the blame on all sorts of other things. The piece of knowledge or foundational truth is protected because these hired hands put the blame on at least five kinds of other things.

The hired hands can attack the connection between the tested hypothesis and the endangered piece of knowledge or foundational truth. The researcher studied the wrong hypothesis. The hypothesis was not logically derived from the foundational truth. The supposedly close and threatening connection between the hypothesis and the foundational truth was in fact only loose or circumstantial, or perhaps was too indirect and specious.

The design and methodology were poor. Look at the sample or at the weak control group. The statistics were not good, inappropriate, not done correctly.

If something has to be sacrificed, there are usually plenty of secondary and auxiliary propositions, corollaries and principles surrounding the foundational belief, and filling the logical space between the foundational belief and the negative findings. Pick one or more of them to sacrifice.

Attack the body of negative studies. There were only two or too few negative studies. You need more. Bring in your own expert researchers to defend the foundational belief. If there are seven negative studies and five friendly studies, claim that the body of studies is inconclusive. No matter how many unfriendly studies are presented, claim that is not enough.

Attack the researchers. They were not sufficiently neutral and objective. They came from an enemy camp. The researchers published their findings in lesser or unfriendly journals. The history of the researchers showed that they were unfriendly to the foundational belief. The researchers were unseasoned, inexperienced, not qualified experts.

With a proper defense team, proponents can easily find other things to blame so that research is unable to remove anything precious from the cumulative body of knowledge.

Is it possible for research to remove anything that is so loose, vague and ambiguous that it virtually defies disproof?

Many of the pieces of knowledge in the cumulative body of knowledge include key words, terms, elements that are so loose, vague and ambiguous that the pieces of knowledge are quite safe. These pieces of knowledge defy research showing that they are wrong, false, disproved. A researcher would almost certainly have such a hard time trying to pin it down, trying to get a real grasp on it, that the researcher understandably gives up in utter frustration (compare Erwin, 1992; Mahrer, 2000a).

It is not so much that these words and terms are unreal, that they are constructs or abstract concepts. The problem is that they are so loose, vague and ambiguous. It is deceptively easy and common to talk about psychoanalytic ego, id and superego. But pity the poor researcher who sets out to question, maybe even to disprove, pieces of knowledge that include elements such as ego, id and superego. 'Freud . . . gives us no rules for actually finding the ego, id, and super-ego as a scientist should. They are not entities occurring in the world like Mendel's genes, or black holes' (Heaton, 1976, p. 81). A researcher is entitled simply to give up on attempts to remove pieces of knowledge that include words and terms such as ego, id and superego.

In much the same way, the researcher is entitled to keep his or her hands off pieces of knowledge including words and terms such as conflict resolution, schizophrenia, identity diffusion, empathy, cognitive permeability, coping skills, locus of control, stimulus salience, ego boundary, unconscious mechanism, quality of the alliance, growth process, autonomy, extraversion, self-concept, perceptual incongruence, maladaptive reaction, evocative unfolding, cognitive map, conflict split, depressive residual, nodal symptom, need for affiliation, ego lacunae, attribution style, character style, working through, narcissistic state, ego state, pathological regression, degree of synergy, stress response syndrome, and many many more.

Quite aside from how these pieces of knowledge managed to get inside the cumulative body of knowledge in the first place, their component parts, elements, words, terms and phrases can be so loose, vague and ambiguous that they successfully defy disproof or even falling inside most researchers' nets (Mahrer, 2000a).

Does research play an important role, or little or no role, in putting something into or removing it from the cumulative body of knowledge? The case I have put together leans hard toward an answer that research plays little or no role at all.

Does cumulative knowledge of research-supported therapies and therapy relationships define what psychotherapy is and is not for?

In recent years, task forces and reviews of research have provided research-based answers to at least two important questions for the field:

1. What are the research-supported therapies and therapeutic treatments (Task Force on Promotion and Dissemination of Psychological Procedures, 1995; Chambless et al., 1996, 1998; Chambless and Hollon, 1998; Chambless and Ollendick, 2001)?
2. What are the research-based therapy relationships, including relevant therapist and client qualities and characteristics (Norcross, 2001, 2002; Steering Committee, 2001)?

As a result, the cumulative body of knowledge now includes research-based 'practice guidelines' for how to do psychotherapy (Barlow, 1994; Hayes et al., 1995; Calhoun et al., 1998; Chambless and Hollon, 1998; Nathan, 1998; Persons and Silberschatz, 1998; Norcross, 2001, 2002; Steering Committee, 2001; Westen and Morrison, 2001).

Perhaps, even more, the cumulative body of psychotherapeutic knowledge now seems to include something that had been missing, namely a research-based identification of what psychotherapy is for, what it can provide, achieve, accomplish. Until recently, there was essentially only a loose and non-research-based answer to the question of what psychotherapy is for, with an almost contentless category of 'improvement' or 'satisfactory outcome', but lacking a clarified, research-based content of the meaning of improvement, satisfactory outcome or what psychotherapy is for. By examining the taskforce reports and their reviews of research, the cumulative body of psychotherapeutic knowledge is much closer to being able to include a research-based, more careful clarification of what psychotherapy is for:

1. Psychotherapy is for 'presenting complaints,' although research has yet to identify and clarify which kinds of 'presenting complaints' qualify or fail to qualify as being within the scope of what psychotherapy is for, e.g. complaints about the rising price of rhubarb at the grocery store or complaints to the mechanic that the car now stalls more than before.
2. Psychotherapy is for 'psychological problems', although research has yet to identify and clarify which problems are or are not especially 'psychological', e.g. an increase of acidity in the local drinking water or a decrease in the value of the national currency in international markets.
3. Psychotherapy is for 'symptoms', although research has yet to identify and clarify what the symptoms are symptoms of, and which symptoms are or are not within the province of psychotherapy, e.g. slurred speech and reduced eye–hand co-ordination after drinking four beers, or a sudden clutching up of throat muscles and inability to breathe after devouring the chicken salad.
4. Psychotherapy is for mental illnesses and disorders as defined by an official diagnostic nomenclature of mental illnesses and disorders.

The other side of these research-based answers to what psychotherapy is for is that psychotherapy is to substantially reduce these states or conditions, with a heavy emphasis on the client's attaining or being restored to what is regarded as a normal range of functioning (Jacobson, Follette and Revenstorf, 1984; Kendall and Grove, 1988; Jacobson and Truax, 1991; Kendall, 1998).

Nor do the task force reports and their reviews of research close the doors to additional possibilities of what psychotherapy can be for, e.g. mention is made of studies using 'general measures of functioning and quality of life' (Chambless and Hollon, 1998, p. 10), although examinations of these studies suggested that the focus was commonly on the more negative side of 'global impairment' (Telch et al., 1995; Gladis et al., 1999). The reports even mention 'enhanced coping with life circumstances', whereby psychotherapy may be conceived as 'a practice composed of sustained conversations with the aim of assisting another to resolve or cope better with circumstances' (Johnson and Sandage, 1999, p. 2; compare Patterson and Hidore, 1997; Lewis, Amini and Lannon, 2000; Bohart, 2002).

In addition, the task force reports and their reviews of research do not wholly exclude what may be called 'personality change', although this is far from a featured research-based answer to what psychotherapy is for, e.g. there are frequent references to Rogers' classic 1957 paper on his enunciation of the necessary and sufficient relationship factors, although it almost seems that research reports fail to acknowledge that the title of his paper cited the necessary and sufficient conditions for 'therapeutic personality change', i.e. 'change in the personality structure of the individual, at both surface and deeper levels, in a direction which clinicians would agree means greater integration, less internal conflict, more energy utilizable for effective living; change in behavior away from behaviors generally regarded as immature, and toward behaviors regarded as mature' (Rogers, 1957, p. 95).

For perhaps the first time in its history, the field can establish research-based boundaries of what psychotherapy is and is not especially for. The field's task forces and reviews of research have established that psychotherapy is mainly for presenting complaints, psychological problems and symptoms, and mental illnesses and disorders, with the aim of providing treatment, and helping the clients to achieve or return to normal functioning. The boundaries are now becoming increasingly clear, thanks to research, about what psychotherapy is and is not mainly for.

For perhaps the first time, many psychotherapies now have research-based grounds for proclaiming that (1) their aims and goals, what they are for and the directions of change they value, fall outside the boundaries of the task force reports and their reviews of research, and (2) these psychotherapies are thereby not bound by the 'practice guidelines' that apply to psychotherapies inside the boundaries.

In other words, the task forces and their reviews of research have essentially defined two systems of psychotherapies, depending on whether they fall inside or outside the boundaries of what the task forces and their reviews of research identify that psychotherapy is for. Perhaps even more important, each system of psychotherapies can have their own valued aims and goals, their own list of valued therapies, their own valued therapy relationships and their own 'practice guidelines'.

My own experiential psychotherapy falls outside the boundaries of what the task forces and their reviews of research identify their psychotherapies are for, their own aims and goals. Their criteria of research-supported therapies, therapy relationships and 'practice guidelines' do not apply to my experiential psychotherapy. My impression is that the same holds for a fair number of other psychotherapies, both in and near the mainstream. In this important sense, we are indebted to the work of the task forces and their reviews of research.

Conclusions, serious problems and suggestions

Doing research to contribute to the cumulative body of psychotherapeutic knowledge can seem to be perhaps the highest and most noble mission of the researcher. One's contribution to this body of knowledge can qualify as an honor, a source of prideful achievement and accomplishment for the research, an inspiration to one's colleagues and young researchers.

And, yet, this chapter has presented a case that doing research for this reason is almost assuredly tied to a relatively unique set of serious problems that effectively block and derail this kind of research, stamp it as essentially fruitless from the start. This is the main conclusion.

Accordingly, for researchers and others who can appreciate such a case, the suggestion is to take some time out in order to solve those serious problems so that researchers can do research for this reason without being effectively road blocked from the start. In addition, solving these serious problems can help to pave the way toward a genuine revolution in the field of psychotherapy. Here is a summary of some of these serious problems:

1. If there is something called a cumulative body of psychotherapeutic knowledge, a serious problem is for the field of psychotherapy to spell out the actual contents. Although there may be frequent allusions to such a cumulative body of knowledge, and although there may be scattered mentions of occasional bits and pieces, it appears that the field

has yet to provide a reasonably authoritative, formal statement of the comprehensive contents, and this seems to stand as a serious problem.

2. A second serious problem is whether a stronger case can be made for (a) a single, grand cumulative body of psychotherapeutic knowledge; (b) relatively separate and distinctive cumulative bodies of knowledge representing different therapeutic systems and approaches; or (c) a somewhat smaller cumulative body of knowledge made up of the common ingredients across the various cumulative bodies of knowledge of the various therapeutic systems and approaches.

3. In its more general form, a serious problem may be stated as follows: 'What are the major determinants of what is included, excluded or removed from the cumulative body of psychotherapeutic knowledge?' Stated in a more specific form, the serious problem is: 'To what extent is research a predominant, moderate or minor determinant relative to such other determinants as the currently fashionable intellectual movements, the currently popular theoretical zeitgeist, commonly accepted psychotherapeutic truths, implicitly assumed psychotherapeutic canons, dictums and axiomatic truths, established and traditional clinical lore, the realistic practicalities of current political, economic and interprofessional forces, and the beliefs of currently regnant psychotherapeutic systems and approaches?'

4. If the cumulative body of psychotherapeutic knowledge is mainly the property of the currently regnant psychotherapeutic systems and approaches, a serious problem may be stated as follows: 'Are therapies falling outside the currently regnant therapies (a) to abide by, accept, conform to and obey the currently fashionable cumulative body of knowledge, or (b) to be welcomed as legitimately falling outside the scope of the regnant therapies' cumulative body of knowledge, i.e. the contents don't apply to them?'

For example, in reviewing research and reviews of research, task force reports have contributed to the cumulative body of knowledge by identifying research-supported therapies and therapy relationships. If the preponderance of the research includes a relatively common acceptance of psychotherapy as treatment of presenting complaints, psychological problems, symptoms and mental disorders, the serious problem is whether or not the cumulative body of knowledge is extended to, and should apply to, therapies with purposes and aims that fall outside the commonly accepted purposes and aims. In large part, the answer depends on whether or not the answer comes from the regnant therapies or the excluded rogue therapies, and therein lies the crux of the serious problem.

5. Through this and the preceding chapters, one common theme is that each reason is neither designed for nor especially able to learn more

and more of what psychotherapy can accomplish, or to learn better and better ways of helping to accomplish what psychotherapy can accomplish. It seems that precious little, if any, research is aimed at discovering what has yet to be discovered, and this applies to research aimed at contributing to a cumulative body of psychotherapeutic knowledge, including research aimed at putting a research stamp of approval on given therapies and therapy relationships.

CHAPTER **10**

The discovery-oriented approach to research on psychotherapy

There are at least three ways of describing this approach to research on psychotherapy, to tell what it is and how it differs from most of the other reasons for doing research on psychotherapy:

1. The discovery-oriented approach is a way of discovering more and more of what psychotherapy can achieve and help to bring about, and better and better ways of achieving what psychotherapy can achieve. In this sense, the title of this chapter may have been 'To discover more and more of what psychotherapy can achieve, and better and better ways of achieving what psychotherapy can achieve'.

   The field has some idea of what valued changes can be achieved by means of psychotherapy, both inside and outside the sessions. The purpose of this kind of research is to search for more and more of what psychotherapy can achieve. The field has some idea of what psychotherapy can do to help bring about these valuable changes. The purpose of this research is to find better and better ways of helping to bring about these valuable changes.

2. The discovery-oriented approach seeks to open new territory, to push the envelope, to keep expanding the frontiers, to explore new ground, to uncover the secrets of psychotherapy, to know what we do not yet know. We have some idea of what psychotherapy can help to achieve. What more can be achieved? We have some idea of how to achieve what we believe we can achieve. What are some better and better ways of achieving what we can now achieve and what psychotherapy is capable of achieving?

   The hallmark of this reason for doing research is to discover, rather than to confirm or check out or put to the test, what we may already believe, think we know and can do. The spirit of the discovery-oriented approach is to complement the other reasons for doing research on psychotherapy, rather than to replace these other reasons.

3. The aim of discovery-oriented research is to help to discover what psychotherapy can become, what it can be and do. The aim of discovery-oriented research is to help foster the genuine evolution of psychotherapy, to foster its development and change. If discovery-oriented research is successful, what psychotherapy can become, 100 years or so from now, may bear only historical kinship with what psychotherapy looks like today. The psychotherapy of today may be the roots of what the psychotherapy of the future can do, achieve and look like. This is the spirit and mission of the discovery-oriented approach to psychotherapy research.

This chapter is longer than the others. Perhaps the main reason is that the 'discovery-oriented approach' to psychotherapy research is relatively uncommon in comparison with the others. Accordingly, in addition to discussing this reason for doing psychotherapy in the same way as I discussed the previous reasons, I want to provide a more detailed introduction for researchers who might find this approach appealing.

There are others who are pioneering this approach to psychotherapy research (e.g. Elliott, 1983a, 1984; Rice and Greenberg, 1984). However, in this chapter I emphasize my own way of doing discovery-oriented psychotherapy research (Mahrer, 1985, 1988a, 1996a, 1996b; Mahrer and Boulet, 1999), although I encourage interested readers to study the versions spelled out in the work of Robert Elliott, Leslie Greenberg, and others.

Do we generally know most of what psychotherapy can be and how to do it, or are there vast undiscovered worlds to explore?

Do you believe that we know perhaps most of what there is to be known about how to do psychotherapy, what happens in fine sessions, what this thing called psychotherapy is? Of course there is always room for finding something new, but do we generally know most of what there is to be known, or do you picture vast undiscovered worlds that we know almost nothing of? This is more than just an interesting topic to talk about, because the picture you have goes a long way to determining whether or not you have the research fire for research to discover how to do psychotherapy. If there is no vast undiscovered world, if we already know most of what there is to be known, you will find it relatively attractive to find some other reason to do research on psychotherapy.

A researcher who believes that we know most of what there is to be known about what psychotherapy is and how to do it can be excused for not rushing into doing research to discover what we probably already know. And we know a great deal. There is no vast undiscovered world of secrets of psychotherapy. We know enough to have lots of courses on psychotherapy. We even divide the courses into how to do psychodynamic therapy, integrative/eclectic therapy and other kinds of therapies. We know what the basic skills are and we have courses to teach them. We have internships and residencies where we train practitioners to do what we know. We have thousands of supervisors and consultants who know what we know about psychotherapy. We have whole libraries of books and journals about what we know, and of research testing what we know. We even have manuals on how to do it. We have diplomas and certificates and ethical codes, all on the firm understanding that we know a very great deal about what psychotherapy is and how to do it. Are we just scratching the surface of what there is to be known about psychotherapy? No. Is there some vast undiscovered world of undiscovered secrets about psychotherapy? Not really. It is always nice to have a few researchers and practitioners out there, peering beyond what we know. But there are better things for researchers to do. It therefore makes sense that there are so few studies that discover what in-session work can be and do, how to do psychotherapy better and better because of what these studies discover (compare Elliott, 1983a, 1983b; Strupp, 1986a, 1989; Goldman, 1989; Imber, 1992).

In sharp contrast, the researcher who does discovery-oriented research can have a whole other picture, a picture of a whole universe of undiscovered knowledge, a world of psychotherapeutic secrets awaiting exploration and discovery. For this researcher, we know almost nothing of what there is to be known about what psychotherapy can be and how to do it. If we could peek 100 or 200 years ahead, we barely have the concepts to enable us to understand what lies ahead. When we look back over the past 100 or 200 years, this researcher's picture is that we have been in a stagnant dead center of a stagnant small pool surrounded by a vast ocean of which we have no knowledge. We are so very ignorant and, worse, we are ignorant about being so ignorant. To the discovery-oriented researcher, what little we think we know can be a justifying springboard for launching us into the vast undiscovered world of what awaits discovery.

The researcher whose picture is that we know most of what there is to be known about what psychotherapy is and how to do it will probably not be especially excited about doing research to discover how to do psychotherapy. On the other hand, this kind of research may well be done by the researcher with a picture of a vast unexplored world of what lies waiting to be discovered.

The characteristics of the discovery-oriented researcher

Hand in hand with a picture of a vast undiscovered world are some other characteristics of the discovery-oriented researcher.

Enthusiasm for discovering more and more about psychotherapy

The researcher wants to know more and more about what psychotherapy can do, and how to do it better and better. Research is, for this researcher, an exciting opportunity to explore, to learn ever more, to open up new vistas of what psychotherapy can be, and to find newer and better ways of how to achieve what psychotherapy can be. This is the main thrust of the discovery-oriented researcher's answer to why this kind of research should be done. This is the researcher's passion, excitement, enthusiasm (compare Goldman, 1977, 1979; Mahrer, 1985; Mahrer et al., 1986a; Hoshmand, 1989; Mahrer and Gagnon, 1991).

Inclination to be part of a team that is rather large and variegated

It is relatively common for psychotherapy researchers to work alone or with perhaps a few colleagues. Often there may be others, frequently students, who serve as assistants, judges, helpers on the study, as people who provide technical help of one kind or another. In contrast, discovery-oriented researchers are inclined to immerse themselves in the actual work, to get down into the data, to get dirty from doing the actual hands-on work. They are the judges. They do the actual technical work. It is here that the action is in discovery.

As there is simply a lot of work to be done in this kind of research, and because most discovery-oriented researchers want to get involved in the actual nitty-gritty work, it is common to have research teams that are relatively large, e.g. 8–12 people or more. With a large research team, there are special times when just one or two notice something that the rest of us have not noticed. We see what they see only after they show us. High interjudge agreement is fine, but the risk is overshadowing the keen observations and ideas of the lone researcher(s) who can see or think what we cannot see or think. This is another reason for having a rather large team of researchers.

When there are just one or two judges, something may well be missed. One or two judges may miss this significant change or some key element when describing what that significant change is like, what it is. Having more judges covers more bases. Still, with a large team of judges, there is always the likelihood that the one or two judges see something that the rest of the judges miss. It works both ways. A large team protects against what the few may not see: 'In searching for clinically significant events, the best hedge against idiosyncratic results is reliance on the agreement of a number of judges who have made independent observations' (Allen et al., 1990, p. 527; compare Horowitz et al., 1989). Similarly, a good bet against losing what the special judge sees is having a large team that can recognize and acknowledge that some judges may be special.

On the other hand, there are often a few researchers on the team who have trouble being purely discovery oriented when studying this therapist and this patient for all sorts of reasons. They are offended by the therapist, the patient, the approach or something. If they were the only researchers on the team, interjudge agreement would be high, and the discovery of what is discoverable would be low. However, if they are only two of 12 researchers, their judgments can be weighted, flagged and set aside (Mahrer et al., 1986a).

To maximize the payoff of discovery, it is helpful if the large research team is representative of a large number of psychotherapeutic approaches and orientations, including researchers who are flag-waving proponents of different approaches and researchers who are avid proponents without being sure what their approach really is. The more varied the approaches the better. It is even helpful if there are researchers who are proud of having no particular perspective at all.

As long as the researchers have a high premium on discovering more and more about psychotherapy, the emphasis on variety means that some researchers are mainly practitioners, some theoreticians, some researchers and some educators/trainers. Some may be identified mainly with psychotherapy-related fields and some may come from fields and disciplines far away from psychotherapy. Some may be older, with lots of experience in psychotherapy, some may be in training, some may be undergraduate students, and some may simply be enthusiastic about studying and discovering more and more about psychotherapy.

Could the discovery-oriented researcher be the actual therapist or patient from the actual session?

Discovery-oriented research usually studies tapes of actual sessions. In studying actual sessions, many researchers find it valuable to have the actual therapist and the actual patient assist in studying the tape (e.g. Elliott, 1983a, 1984, 1985; Barkham and Shapiro, 1986; Elliott and Shapiro, 1988, 1992; Hill et al., 1988; Llewelyn et al., 1988; Martin and Stelmaczonek, 1988; Cummings et al., 1992; Cummings, Hallberg and Slemon, 1994; Goldfried, Raus and Castonguay, 1998; von Knorring-Giorgi, 1998).

I have had some experience of having the actual therapist and the actual patient participate as researchers. This limited experience seems to suggest that the actual therapist and the actual patient could be, but usually are not, members of the research team. At least three considerations point toward this conclusion. One practical consideration is that it is hard to get them on the team. They usually live far away, typically in another country. The few I have contacted were not especially interested in studying the tape, though they were often quite interested in what we found. Indeed, I have spent many hours, visiting cities where the therapist lived, going over tapes of sessions of theirs which the research team studied. Another practical consideration is that we have little or no idea who the patient is, and our very interest in protecting confidentiality worked against being able to invite the patient to help as a researcher.

A second consideration is that when the therapist was available locally, and did participate as a part of the research team, the therapist did not seem to add much that was especially helpful, over and above what was provided by the rest of the team. For purposes of our work, this seems to suggest that the therapist might well be a member of the research team, but it does not add much.

A third consideration is that the actual therapist and patient were not especially driven by a desire to discover more and more about psychotherapy. Instead, in playing the tapes of their sessions, they were far more drawn toward talking about what was compellingly personal to and for them. What they wanted to talk about was intriguing, but only bordered on discovering what the research team was intent on discovering. And they had far less interest in helping to study tapes of other sessions.

In general, the actual therapist and patient might be part of the research team, but they have usually been interested in what was found rather than in being members of the team.

What are the discovery-oriented research questions?

One of the important things that distinguish discovery-oriented research from most other kinds of research, and reasons for doing research, is its research questions. Its questions arise mainly from a quest to discover what psychotherapy can be, and how to enable psychotherapy to help achieve what it can achieve, rather than mainly from a concern with testing, checking out, verifying what researchers believe we know (compare Maccia, 1973; Gelso, 1979; Anderson and Heppner, 1986; Hitchcock, 1986; Howard, 1986; Polkinghorne, 1988; Talley, Strupp and Butler, 1994).

Here are some of the research questions that identify, characterize and distinguish discovery-oriented research.

1. What are the impressive, significant, valued changes or events that can occur in psychotherapy sessions?

When a discovery-oriented researcher studies a psychotherapy session, picture the researcher as eager, poised, ready, receptive, open to something prized. What might there be here that is impressive, significant or valued, some change that is exciting? What the researcher finds may be familiar, something already known, or it may be somewhat new, or it may be almost utterly new, at least to this researcher. This is the first question the discovery-oriented researcher seeks to answer.

Researchers acknowledge that such important and impressive events can occur in psychotherapy sessions. They have used lots of terms and phrases in acknowledging that such good things can happen in actual sessions. Here are some of these terms and phrases: indications of movement, progress, process, improvement; significant change events; critical moments; critical incidents; peak in-session events; facilitating therapeutic episodes; auspicious moments; valued or prized in-session changes; in-session outcomes, sub-outcomes; turning points; significant shifts; helpful impacts; good moments, very good moments; key in-session events; moments of significant change (Standahl and Corsini, 1959; Orlinsky and Howard, 1967; Auerbach and Luborsky, 1968; Duncan, Rice and Butler, 1968; Kelman, 1969; Goldfried, 1980; Hoyt, 1980; Stiles, 1980; Stone, 1982; Elliott, 1983a, 1983b, 1985; Luborsky et al., 1984; Mathieu-Coughlan and Klein, 1984; Rice and Greenberg, 1984; Elliott et al., 1985; Mahrer, 1985, 1988b; Greenberg and Pinsoff, 1986; Mahrer and Nadler, 1986; Elliott and Shapiro, 1988; Martin and Stelmaczonek, 1988; Cummings et al., 1992; Mahrer et al., 1992a; Elliott and Wexler, 1994).

Some psychotherapy researchers acknowledge that there can be in-session changes that are impressive, significant, valued. Researchers are ready with the labels. On the other hand, there are virtually no studies where the main intent is to study these sessions to see, to discover just what these impressive and valued changes can be. This is the explicit question guiding the discovery-oriented researcher. Is some impressive change happening here? Is there a significant change in this session? If so, what is it, how can it be described? It would be nice to review studies that answer these questions, but there are very few of them.

Researchers have found it sensible and useful to learn more about what happens in sessions by turning to the patients themselves. The methods have ranged from traditional to qualitative and phenomenological. However, in almost all of these studies, the main intent was rarely to discover, and nor did many studies come up with, new kinds and categories of important, significant, impressive, in-session changes.

In virtually all of these studies, patients helped to identify where and what the important, impressive, helpful, in-session events were (Wilson and Evans, 1977; Kazdin and Wilson, 1978; Elliott et al., 1982, 1985; Elliott, 1983a, 1984, 1985; Barkham and Shapiro, 1986; Elliott and Shapiro, 1988, 1992; Hill et al., 1988; Llewelyn et al., 1988; Martin and Stelmaczonek, 1988; Elliott and James, 1989; McLeod, 1990; Cummings et al., 1992; Heppner, Rosenberg and Hedgespeth, 1992; Cummings, Hallberg and Slemon, 1994; Sexton and Whiston, 1996; Hardy et al., 1998). However, what the patients said, in seeking to say that here was an impressive change event, was rarely if ever used to discover the nature or content of an impressive change event. Instead, the common practice was to feed or code what patients said into a predetermined category system. Relying on what patients said was helpful, except in discovering the nature and content of new in-session change events.

Although phenomenological, hermeneutic and related strategies have been groomed as fitting for such uses, a review of studies aimed at un- covering impressive, significant, in-session events found no studies that used phenomenological or phenomenologically related research strategies (von Knorring-Giorgi, 1998). Interestingly, in her own phenomenological analysis of a patient-located, significant, in-session event, von Knorring- Giorgi was successful in yielding a description that departed to some degree from more or less traditional categories, namely a pivotal challenge to old and problematic patterns of feeling, perceiving and behaving. This was one of the few studies able to come up with relatively new descrip- tions, kinds and categories of significant in-session change events.

Indeed, most studies of in-session change events used predetermined kinds and categories of these in-session change events, regardless of the strategies used to locate the actual change event in the session. Some stud- ies combined reasoning down from theory and back from outcome to locate the in-session change event (Curtis and Silberschatz, 1986; Lambert, Shapiro and Bergin, 1986; Silberschatz and Curtis, 1986; Weiss, 1986; Safran, Greenberg and Rice, 1988; Silberschatz, Curtis and Nathans, 1989; Muran et al., 1995; Clarke, 1996). Some studies started by flagging a ses- sion as a 'good' session, and then seeing which in-session change events seemed to contribute to the session being deemed a good one (Stiles, 1980; Stiles and Snow, 1984; Friedlander, Thibodeau and Ward, 1985).

Many studies start with a predetermined idea of what is to be con- sidered in-session significant change events, e.g. if the patient seems to indicate that she has some problem, the good change is when the prob- lem seems to be resolved, or at least substantially reduced. If the patient seems to be abnormal, either way below normal, as in rate of speech, or way above normal, as in loudness of voice, a significant change event is when the patient is being much more normal. A good change event can be when the patient is showing signs of a good patient, a satisfied patient, a person who is adjusted, treated, functioning well, like saying how good he feels, how much he has changed, how helpful therapy has been. Again, these are examples of predetermined kinds and categories of significant in-session change events.

Although there are many studies on in-session change events, virtually all of these studies already had predetermined categories of in-session change events embedded into their designs, hypotheses and measures. It is the rare study that sought to discover what in-session change events may be found. Yet this is the opening question for the discovery-oriented researcher.

2. Do impressive, significant, valued, in-session changes or events occur in some sequence(s)?

The first question is whether we can find and describe these impressive in-session changes. If we can, other questions can be asked. Do they occur in some kind of sequence or order? The researcher is looking for stages, steps, patterns, programs of in-session valued changes. These may occur across a session or a number of sessions. The researcher is open to sequences that may be simple or complicated, tightly connected or loosely interwoven. Yet the guiding concern is whether one kind of impressive change seems to precede or follow some other kind, perhaps paving the way for or being helped by the occurrence of some other kind of impressive in-session change.

Researchers have found it attractive to study in-session sequences of events, but they rarely if ever look for sequences of impressive and valued changes. Some researchers are drawn toward language-related events, perhaps because, in part at least, they are rather easily objectified and quantified, e.g. researchers have studied sequences of speaking turns, units of word frequency, changes in topic initiation and following, ratios or self-reference to other reference, proportions of nouns and verbs (e.g. Tracey and Ray, 1984; Tracey, 1985, 1987; Russell and Trull, 1986; O'Connor et al., 1992; Sexton, 1993, 1996; Milbrath et al., 1995; Reynolds et al., 1996; Richards, 1996; Sexton, Hembre and Kvarme, 1996).

Some researchers have started with a predetermined model of how change occurred, and studied how this model plays itself out in terms of in-session processes and patterns. These studies include, for example, a model of Piagetian and Rogerian processing of painful experiences (Stiles et al., 1990), a model of evocative unfolding (Watson and Greenberg, 1996), and models emphasizing linkages between in-session processes and post-treatment outcomes (e.g. Prochaska and DiClemente, 1984; Safran, Greenberg and Rice, 1988; Stiles et al., 1990; Gray, 1993; Muran et al., 1995; Kolden, 1996).

A third body of studies selects a particular kind of impressive in-session event, and looks at the sequences or programmatic ways that it plays itself out across a session, e.g. a group of studies focused on the sequential playing out of valued strong feelings, or particular kinds of valued strong feelings, over psychotherapy sessions (Mahrer et al., 1986a, 1986b, 1987, 1991a, 1991b, 1992b, 1999). Another series of studies predetermined to look at the degree the patient addressed significant issues, and the degree the patient made use of the therapist's interventions, paying especial attention to the increases, decreases and shifts over a session (Frieswyk, Colson and Allen, 1984; Gabbard et al., 1988; Allen et al., 1990).

It is interesting that the methods of studying this question outstripped the quality and sophistication of the findings. From early on, researchers counted on the use of methods of sequential analysis (e.g. Snyder, 1945), and later improved this with such methods as time-series analysis (Glass, Wilson and Gottman, 1975), cross-lag time-series analysis (Gottman, 1979) and stochastic process analysis (Hertel, 1972; Lichtenberg and Hummel, 1976; Benjamin, 1979; Lichtenberg and Heck, 1979), wherein predetermined categories of therapist methods and significant client change events identify interrelated couplets of therapist and client statements organized into a Markov chain (e.g. Friedlander and Phillips, 1984; Mercier and Johnson, 1984; Tracey and Ray, 1984; Tracey, 1985; Wampold and Kim, 1989).

In-session sequences have been studied, but not in-session sequences of impressive, valued, in-session changes. Once we can identify the impressive changes in sessions, the question is whether or not these impressive changes occur in some sequences and, if they do, what these sequences are. Unfortunately, we do not have much of a body of studies that have sought to answer this question.

3. How can these impressive, significant, valued, in-session changes or events be brought about?

First the discovery-oriented researcher finds a change that occurs in the session, a change that the researcher regards as impressive, significant, valued. The researcher can then be interested in how this impressive change came about. How did this nice change happen? What helped bring it about? What did the therapist do? What did the patient do? What did they do together? Whatever it was, I like this change, so how can I bring it about in my therapeutic work? Schon (1982, p. 299) portrays the spirit of this third research question: 'Indeed, it can be liberating for a practitioner to ask himself, "What, in my work, really gives me satisfaction?" and then, "How can I produce more experiences of that kind?".'

This third question starts with the impressive in-session change, and looks to see how it was helped to occur. A more common research strategy is to start with a predefined, valued, in-session change, a predetermined method that is thought of as helping to bring it about, and to answer these questions: 'Does it hold up that this particular method is effective in bringing about this particular in-session change?' 'Does this method work to achieve that change?' Such a research strategy tests whether predetermined methods are effective in reducing resistance and promoting insight understanding (Patton, Kivlighan and Milton, 1997), resolving splits or conflicts in the self (Greenberg, 1980), bringing up previously warded-off material (Silberschatz and Curtis, 1993), confronting new material (Horowitz et al., 1975), heightening insight understanding (Garduk and Haggard, 1972; Elliott, 1983a; Hill, Carter and O'Farrell, 1983; Elliott et al., 1985), greater depth of experiencing (Greenberg and Clarke, 1979; Greenberg and Higgins, 1980; Greenberg and Dompierre, 1981; Hill, Carter and O'Farrell, 1983; Wiseman and Rice, 1989; Watson and Greenberg, 1996), greater responsivity to hypnotic material (Vickery et al., 1985; Council, Kirsch and Hafner, 1986) and a good therapist–client relationship (Garduk and Haggard, 1972; Foreman and Marmar, 1985; Kiesler and Watkins, 1989; Kivlighan and Schmitz, 1992).

The strategy used in these and similar studies is designed to test, check out, whether this predetermined method is really effective to help bring about this predetermined kind of impressive change. This strategy is not designed to answer, and is actually poorly designed to answer, a question that seeks to discover how to bring about some impressive, significant, valued, in-session change or event. Yet this is the third question in the discovery-oriented research approach.

It is hard to find studies aimed at answering this question. Perhaps one reason is that, instead of seeking to discover what may have helped to bring about this impressive in-session change, researchers skip to some predetermined method, and do a study to check out what they hypothesize.

Nevertheless, there are some studies that open the discovery-oriented window a little bit, e.g. Greenberg and his colleagues already predetermined to study a particular method or technique, but took the nice step of inquiring into what seemed to occur when the two-chair technique was effective in helping to attain the impressive change (Greenberg and Clarke, 1979; Greenberg and Higgins, 1980; Greenberg and Dompierre, 1981; Greenberg and Webster, 1982). Opening the window even further, Elliott (1983a) looked for ways that seemed to be helpful in achieving a given instance of insight understanding.

The discovery-oriented question leaves wide open the ways of answering the question: 'How can these impressive, significant, valued in-session changes or events be brought about?' Very few studies salute this question directly and in a way that allows for a wide open discovery of answers.

4. How can the therapist use these impressive, significant, valued, in-session changes or events when they occur?

Suppose that an impressive change has just occurred in the session. Then what? What does the therapist do? How does the therapist use the occurrence of this valuable change? In a sense, the spirit of this question is answered in a general way by the second question: 'Do impressive, significant, valued, in-session changes or events occur in some sequence(s)?' If this impressive change is followed by this other impressive change, the general answer is that the therapist uses this impressive change by moving toward that subsequent impressive change. Here is a general answer. But maybe it helps to get a little more specific.

Right after the impressive change happens, and perhaps a little further along, suppose we take a closer look. What does the therapist do? Does the therapist seem to use it in some way or not especially? The therapist is almost certainly going to do something. If the therapist seems to use it, the question is how, for what purposes?

Although practitioners have to have an answer to this question every time an impressive in-session change takes place, it seems to be that researchers rarely if ever focus on this question. The few studies that shed a little light on this question usually did so as a sidelight to some more important other research matter. Still, there are some hints. When the therapist seemed to think of the client in-session change as welcomed and desirable, the likelihood was that the therapist used this by expressing the therapist's pleasure and satisfaction (Mickelson and Stevic, 1971). When the impressive in-session change involved the client's offering of important and especially meaningful material, the therapist can use this to offer an exchange in kind, namely the disclosure of some of the therapist's own personal material, and the consequence was further impressive client changes such as heightened insight or a carrying forward of the client–therapist relationship (Knox et al., 1991). When there seemed to be an impressive reduction in the clients' demandingness and efforts to control, one way that therapists can and do use this is by tending to reduce their own demandingness and efforts to control the client (Lichtenberg and Barké, 1981).

When there seemed to be an impressive reduction in some problem, or when some deeper inner quality seemed to open up and come forth, one way that therapists capitalized on these changes was to seek to extend them out into the post-session real world by means of homework assignments (Mahrer et al., 1994; Mahrer, Nordin and Miller, 1995). When the impressive change consisted of the occurrence of quite strong feelings, some therapists seemed to use this by intensifying the already strong feelings even further, and proceeded toward particular kinds of further impressive changes depending on the nature of the initial strong feeling (Mahrer et al., 1999).

The purpose of this fourth question is simply to inquire into the various ways that impressive in-session changes can be used when they do occur.

Is a justification for framing and answering these questions to discover what psychotherapy can be and do, and how to do it better and better?

Most studies find it important to justify how and why what they study is worthy of study. The texts usually show how their studies can shed light on bigger and more important matters, larger and deeper issues. The studies are justified because their findings will bear on important applied matters, have important practical applications and implications. The studies are justified because some important matter is insufficiently studied, or what we do seem to know is conflicted and equivocal.

One way of justifying these four discovery-oriented research questions is that they are the best way we have of formulating and framing research questions, the answers to which seem to be able to help us discover what psychotherapy can be and do, and to discover how to do this thing called psychotherapy better and better. It would be better if we could formulate and frame even more helpful research questions.

One way of justifying research to answer these questions is to say that answering these questions is the best way we know to help us discover what psychotherapy can be and do, and to discover how to do psychotherapy better and better (Mahrer, 1985, 1988a, 1988b, 1996a, 1996b; Mahrer and Boulet, 1999).

Should the discovery-oriented researcher study tapes from a research library of taped sessions?

Almost from the very beginning of psychotherapy, there has been a sprinkling of researchers who wanted to learn more by studying what actually seemed to happen in actual sessions. Carl Rogers pioneered this by careful study of recordings of actual sessions in the 1940s and 1950s. However, researchers had paved the way by studying recordings of actual psychotherapy sessions almost from when the technology was available, certainly in the 1920s and 1930s (Dittes, 1959). The discovery-oriented researcher merely continues the tradition: discover more and more about psychotherapy by close and careful study of what happens in actual sessions. The picture is of a rich research library of tapes of psychotherapy.

What kinds of tapes are useful for such a psychotherapy library?

It would be nice to have a centralized library of psychotherapy tapes, but whether the research library is centralized or local, decisions have to be made about what kinds of tapes may be especially useful. These are some of the guidelines that have helped in building my own research library, which now includes approximately 500 tapes:

- Tapes are added each year. Beginning in 1954, I have continuously added to the holdings, and continue doing so today.
- Videotapes have advantages over audiotapes, such as being able to see facial expression, non-verbal behaviors, and so on, but audiotapes are much easier to get from psychotherapists. With only some exceptions, virtually all the tapes in my library are audiotapes.
- The premium is on actual sessions with actual patients or clients. Demonstration sessions in front of a group, with or without a volunteer from the group, are much less valuable. Prepared sessions, somewhat scripted by a volunteer or actor or proxy patient, are not especially valuable. Sessions using volunteer subjects, usually for some research project, with subjects being paid or getting some sort of credit, are not especially valuable.
- It is important to elicit tapes from a wide range of practitioners. This refers to the nature of their approach, orientation, school of psychotherapy, and to country. Tapes are from many countries, although almost all of the sessions are in English. This refers to profession. Tapes are from practitioners from virtually all the psychotherapy-related professions, and some practitioners who may be outside the usual psychotherapy-related professions. This refers to length of experience. Some of the psychotherapists are in training, most have 5–20 or so years of experience, and some have lifetimes of seasoned experience. This refers to almost any meaning of psychotherapy. Tapes are from counselors, case workers, psychoanalysts, healers, virtually anyone who falls within or near a stretched meaning of the word psychotherapy.
- I am grateful to the well-known developers and leaders of various approaches who were willing to let me study their audiotapes. Here I think of gracious and helpful people such as Dr Albert Ellis and some others who sent me their tapes right away, and who even sent me one or more series of tapes of sessions with the same person. I am thankful.
- I am grateful to those who wrote about their psychotherapies, and who were willing to send me tapes of their sessions. It is exciting to read

about a new therapy and to get tapes from the proponent, or to come across proponents of established therapies who are willing to send me tapes of their sessions.

- I am grateful to those practitioners whose names are not especially well known, who do not write about their work, who do not give workshops at conventions and conferences, but whose tapes are precious, on the forefront of what is there to be discovered. How did I get these tapes? It was simply by asking colleagues for the names of practitioners who are special, gifted, masters of their craft, the therapists who do not especially seek the spotlight by writing, giving workshops or holding positions of leadership. They are simply wonderful and gifted practitioners who were willing to give me the gift of some audiotapes. I am so grateful.

- The emphasis is on any and all kinds of 'patients' or 'clients' whose concerns are with any and all kinds of issues, problems, changes, worries, things to talk about, states, conditions. It is fine if the people are in fine shape or in awful states of distress and pain. No matter what category system is used, the emphasis is on people of all kinds. Any label will do. Any category is acceptable. Any kind of mental illness is just fine. I suppose the emphasis is on a broad representation of people and concerns, no matter how these are labeled or categorized.

- Tapes are sought where the therapist is working with individuals starting from about 10–12 years of age and on up. My interest is not especially with very young children, couples or groups.

- Almost all the tapes include a therapist. However, I am starting to include tapes of people who have their own sessions, by themselves. Most of these people are having their own experiential sessions, but I would welcome tapes of sessions by oneself, no matter what the 'practitioner' is doing in the session.

- I welcome tapes of initial, middle or final sessions. It is fine if this is the only session, or if this is one of a fair number of sessions.

- I am not especially interested in tapes of sessions where there is a single client and several therapists, co-therapists.

- Having one taped session is just fine. It is a welcome gift to have several sessions with the same person, even just a few. Having a fair number of sessions with the same person is a boon.

- When therapists ask me for the kind of session I am looking for, I generally name several kinds. One is that I value sessions that are reasonably illustrative of the way the therapist works. Just a modest ordinary session would be just fine. Second, I value sessions where the therapist considers the session to be a good one, rather effective (compare Garfield, 1981). It is probably not one of the therapist's greatest feats, but things went rather well in the session. Third, I especially value those extraordinary sessions where there was some remarkable change. The session almost begs careful study. It is almost as if the therapist were privileged to have been the therapist in this extraordinary session. Something magical seemed to happen in and to the person. This is the kind of tape the therapist may be embarrassed about contributing, partly because the therapist is so proud of that tape. Finally, I value tapes containing something strange, unusual, hard to fathom, uncanny, hard to understand. It may have been good or bad, or simply extraordinary, compelling.

These are the kinds of tapes that I hope can be included in the ever-growing research library. In addition, there is one more kind of tape:

- When practitioners try out what the research discovers, and their tapes are added to the continually enriched tape library.

The research aims at discovering new things about how to do psychotherapy. One rather practical test of the usefulness of the findings is that the practitioners on the research team, and the practitioners who read the published studies, are inclined to try out what was discovered. Most of the publications invite readers to send tapes and, when they do, and when practitioners on the research team do, their tapes are added to a continuously richer tape library. Here is a valuable way of continually enriching the tape library.

The better the tape library, the better the discoveries

Seasoned and experienced researchers generally know that if the data they study are interesting, rich and of high quality, their findings are likely to be interesting, rich and of high quality. If you study garbage, you get garbage. The research library is like a fascinating pool containing fascinating things to study, to discover. It is a wonderful adventure to see what new and special discoveries may be found in studying this next tape.

Many of the tapes are from practitioners who regard their tapes as rather ordinary. However, a large proportion of these tapes contain precious discoveries when they are studied closely. Often the practitioners are surprised when I tell them what marvelous discoveries were found in their work. Of course, many of the tapes seem to contain little or nothing that the research team finds important, useful, new discoveries. Nevertheless, the tape library is special, and the general guideline seems to hold: the better the tape library, the better the discoveries.

What are the steps in doing discovery-oriented research?

The general aim of discovery-oriented research is to discover more and more about what psychotherapy can accomplish, and how to do psychotherapy better and better. One way of doing this is to do research to answer these questions:

1. What are the impressive, significant, valued changes or events that can occur in psychotherapy sessions?
2. Do impressive, significant, valued, in-session changes or events occur in some sequence or sequences?
3. How can these impressive, significant, valued, in-session changes be brought about?
4. How can the therapist use these impressive, significant, valued, in-session changes or events when they occur?

Here is one way of doing discovery-oriented psychotherapy research. It is only one way of trying to answer the four questions. The research program is rather careful, somewhat precise, reasonably rigorous and follows a series of steps.

1. Study the tape to determine if there are any impressive changes

A few of the team members have already done a very provisional labeling of a next tape as perhaps containing one or more impressive changes. Starting with that tape, each team member is to study the tape independently to answer this question: 'Do you believe this tape contains any changes that seem impressive, significant, valued, or none at all?' Judges are simply to decide if the answer is yes or no. Although judges are provided with lists of various kinds of impressive, significant, valued, in-session changes from comprehensive reviews (e.g. Mahrer and Nadler, 1986; Mahrer et al., 1992a), the following working guidelines are helpful:

- It is impressive in relation to the way the person or patient seemed to be earlier. The baseline is the person's earlier state or condition, or what seemed central, important, of concern, bothersome, troubling before this change.
- Its impressiveness is not necessarily restricted to any particular list of kinds or categories of impressive, significant, valued, in-session changes, or any particular approach's set of valued impressive changes.
- It can be judged as impressive because it is a step toward, it is instrumental for, it opens the way toward a subsequent impressive change. It is important because of what it leads to. It is a helpful process or means toward a more important, valued consequence or outcome.

- It can be impressive because it is a preview appearance of the post-treatment outcome, of whatever would be regarded as an indication of successful and effective post-therapy change.
- It can be impressive because it is a substantial reduction or absence of whatever was identified as the problem, trouble, difficulty, pain or hurt, problematic condition or state.
- It can be impressive because it indicates substantial movement toward a state that may be regarded as valued, welcomed, desired, positive, optimal, what the person is capable of becoming.
- It can be impressive because judges simply found, recognized, acknowledged it as having the qualities or characteristics of being valued, significant, impressive, i.e. it is judged impressive because the judge judged it to be impressive, even though the reason for being impressive is not nicely given in the above reasons.

Most judges operate from a personal list of significant, impressive changes that are nevertheless unarticulated, explicated, unformulated. But, if it is there in the session, they will usually spot it. The problem is how to enable judges to spot significant changes that are not on their highly personal lists. It sounds helpful to ask judges to set aside their personal lists, their predetermined and pre-established notions and ideas about significant changes. However, it is exceedingly difficult to ask judges to set aside notions and ideas of which they are essentially unaware but which nevertheless play a large hand in determining what they do or do not spot as significant changes. What may help is for judges to accept a few additional guidelines.

One additional guideline is to be open to and value a sense of being surprised. Here is something unexpected, out of the ordinary, different, perhaps perplexing, bewildering. If judges can allow themselves to be open to a sense of surprise, even if it comes and goes in a flash, they may be on track toward finding a significant change that is not on their unformulated personal lists. In this first step, judges need not decide whether or not the event is a significant change. They can arrive at that determination in step 2. Just give a little acknowledgement to what may have brought about the sense of surprise.

A second additional guideline is to be open to a sense of being bothered, troubled, drawn up against, disliking, disturbed. Something here gets to the judge even before the judge is able to formulate what it is that is bothersome, troublesome. It is this vague and unexplicated sense of unease, of drawing away, that may well signal some significant change that is beyond or even violates the judge's own personal unexplicated hazy list of significant changes.

If judges are ready and able, they may well use these two additional guidelines to signal the possibility of significant changes in the tape. It helps that the judges know that the more careful and stringent determination will occur in step 2.

At the next team meeting, after hearing the yes or no judgments of each team member, the team as a whole determines whether to study that tape or to go through step 1 with some other provisionally stamped tape.

2. Study the tape to flag where the impressive changes seem to be

Once the team has decided that this tape seems to contain an impressive change, the homework is to answer this question: 'Where and when, on the tape, do you believe an impressive change started and when and where does it seem to end?' During the week, each team member individually listens to the tape to answer the question in writing. Once again, the judge is to be as open as possible to any sign of an impressive change, and to determine if there is one or several impressive changes, the counter numbers of where each begins and ends, and some of the verbatim words to help identify the beginning and end of each impressive change. Some impressive changes are relatively short, and some are rather long, involving a fair number of both patient and therapist interchanges.

In this way, the door is open to admit any and all kinds of changes that impress any judges, rather than preselecting your own particular categories of valued changes such as insight, conflict reduction or symptom reduction. The emphasis is on whatever touches you as something impressive happening here, rather than relying on your theory, your knowledge, your being on the lookout for particular kinds of traditional significant in-session changes.

In the next team meeting, each judge's answer is given, and the team determines how many impressive changes there were on this tape and exactly where each began and ended.

3. Describe the impressive change and what qualifies it as impressive

Starting with the first identified impressive change, the homework is to answer this question: 'How would you describe what is happening in this impressive change, and what do you believe qualifies it as impressive, significant, valued?' Each judge is to listen individually to the tape, to answer the question in writing and to emphasize the use of simple, concrete, non-technical, non-jargon words (compare Schutz, 1964; Glazer and Strauss, 1967; Spiegelberg, 1972; Keen, 1975; Fiske, 1977; Glazer, 1978; Valle and King, 1978; Giorgi, 1985). The words should emphasize being simple and concrete, rather than high level and abstract, and the words should be more from the common marketplace, rather than spotted as the technical jargon terms of some particular vocabulary.

The same words can just about describe what is happening in this impressive change, and also serve to answer the question of what qualifies this change as impressive. Just keep the words simple and relatively low level enough to answer the question. So a particular judge may write down: 'Up to now, the patient seemed so depressed and gloomy, giving up, and now he seems so happy, laughing, on top of things' or 'From the very beginning, he was stuttering on lots of words, but here he isn't; he talks just fine. No stuttering at all!' or 'She started out with her voice so dead, no feeling, neutral, and long silences, but here she's talking with real feeling, like she's got some real interest; she's like a different person in her voice and how she talks.'

It is always possible to rise to higher and higher levels of abstraction by, for example, asking why that particular answer can be justified. 'Now she is talking with real feeling, like she has some real interest. But why is that such an impressive change?' The higher and higher levels of answers can easily get into notions of voice quality and emotionality, levels of particular blood chemicals, ego control and depressive psychopathology. One problem in rising to such higher levels of description is that the high-level answers are almost certainly going to have to dip into some particular vocabulary. Another problem is that the high-level answers will increasingly fail to answer the initial question we started with, namely 'How would you describe what is happening in this impressive change, and what do you believe qualifies it as impressive, significant, valued?'

All in all, it is most helpful if the judges answer the question by using words that are relatively simple, concrete, non-technical and non-jargon.

Collate the individual descriptions into a single composite description

At the next team meeting, each judge reads, and the team discusses and then hands in, his or her written description. The task is to collate the individual judges' written answers into a single composite. This is done by having two researchers independently organize the components of each judge's answer into a single composite, using guidelines for mapping, clustering and organizing components (e.g. Glazer and Strauss, 1967; Holsti, 1969; Conrad, 1978; Glazer, 1978; Viney, 1983; Hycner, 1985; Lietaer, 1992).

The first step here is to map each element of each judge's answer on a spreadsheet. The second step is to organize and cluster the elements as is done in some forms of content analysis or theme analysis (e.g. Holsti, 1969; Schofer, Black and Koch, 1979; Taylor and Bogdan, 1984). Higher-frequency elements generally occur as clusters. Lower-frequency elements may either be determined as essentially non-contributing, or as possessing qualities of being unique, singular, sensitive, useful, creative, accurate, correct (compare Mahrer et al., 1986b; Mahrer and Gagnon, 1991). The third step is for each of the two researchers to formulate a specific wording of the composite description, and to compare and refine the two into a single composite description, which is presented to the entire team at the next meeting, for their final refinement or approval. Here is a verbatim example of a final team-approved composite: the patient has moved into a new state of openly undergoing a feeling of genuine, real strength, and certainty about his or her self and ability to deal with problematic matters.

4. Study what the therapist and patient seemed to do to help bring about the impressive change

Once the team arrives at a description of what the impressive change is and what makes it impressive, the next question is: 'What did the therapist, the patient, or therapist and patient together, seem to do to help bring about this impressive change?' Each judge listens to the tape individually, starting from the impressive change, and going back as far as the judge feels is helpful to answer the question. Judges are free to go back to the beginning of the session, especially if this is the first impressive change or, usually, to the antecedent impressive change on the tape.

Identify the patient's state or condition

In studying what happens in sessions, most researchers almost completely bypass the patient and instead focus on therapist 'interventions'. Impressive in-session changes occur, according to this common mind-set, almost exclusively because of what the therapist did in applying interventions. In this mind-set, the patient's role is mainly that of the subject or object of therapist interventions. Except when things go wrong. Then therapists and researchers often turn automatically to the patient. The patient lacked motivation, had poor defenses, was too resistant, had a borderline disorder. The patient's contribution is generally regarded as rather robust when things go wrong and as rather skimpy when things go well.

To acknowledge the patient's contribution to bringing about the impressive change (Elliott, 1983b; Martin, 1992; Messer, Tishby and Spillman, 1992; Strupp, 1994), and also the role of the patient's state and condition, the more stringent question that the judges answer is: 'Under what explicit patient conditions, when the patient is in what particular state or is being what particular way, what does the therapist or what do the therapist and patient do to help bring about this impressive patient change (Mahrer, 1985, 1988b, 1996b; compare Hempel and Oppenheim, 1953)?'

Including the patient's state or condition is a way of handling an acknowledgment that what happened earlier, perhaps across earlier sessions, may well play a substantial role in understanding how and why what the therapist did seemed to be able to work. These earlier influences can be subtle, perhaps cumulative, and hard to gauge, e.g. the impressive change may be that the patient cried, for perhaps the first time, when the therapist simply said, quietly, 'Go ahead'. Including the patient's state or condition can help to incorporate and acknowledge these subtle cumulative earlier influences. Accordingly, the judge's description, the judge's answer to the question, may begin: 'When the patient seems to be fully engaged in telling a painful, highly meaningful, childhood experience, and seems to be on the verge of tears, and then when the therapist quietly says, "Go ahead" . . .'. What seemed to help bring about this impressive change takes into account both what the therapist did and the patient's immediate state or condition.

Use simple words and terms

In addition, it is not especially helpful to describe what therapists do in such traditional terms and phrases as interpretation, problem exploration, advisement, desensitization, support, clarification, guided imagery, and so on. Judges should decline the use of stock jargon terms and phrases drenched in the giveaway vocabulary of any particular approach, e.g. conditioned inhibition, resolution of splits in the self, gestalt two-chair, analysis of the transference neurosis, discrimination training, attacking irrational cognitions, intermittent reinforcement, genetic interpretation, systematic desensitization, stimulus control. Instead, judges should emphasize simple, concrete, close-to-the-event descriptions of what this particular therapist and patient seemed to do in this particular instance (Glazer and Strauss, 1967; Strupp, 1971; Glazer, 1978; Kazdin and Wilson, 1978).

Arrive at composite answer

At the next meeting, each judge reads their written answer, it is discussed by the team, and handed in. These are again collated by the two researchers who work to arrive at a single composite answer that is presented to and discussed by the team at the next meeting. Here is the final, composite, verbatim answer to the way in which the earlier cited impressive change was found to be brought about: when the patient is predominantly living and being in a scene that is fraught with feeling, the therapist (1) speaks with the voice of key other persons in the scene, and also speaks with the voice of relevant other parts of the patient, while (2) continually pressing the patient to undergo stronger and stronger feeling.

5. Study how the therapist uses the impressive change once it occurs

The next question for the judges to answer is: 'How did the therapist seem to use this impressive change once it occurred?' Each judge individually studies the tape, concentrating on what happens after the impressive change. The judges are free to study as far forward as each judge deems useful in order to answer the question. The judge may focus on a relatively immediate use or perhaps one further along, on a single apparent use or on a series or sequence of uses, a use that seems rather simple or somewhat complicated, or even to conclude that there seems to be no apparent use at all. In any case, the written answer is to emphasize words that are simple, concrete, and not especially abstract or couched within the vocabulary of any particular approach.

At the next team meeting, each judge presents his or her answer, it is open for discussion, handed in, and the two researchers follow their procedure to arrive at a single composite answer which is presented to the team at the subsequent team meeting. Here is the verbatim example of the composite team answer to how the therapist seemed to use the impressive change in which the patient has moved into a new state of openly undergoing a feeling of genuine, real strength and certainty about his or her self and ability to deal with problematic matters: the therapist uses this impressive change by encouraging the patient to find previous situations in which the patient was this way with satisfaction and pleasure.

6. Repeat steps 3–5 for each impressive change in the session

If there were several impressive changes in the session, the team repeats steps 3–5 for each of the impressive changes in turn, i.e. first the judges describe the impressive change and what qualifies it as impressive, then they study what the therapist and patient seemed to do to help bring about the impressive change, and finally they study how the therapist seemed to use the impressive change once it occurred. This completes the study of this particular session.

7. Continuously develop and refine the categories of impressive changes, how to help bring them about and how to use them when they occur

After studying a small number of sessions, e.g. three or five or so, the researcher has accumulated a number of composite descriptions of impressive patient changes, ways of helping them to come about and ways of using them once they occur. Several researchers can organize these composite descriptions into a small number of provisional categories (e.g. Lietaer, 1992). In other words, the researchers have come up with an initial provisional set of categories, a category system, of impressive patient changes, of ways of bringing each about and of using them. Each category in each system can be given a title, a heading, a label, together with a few sentences to fill out the meaning of each category, sentences from the composite descriptions.

Once the provisional category systems are established, each subsequent tape that is studied yields composite descriptions that either fit nicely into the provisional category system, call for some modification or refinement of the category system, its label or description, or call for a major reorganization of the category system. By following this procedure, the category system of impressive changes can be continuously improved.

By following this same procedure with the findings from how the therapist and patient helped to bring about the impressive change, and from study of how the therapist uses the impressive change once it occurs, a continuously more careful and useful matrix develops. This matrix says that, for this particular category of impressive change, here are some useful ways to help bring it about, and here are some useful ways to use this impressive change once it occurs. Here is a continuously richer marketplace for practitioners to shop, generated from the continuous products of discovery-oriented psychotherapy research.

8. Continuously develop and refine in-session sequences of impressive changes

Some sessions may have just one impressive change. Most sessions will probably have several impressive changes. Suppose that the research has accumulated 20, 50 or more sessions with multiple impressive changes, and that each of the impressive changes has been placed into the developing category system of impressive changes. It is then possible to examine the sequences of categories of impressive changes over each of the sessions to discover various sets of in-session sequences of impressive changes (e.g. Cashdan, 1973; McCullough, 1984; Mahrer, 1996a, 1996b). It is possible to see which categories of impressive change seem to precede and to follow other categories of impressive changes, and to see the various sequences of in-session changes that can occur over a session.

In other words, if a practitioner wants to get impressive change z, this research can suggest that one way is first to achieve impressive change y, and that another way is first to achieve impressive change m, then impressive change n. In still other words, this research can offer practitioners choices of various in-session programs to follow, sequences of in-session changes, either within a single session or over a series of sessions. In essence, practitioners can be offered a relatively solid basis for choosing a way of doing psychotherapy, a sequence of impressive, valued changes that the practitioner may like, and that can essentially become that practitioner's own preferred brand of psychotherapy.

Determine the continuously modified conditional probabilities of connections between impressive changes

The data may be used to determine the strength or confidence of connections between each antecedent-consequent pair of impressive changes. The probabilities can be calculated from the observed frequency of a given connection in relation to the observed frequencies of all connections. Accordingly, as more antecedent-consequent pairs of impressive changes are continuously added to the cumulative body of findings, there can be continuously careful modification of the conditional strength or confidence in the connection between each pair of impressive changes, and thereby in the sequencing of impressive changes over the session(s).

9. Complete the circle: actually try out what the research has discovered, and add the tapes to the library

The progressively cumulative findings essentially offer a continual series of invitations to the members of the research team, and to those who read the published studies: are any of these findings of interest to you? Would you be interested in obtaining any of these kinds of impressive in-session changes, in adopting this program of steps in doing psychotherapy, in these methods of helping to bring about and use these impressive changes? Experiential psychotherapy (Mahrer, 1996/2004) came about in large part by nodding yes to these invitations, by letting discovery-oriented research findings determine what a psychotherapy could look like, what it could do and how it could do it in a session.

The actual adoption and trying out of what the research discovers is probably best done by practitioners who, on their own and without being told to do so by some research design, find the particular findings to be exciting, sensible, appealing, attractive, meaningful, workable and useful (Shapiro, 1957, 1964, 1969; McCullough, 1984). The circle is completed when these tapes are then fed back into the library of tapes to be studied, and we begin once again with step 1, in which the judges study the tape to determine if there are any impressive changes.

These nine steps are one way of carrying out discovery-oriented research. They may be taken as one concrete meaning of discovery-oriented research.

Is discovery-oriented research elegant?

I don't know if the word 'elegant' is the most fitting word. I am not quite sure what 'elegant' means in regard to a reason for and a way of doing research. However, I gradually saw and appreciated what this approach looked like as it emerged over a fair number of years. I also came increasingly to appreciate how it stacked up next to other research approaches, how it was able to reveal secret after secret of psychotherapy, how rigorous and systematic and yet careful and sensitive it was, and perhaps, above all, how this approach rose to mastering issues dealing with sophisticated conceptualization, careful reasoning, resolution of many of the esoteric questions in the field, helping to elevate the science of psychotherapy research and paving the way toward high-level advancement of the field.

The more I observed the discovery-oriented approach in action, the more I came to appreciate that it seemed to have a special characteristic of, well, 'elegance'. I hope that this section can help clarify what I mean. Perhaps you can provide a more fitting and appropriate word or phrase.

It is common to think of most traditional research as perhaps starting with a phase that is frequently looked down on as exploratory, pilot, observational, soft, naturalistic, preliminary. It is a way of coming up with ideas that rigorous research turns into testable hypotheses to be subjected to superior, careful, precise, scientific, controlled experimental testing, verification, confirmation and disconfirmation. The preliminary discovery-oriented phase can be of some use, but it is not the real thing.

The idea is to relax scientific standards and to poke around, do a little exploration, perhaps a pilot study or two, and come up with a respectable hunch. Then put the rigorous standards back in place, carefully frame a testable hypothesis, and subject the hypothesis to scientific confirmation and disconfirmation. 'Typically, the discovery context is the source for our concepts and hypotheses and the justification context is the warrant for their confirmation or their disconfirmation' (Borgen, 1992, p. 113; compare Reichenbach, 1938; Gelso, 1991).

Research is commonly thought of as having a mission, but the mission is not to discover. Research has a hallowed role to fulfill in developing and advancing the science of psychotherapy, but the role does not feature discovery. 'The hallmark role of research is *not* to innovate, *not* to discover exciting new therapeutic techniques or interventions' (Kiesler, 1994, p. 143). I disagree.

The purpose of this section is to outline a case that discovery-oriented psychotherapy research can be elegant, rigorous, elevated, polished, refined, that it can be far superior to ordinary, hypothesis-testing research in terms of sheer elegance (Mahrer, 1988a). If the goal of research is to discover more and more of what psychotherapy can do, and more and more about how to do it better and better, the ordinary scientific method may not be the ticket. It is neither designed for nor useful for such discovery (Polanyi, 1962). But the discovery-oriented approach is explicitly designed and useful for such purposes. It is a stringently careful, rigorous, scientific, elegant method of research.

An elegant way to find and describe an in-session impressive event, change, phenomenon

The most common way of finding something impressive, interesting, valuable to study in a session is to start from some preselected list. Look for indications of insight and understanding, symptom resolution, a good helping alliance. One problem is that using such a list almost forecloses the likelihood of discovering new ones. Another problem is that each item on the list was almost certainly put there by someone who decided the particular event or in-session change is one that is impressive, important, valued; it was not arrived at in a way that seems especially careful, rigorous, elegant. A third problem is that the description or nature of the supposedly impressive, valued, in-session event was determined before the event was carefully studied in actual sessions; it could be much more elegant to arrive at its careful description by studying what it actually looks like in actual sessions.

When the explicit aim is to see whether the session contains impressive and significant changes, it is not especially helpful to use common methods that are mainly designed to uncover the meaning of a text or a discourse. The question is 'are there any impressive changes in this session, and if so, what are they?'. The question is not 'how can we arrive at some meaning in this text or discourse?'. Therefore, it is not especially useful to turn to such methods as contextual analysis, thematic analysis, communication analysis, discourse analysis, text analysis, semantic analysis, content analysis or linguistic analysis.

These methods were not especially developed to find impressive in-session patient changes. What helps to make our method elegant is that it consists of a series of steps, each one getting closer to finding and identifying the impressive in-session change. Elegance is enhanced by means of the three steps:

1. Judges study a tape to determine if the tape does or does not contain impressive in-session events. Among the helpful guidelines are lists of previously determined, impressive in-session events, and suggestions of the kinds of personal cues that signal the presence of impressive

in-session events. But judges are quite free to go well beyond these merely helpful suggestions. This first step culminates in a simple judgment of yes or no.

2. If the judgment is yes, judges study the entire tape to locate where impressive events seem to be on the tape, where each starts and ends. There is no further description of the impressive event itself.

3. Judges then study the impressive event to arrive at a careful description of its nature, content, characteristics.

By carefully proceeding through these three steps, the challenge is that the discovery-oriented approach is a superior, rigorous, elegant way of finding, discovering and providing descriptions of in-session events, changes, phenomena that are impressive, important, valued.

Is the three-step method of discovering impressive change events superior to imposing predetermined large categories?

It is relatively common to look for impressive, significant, valued, in-session events by starting with a system or list of predetermined large categories such as insight and understanding, transference analysis, symptom reduction, and so on. There are at least two ways in which the three-step discovery-oriented method seems to be superior.

One is that the three-step method is far more likely to discover new impressive in-session changes that would be lost by merely imposing some list of predetermined kinds of impressive changes. The first step invites judges to go through a whole session to determine whether or not there might be one or more impressive changes, without restricting these to any predetermined list. The second step enables judges to locate where the impressive change(s) might be, again quite aside from their nature or content. These two steps allow for the discovery of impressive changes that would probably fall outside the ones that would be found by using any predetermined list of large categories.

The idea is simple, avoids the problem of being restricted to the predetermined, pre-established categories of some system and yet it is rarely used in psychotherapy research (compare Walsh, Perrucci and Severns, 1999). Essentially, judges are asked if there are any significant changes here in the session, where they are and what it is that seems to make them significant. Here is one way that the discovery-oriented method seems to be superior.

Second, once an impressive change is found, the description of its nature and content emphasizes simple, concrete, descriptive words and terms, non-jargon terms. The emphasis is much more on phenomenon-inspired description rather than inserting the impressive change event under a predetermined large category (von Eckartsberg, 1971; Giorgi,

1975, 1985, 1986, 1997; Strauss, 1980; van Zuuren, Wertz and Mook, 1987; Wertz and van Zuuren, 1987). In at least these two ways, the three-step method is superior to the more common method of using a predetermined list of large categories.

Elegance: a sensitive careful way of determining whether this is interesting to study, rather than identifying the objective truth

It is exceedingly common to assume that there really is an objective truth, and that a rigorously scientific procedure can spot the objective truth or at least come very close to approximating that objective truth (Mahrer, 2004). When this way of thinking is followed with regard to impressive, valued, significant changes, the question is 'how can a judge or judges identify the actual, veridical, objectively true impressive changes in this session?'.

According to this way of thinking, with a truly objective measuring tool or instrument, a single judge ought to be able to spot the objectively present impressive change. If the researcher wants to be quite safe, use a number of judges, and determine whether the team of judges meets some scientific criterion of agreement, e.g. two-thirds or three-quarters of the judges agree.

The discovery-oriented research strategy accepts a different way of thinking. Instead of accepting the idea of some objective truth that can be spotted by a scientific judge, the question is 'what careful, sensitive, rigorous method can enable a team of judges to determine if they have something interesting to study?'. If this team wants to study what it regards as impressive in-session changes, how can the team determine if there are impressive changes on this tape, where they are, how they can be described, and whether or not they want to study those impressive in-session changes? The discovery-oriented question is quite different from the question posed by the objective research team whose mind-set thinks in terms of objective truths.

Suppose that the research team consisted of 12 judges, and seven of the judges found what they believed to be an impressive change and were enthusiastic about studying that impressive change. Should they go ahead and study it? The discovery-oriented answer is that, if the seven judges are enthusiastic enough to study that impressive change, go ahead. The other kind of research team might be more concerned whether 58.3 per cent interjudge agreement is high enough to say that the impressive change is really an impressive change.

There can be lots of reasons for using a rather large team of judges (e.g. Pittenger, Hockett and Danehy, 1960; Luborsky and Auerbach, 1969; Labov and Fanshel, 1977; Elliott, 1983a, 1983b; Greenberg, 1984;

Marmar, Wilner and Horowitz, 1984; Mahrer et al., 1986a). One reason is to enable the team to find and study impressive changes that some of the team are quite entitled to decline seeing as impressive changes.

It is interesting to note that, in almost every instance, a surprisingly high proportion of team members agreed on the impressive change, and that the non-agreeing judges (1) were quite free to take a vacation on that impressive change and (2) to think of themselves as simply not agreeing rather than as failing to spot the impressive change that was determined by their colleagues to be objectively present.

Does the elegant replicability of the discovery-oriented strategy invite different teams to arrive at different impressive changes?

Not only that, this way of thinking invites the two teams to be proud that they came up with different impressive changes, perhaps at different places, using the same tape. The three steps used to arrive at the impressive change are careful and precise, and thereby can allow each team to be reasonably confident in the impressive changes that it came up with, even though the changes may differ from one team to the next.

Picture a team of psychoanalytic judges, another team of cognitive–behavioral judges and a third team of a healthy mix of well-known and less well-known approaches. Each team starts by determining whether or not the session seems to contain impressive changes. There is a rule that each team is to carry out this first step carefully and rigorously, but there is no rule that each team has to come up with the same answer.

If any of the teams said yes, the second step tells the judges to determine where the impressive changes are located on the tape. Once again, the different teams, using the same careful and rigorous procedure, will probably arrive at different places where the different impressive changes occurred.

The third step involves describing the impressive change and what seems to qualify it as impressive. On this third question, if two or three of the teams saw impressive changes occurring at the same places on the tape, they ought to come up with similar descriptions by following the guidelines for this third step.

The very elegance of the discovery-oriented strategy makes it understandable that different teams will arrive at different places where impressive changes occurred, if any, because of the first two steps. The first step asks if there are any impressive changes and the second step asks where they are located on the tape. The test of elegance is whether the teams followed the first two steps carefully and well, not whether they came up with the same answers.

What is an elegant alternative meaning of outcome and the ways of finding and describing outcomes?

The discovery-oriented research question is: 'What are the impressive, significant, valued changes or events that can occur in psychotherapy sessions?' The notion of 'outcome' comes when the following is the research question: 'What are the impressive, significant, valued changes or events that can occur after psychotherapy sessions?'

The field of psychotherapy has a relatively accepted meaning of what an outcome is, and how to tell if a good outcome has been achieved from a list of good, successful, impressive, significant, valued outcomes. Researchers give a battery of tests to patients before and after therapy. Researchers interview therapists and clients before and after application of a therapeutic program.

And yet, the meaning of outcome was not especially arrived at by elegant research. The categories of outcome were not especially arrived at by elegant research. The way of finding an outcome was not arrived at by elegant research. The description of what outcomes are did not especially come from elegant research. Once the meaning was accepted, once the way of finding and describing outcomes was accepted, researchers can use their tools to do a good or sloppy job of seeing whether or not this series of sessions ended with good outcomes.

It would be an interesting exercise to apply the careful discovery-oriented method to arrive at an elegant alternative meaning of post-session outcome, a way of finding outcomes and a way of describing outcomes, i.e. judges would carefully study what happened after the sessions to determine whether there were any impressive changes, to flag where the impressive changes seem to have occurred, and finally to describe the impressive changes and what qualifies them as impressive. It would seem that this would probably result in a more elegant meaning of outcomes and a more elegant set of descriptions of what the outcomes are.

How to bring about, use and program in-session impressive changes elegantly?

There are some questions that many practitioners face and that most researchers do not study (e.g. Spence, 1994). Here are a few of these questions:

- How can I help to bring about these impressive in-session changes?
- How can I use these impressive in-session changes once they occur?
- How can I program, organize into steps, these impressive in-session changes?

In general, most studies of what happens in therapy sessions, how therapy works, how psychotherapeutic change occurs, start with some predetermined notions, ideas, conceptualizations, theories. The studies are inclined to clarify, confirm or perhaps even cast some doubt on what the researcher already seems to believe. It is relatively rare that the researcher sets out with a genuine willingness to see, discover, be surprised by, what answers may be found to a question of what seems to happen in therapy sessions, how therapy seems to work, how psychotherapeutic change seems to happen. The spirit is one of being surprised by what you discover, rather than checking out what you believe is true.

Researchers have little trouble finding category systems of things that therapists do, or ways that therapists and patients are with one another, that therapists respond to clients, important, valued and good things that happen in psychotherapy sessions. One trouble with these category systems is that they begin their work with categories that are already predetermined, pre-established. This makes it very hard to discover new categories of good and significant in-session changes and how to bring them about and use them once they occur. Using category systems is bad for researchers who are dedicated to discovering new categories (e.g. Walsh, Perrucci and Severns, 1999), who want to discover new and better answers to questions of how to bring about, use and program impressive in-session changes.

The exciting challenge is that the discovery-oriented method of doing research is an elegant, useful, effective way of answering these questions. Indeed, the tough, bold challenge is that the discovery-oriented way of doing research is superior to virtually all other ways of doing research to answer these questions.

A grand matrix for selecting how to do psychotherapy

Each batch of findings adds to an ever-growing, ever-clarified, more comprehensive matrix of impressive changes, sequences in which they occur, how to help bring them about and how to use each impressive change. Here is perhaps an elegant gift of practitioner-relevant findings, a gift that practitioners can find useful.

Picture a practitioner as first selecting the kinds of impressive, valued changes that are important to that practitioner. Then picture the practitioner as selecting, from the matrix, the sequences of impressive changes that provide the practitioner with a programmatic series of steps of impressive changes. This programmatic sequence tells the practitioner the steps to follow in achieving the impressive changes that are deemed important by and for the practitioner, either in general or for this patient or these patients. Finally, the matrix provides the practitioner with the concretely specific methods of helping to bring about each impressive change in the sequence, and how to use each impressive change, once it occurs, in order to move toward the subsequent impressive change in the programmatic sequence.

In essence, the grand matrix of findings provides practitioners with a way of selecting how to do psychotherapy, both in a programmatic sequential way and in more concrete, specific, working ways. Make your selection and you have virtually selected your way of doing psychotherapy.

Is starting from in-session impressive changes superior to traditional ways of studying how to do psychotherapy?

One traditional way to study what happens in psychotherapy sessions, to find out what in-session work can be like, is to test predetermined hypotheses. If the therapist does this or that, under these conditions, this valued patient change should occur. If you do good interpretations, here is the good patient change that ought to happen. The researcher ordinarily tests this hypothesis and then leans toward saying, yes, that seems to be the case, or leans toward having some doubts.

Another traditional way is to wait until sessions between patient and therapist are over, either a single session or the whole series of sessions, and do one of two things. One is to ask the therapist or patient if the session was a good one and what they liked in the session, something that seemed good. The second is to decide that the patient is now much better, and to study lots of connections between what you think happened in the session and the impressive post-treatment outcome assessment.

One of the troubles with traditional ways of studying how to do psychotherapy is that they are not especially designed for, or very good for, finding out much about how to help bring about specific kinds of impressive in-session changes or how to use them once they occur. In addition, these traditional ways of studying psychotherapy are very weak both in discovering the impressive and valued in-session changes that occur and can occur, and in helping to discover the sequences in which these impressive changes occur.

It seems that a much more superior way of answering these questions is to start by locating and finding the impressive changes in the session. Not only do these impressive changes enable you to find the sequences in which they occur, across a session or a series of sessions, but each impressive change serves as an anchor point, a starting place. Once an impressive change is located and described, it is relatively easy to examine what the therapist and patient seemed to have done to help bring it about, and to examine how the therapist seemed to use that impressive change once it occurred.

The challenging case is that starting from in-session impressive changes is superior to traditional ways of studying how to do psychotherapy, how to help bring about, use and program in-session impressive changes.

Elegant ways of discovering far more than just the sum of what is discoverable on each tape

It is perhaps easy to think that this research strategy is limited to what was discovered on each tape, or even to a kind of pooling, combining or adding up of what was discovered on each tape. In contrast, the discovery-oriented strategy includes some elegant ways of discovering much more.

Creating categories from components of the tapes

The discovery-oriented strategy includes the creation of categories: categories of impressive changes, methods, how to use impressive changes. Studying each session culminates in the continuous modification of the system of categories. However, in an important sense, the categories are more than what is found on any tape, or even the sum of what is found on all of the tapes.

For example, in one session, an impressive change was identified as the patient's decision to leave her parents' home and talk with her friend about finding an apartment. In another session, the impressive change consisted of the patient's excitement about giving his neighbor a gift of roses and his intention to do this tomorrow. A third impressive change, in another tape, was the patient's resolve to go home and tell his wife the truth about his mother and how she died, even though he had essentially lied about this throughout their marriage. The method of creating and revising categories brought these three impressive changes together into a single larger category described as a state of readiness for new ways of being and behaving in the world. Rather than the mere sum of what was found in the three impressive changes from three different patients, categories are created over and above the actual components from which the categories emerge.

Which methods can go beyond the sum of what is discoverable on each tape?

Consider three tapes where the same kind of impressive change is achieved. In one tape, method x seems to work; in a second tape, method y seems to work; and in a third tape, method z seems to work. Careful

study of what occurred on each tape seems to indicate that the same
patient condition or state characterized the first two tapes, but was absent
in the third tape. Accordingly, the provisional description of how to
achieve the impressive change goes along these lines: when the patient is
in condition or state a, methods x or y may be useful to help achieve the
impressive change; however, when the patient is not in condition or state
a, method z may be useful to help achieve the impressive change. This
working principle can emerge from careful study of what was found on
each tape, but is more than the mere sum of what was discoverable on
each tape.

What sequences of impressive changes are beyond what was found on the individual tapes?

Perhaps one of the most powerful and far-reaching gifts of the discovery-
oriented research strategy is that of in-session sequences, programs or
steps of impressive changes. What seems elegantly exciting is that these
sequences or steps may not be present in any of the tapes, and yet can
emerge from discovery-oriented study of all the tapes.

A simple example is when impressive change x was followed by impressive change y, perhaps in a number of tapes. In other tapes, impressive
change y was followed by impressive change z. The emergent discovery is
a more comprehensive in-session sequence of steps starting with impressive change x, proceeding to impressive change y, and culminating in
impressive change z, yet this sequence of steps did not occur in any of the
tapes.

Enlarging the scope of the discovery to reach a big principle

Once the discovery-oriented strategy finds something new, another elegant way of discovering far more than just the sum of what is discoverable
on each tape is to keep enlarging the scope of what was discovered. Keep
pumping it up. Keep seeking bigger and bigger implications until the
scope runs into some big principle, some standard and accepted principle
in the field of psychotherapy. This procedure is to be carried out carefully,
logically, conceptually, elegantly.

For example, suppose that a discovered method consisted of inviting
the patient to close her eyes and do her best to allow whatever feeling was
here to become as powerful as it can. The limited implication may hold
that here is a method of achieving a higher state of feeling. If the
researcher kept enlarging the scope, kept thinking bigger and bigger until
it bumps up against, collides with, challenges a much bigger and broader
principle, an established way of thinking about and doing psychotherapy,

what might be the newly discovered notion, idea, possibility? The discovered principle may be stated as follows:

> In therapies for which this way of thinking is suitable, virtually every session may begin by inviting the patient to close the eyes and to allow whatever bodily felt feeling is present to become substantially stronger, more intense, more powerful.

Here is another example. Suppose that a number of effective methods for achieving a number of kinds of impressive changes included the component of the person's attention being directed toward personally important centers of attention such as the cancer in the lungs, the special look on her mother's face, the rippling reflections on the water. If this finding is enlarged until it challengingly collides with a generally accepted basic principle, the newly created discovered principle may be stated as follows:

> To attain these particular kinds of impressive changes, it is helpful if the person's attention is predominantly directed toward and focused on elements that are personally important and significant, rather than the person participating in the traditional patient–therapist relationship in which their attention is predominantly directed toward and focused on the other.

The elegance lies in careful and rigorous enlargement of the discovered finding until it bumps up against, challengingly collides with a principle that is relatively important, generally accepted and regarded as part of what is traditionally taken for granted in the field of psychotherapy.

Is discovery of a better way perhaps more elegant than showing that a way works?

One of the nagging problems in the traditional research strategy of trying to prove, confirm, verify, uphold a hypothesis is that the very attempt is fruitless. It is, philosophers of science contend, impossible to show that all reasonably possible instances will confirm a hypothesis. At the other end, it takes only a few strong instances to disprove, disconfirm, falsify the hypothesis. Popper (1980) went a long way in solving the problem by showing the conceptual power and elegance in researchers actually trying to disconfirm, disprove, falsify a hypothesis, in showing how theories can grow, develop, improve when researchers shifted from trying to confirm and verify a hypothesis to trying to disconfirm and falsify a hypothesis.

In an extension of the spirit of this Popperian shift, discovery-oriented research invites researchers to look for better and better ways of achieving some goal, aim, use, rather than doing research to show that some particular way works. In this sense, discovery-oriented research is more elegant than most traditional strategies aimed at verifying, proving, confirming that this particular way works and is effective, successful or more so than some other way.

Avoiding many of the problems of trying to test imprecisely vague categories of therapeutic methods

The search for ways of helping to bring about and use impressive changes puts a high premium on discovering methods described rather carefully, concretely. Furthermore, the methods are also described by carefully describing the patient conditions or states that provide the explicit helpful contexts. Picture a method as consisting of a clause, 'when the person is being this way or that way, or is in this or that condition', followed by about 30–50 or so words laying out much of what the therapist actually does in carrying out the method. This way of describing a method is in some contrast with the common use of big, loose categories so that researchers say that the therapists are using methods of interpretation, empathy, paradoxical intention, self-exploration, alliance development, guided imagery, two-chair technique, empowerment, desensitization, relaxation, heightening of experiencing.

When methods are described carefully, rather than lumped under big, loose categories, and when the emphasis is on discovery of new and better ways, rather than on showing that a method works, you are minimizing or avoiding some tough problems that researchers can easily run into: when the category is big enough, loose enough and able to stretch far enough, it is easy to drain any new method of its newness. Fresh new discoveries quickly lose their distinctiveness when they are dressed in the uniform of the masses: 'Oh, that is self-exploration. . . . Of course, that is experiencing heightening. We already got that.'

It is easy to presume that two therapists, or all the therapists, are using the same method. 'Therapists in the experimental group used interpretation.' The therapists are indeed using the same method when what they are doing is encompassed by a large and loose category labeled interpretation. However, when methods are described carefully, as emphasized by the discovery-oriented strategy, few if any of the therapists in the experimental group were using the same method at all.

When therapist methods are packaged in large categories, it is hard to tell if the therapist is carrying out a method inadequately, barely adequately, in a satisfactory way or in a most elevated manner. It is a good idea to check. Manuals won't help much because they generally emphasize what is adequate. With or without manuals, usually there is a problem of just how well or how poorly the category was carried out, both by the same therapist in different places and by different therapists, all supposedly using the method of alliance development. This problem tends to be sharply minimized when the method is described carefully, so that there is much less room for sloppy inclusion and it is much easier to say that what the therapist is doing does not qualify.

When researchers pronounce that the therapists are using interpretation or empathy or self-exploration, the typical heavy emphasis is on what the therapists are doing. What is almost always omitted is a careful description of the patient condition or state, and the patient's participation and helpful assistance in carrying out the method. This rather common and seemingly serious problem is minimized or avoided when the researcher uses the discovery-oriented procedure of describing the therapeutic method.

All in all, the search to discover new carefully described methods seems elegantly superior to, and avoids some serious problems of, trying to test imprecisely vague categories of therapist methods.

If the session is effective, how can this therapy become more effective?

It is relatively common for many psychotherapy researchers to try to determine if a particular treatment is effective, or effective for this problem in particular. I am inclined to believe that a more elegant research quest is to discover better and better ways to help a psychotherapy become continuously better and better, e.g. each session of experiential psychotherapy has two aims or goals (Mahrer, 1996/2004, 2002). One is to enable the person who began the session to become a qualitatively new person, based on and including a deeper potentiality discovered in the session. The other is for the person to be free of the painful scenes that were front and center for the person in the session.

The session is effective if these two goals are achieved by the end of the session, and can be shown to be achieved in the beginning of the next session. If the session is an effective one, the session can be examined to see if more can be discovered about how to achieve the two goals of the session. The spirit is that it is more elegant to discover more and more about how to make each session better and better than it is to show that some treatment is effective.

Three reasons why discovery-oriented research is elegant

Compared with the common preference for doing hypothesis-testing research, discovery-oriented research can be more elegant because it allows for the testing of hypotheses as well as at least three things that hypothesis testing has less of, namely discovery of new things, the adoption and use of what was discovered by practitioners who find the discoveries appealing and useful, and the continual feeding in and study of further instances.

Suppose that the study of one impressive change finds one way of helping to achieve that change. As additional instances of that kind of impressive change are studied, the further findings allow the researcher, at the same time: (1) to clarify the confidence of previously found ways of helping to achieve that impressive change; (2) to refine, modify and advance the previously found ways of helping to achieve that impressive change; and (3) to discover alternative and additional ways of helping to achieve that change (Roos, 1979; Mahrer, 1985, 1988a, 1996b; Hoshmand, 1989). The combination of hypothesis testing, confidence building and further discovery seems elegant (compare Shapiro, 1951; Edwards, 1998), and applies not only to ways of helping to achieve impressive change, but also to developing categories of impressive changes, sequences of impressive changes and ways of using impressive changes.

The case for elegance holds that hypothesis-testing research is weaker than discovery-oriented research because it is not designed to include further discovery, whereas discovery-oriented research is more powerful than hypothesis-testing research because it is designed to include both further discovery and the checking out of what had been discovered.

Is it more elegant to invite interested practitioners to try the hypothesis out than to test it?

Suppose that the research finds a particular method of helping to achieve this particular impressive change. A common research strategy is to test out the finding, e.g. get some therapists to use the method and see if the method is effective in getting the hypothesized consequence, i.e. the particular impressive change.

The discovery-oriented strategy is, in contrast, to put the finding into the public marketplace, to invite interested practitioners to try using this method if they are indeed interested in helping to bring about this particular impressive change. The invitation includes a careful description of the method, and how and when to use this specific method to help achieve this particular impressive change. The research plea is for these practitioners to contribute their attempts at using this method to the library of tapes that are studied.

In a sense, the discovery-oriented procedure seems more honest. The practitioners who actually use the method are practitioners who are drawn toward the method, like it, want to use it, and tend to find the method and the impressive change sensible and valued. This has some preferential features over finding a group of therapists with varying interest in using the method, varying value in the impressive change, varying eagerness to find some new way of getting that impressive change. Instead of recruiting and training a group of therapists in using this method, it would be an interesting challenge to see what proportion of these therapists would choose to read about the method on their own, register for a workshop on the method, naturally seek out and use this method on their own. I doubt if the proportion is high in most hypothesis-testing studies.

There is an additional way in which the discovery-oriented procedure can be more elegantly sensitive, powerful and richer. It allows the researcher to study the new tapes to see whether the specific method, used under the specific patient state and condition, results in the impressive change or some other impressive change. It opens the door to studying variations and improvements on the particular method. It allows the researcher to see if this particular method shows up in studying what therapists seem to do in helping to bring about other kinds of impressive changes. In general, it seems that inviting interested practitioners to try out the discovered method is, in many ways, more elegant than traditional testing of the hypothesis.

Discovery-oriented research elevates the search for knowledge above the validation of what the traditional researcher already believes is true

There is a kind of elegance in the researcher using careful methods in the scientific adventure of discovery, exploration, and pursuit and extension of knowledge. There is a kind of elegance in the researcher's discovery of the secrets of psychotherapy by asking what are the impressive changes to be found in this tape, do the changes fall into identifiable sequences, what are the ways of helping to arrive at these changes and how may these changes be used once they occur. Asking these questions in a spirit of discovery provides a way of continuously advancing not only the actual methods, but also what can be achieved in psychotherapy, as well as the conceptual sense-making of what is discovered.

The discovery-oriented strategy is hopefully a careful means of discovering new knowledge. It is a systematic way of engaging in the sheer adventure of discovering what we can learn. The discovery-oriented researcher has an eagerness and a readiness to find out more, to discover more. It is as if the researcher merely begins with what we believe we know, and has a picture of whole new universes of what is out there to be discovered.

Discovering or coming up with new ideas, the creative phase of research, is usually thought of as somehow happening before the researcher does the scientific study. It is almost looked down on as not actually or really doing research, but exploratory, pilot, observational, soft, naturalistic, preliminary. A non-rigorous study may perhaps be called one of these words and have a fair chance of being published. Yet it is one source of what researchers salute as hypothesis derivation. Another source is theory deduction, carefully and logically deducing down from a theory to a hypothesis to be tested. The trouble is that few researchers are rigorous and sophisticated in the creative phase of research, coming up with hypotheses, arriving at creative hypotheses (McGuire, 1989, 1997). It is here that discovery-oriented research can be elegant in blending the discovery-oriented outlook, the search for what is new, the careful, rigorous framing of research questions and perhaps even creative, new, discovery-oriented hypotheses.

In contrast, most traditional research consists of the testing of hypotheses, mainly to show the truth of what the researcher already believes is true. The hypothesis is usually dressed in null language, but the vocabulary rarely disguises what the researcher believes. Indeed, whatever creative thinking might have been involved probably took place in arriving at the hypothesis to be tested, rather than in the course of the study. The case is that elegance resides more in the discovery of what is new than in the testing of what is already believed.

Use of the common scientific or discovery-oriented methods

The common scientific method has some identifying features. It usually includes an hypothesis that is to be tested, confirmed or disconfirmed. It usually involves an experimental group and a control group. The common scientific method has an admirable public relations, marketing label because calling it 'scientific' gives the impression that it is used when you want to do research that is scientific, careful, rigorous, and that some other method would therefore be less scientific. Actually, the experiment–control method is just fine for checking out what you believe is true. If you believe it is true, and you want to see if it is really true, use the scientific method of experiment and control.

On the other hand, if your aim is mainly to discover, to explore what you don't know but are curious to know, use the discovery-oriented method. The two are different, and they have different aims, purposes and uses.

The scientific method can do a little discovery, but it was not built for discovery as its main use. It is best used to check out what you believe is true. In the same way, the discovery-oriented method can check out what you believe is true, but that is not its main job. Its main job is to enable you to discover new knowledge.

The secrets of change through direct study of the actual change phenomenon

There seems to be a kind of simple and pure elegance in discovering the secrets of wondrous change by a straightforward, simple, pure, direct focus on the prized change phenomenon itself (Schutz, 1964; Spiegelberg, 1972; Keen, 1975; Valle and King, 1978; Giorgi, 1985). You may be intensely interested in the working practicalities of how to help bring about a particular change, or your special interest may be in making conceptual sense of how and why change occurs. In either case, perhaps the most fruitful and elegant way is to be curious and fascinated with a careful and close study of this wonderful change, of that wonderful change, and of what seems to occur inside and between each of these wonderful changes. Elegance lies in the up-close, in-depth, naïvely open study of the actual change phenomenon.

Faced with what seems like a genuine in-session change, the discovery-oriented researcher is somewhat like the naïve child who simply rushes into the phenomenon, excited to probe into it, see how it works. This rushing in is in contrast to a way of studying psychotherapeutic change by first selecting or developing a theory of how psychotherapeutic change occurs (Kiesler, 1973; Marmar, 1990). Where does the elegance lie? I believe it lies in the energetic rushing down into the phenomenon to see how it works, rather than in the backing away and thinking about some conceptual way of making sense of the removed phenomenon.

Instead of directly probing into the actual change phenomenon itself, elegance is lost when the researcher transfers the focus of study to whatever is regarded as outcomes at the end of treatment, miles away from the actual change phenomenon itself.

Elegance is sacrificed when the researcher rises far above the actual change phenomenon into a high level of abstraction, and views the actual change phenomenon through distancing and distorting conceptual lenses such as egocentrism, helping alliance, borderline condition, regression, or any of the thousands of abstract conceptual lenses.

Elegance is sacrificed when the researcher inserts an opaque barrier between the researcher and the actual change phenomenon by instead studying test scores, measures, questionnaires or interviews between an interviewer and the clients or therapists (compare Kagan, Krathwohl and

Miller, 1963; Andreozzi, 1985; Elliott, 1985, 1986; Martin, Martin and Slemon, 1987; Elliott and Shapiro, 1988, 1992; Kivlighan and Angelone, 1991; Lietaer, 1992). Not only does this situation open the door to inter- viewer-driven data, biases and responses, but it replaces careful study of the actual change phenomenon with interviewer–interviewee interactions, rela- tionships, situational contexts and conjointly determined mutual effects.

Elegance is also sacrificed when the researcher concentrates much more on the therapist's subjective reports or on the patient's subjective reports than on the actual in-session change phenomenon itself. Qualitative researchers have mined a rich lode by interviewing therapists and patients, and by focusing their analyses on these data rather than on the actual in-session change events themselves. For a review of these stud- ies and their findings, see Maione and Chenail (1999).

Is it more elegant if research questions beget research methods rather than research methods begetting research questions?

Most fields of study start with research questions and then develop research methods to help answer the research questions (Koch, 1959; Feyerabend, 1972; Chalmers, 1982; Slife and Williams, 1995). However, to a large extent, the field of psychotherapy has reversed the matter by first embracing research methods, largely those dictated by experimental psy- chology, with the unfortunate consequence that the research methods determine, limit, restrict the allowable research questions. It is almost as if a person approaches the field of psychotherapy by first checking out the toolbox of research methods, and then reasoning like this: 'Given these research methods, what kind of problem do they let me study or what kind of question do they allow me to ask?'

Almost without exception, most new research methods were devel- oped as a helpful means of examining some research problem or answering some research question. However, when psychotherapy researchers include these new methods in their toolbox, these new methods come stamped as scientifically approved, and take their place as defining what kinds of problems may be studied and what kinds of ques- tions may be asked. The discovery-oriented strategy seems more elegant by allowing the research questions to help determine what research meth- ods are useful, and to invite the researcher to develop research methods that are useful in trying to answer these research questions.

As a rather undramatic, small example, almost from the beginning of research on psychotherapy, relatively sophisticated methods of sequential analysis were available (Snyder, 1945), and these were developed into time-series analysis (Glass, Wilson and Gottman, 1975), cross-lag time-series analysis (Gottman, 1979) and stochastic process analysis (Hertel, 1972; Lichtenberg and Hummel, 1976; Benjamin, 1979; Lichtenberg and Heck, 1979) of sequential events, usually organized into Markov chains (e.g. Friedlander and Phillips, 1984; Mercier and Johnson, 1984; Tracey and Ray, 1984; Tracey, 1985; Wampold and Kim, 1989). When researchers started with these sophisticated methods, the problems they found appropriate to look at were limited to things such as sequences of the ratio of self-directed words to other-directed words, pronoun–verb couplings, and sequences of topic initiation and topic following. In contrast, the discovery-oriented researcher is freer to start with the question 'Do impressive, significant, valued, in-session changes or events occur in some sequence or sequences?' and to let this research question help seek out the more useful research methods, and even to guide or invite the researcher to figure out more useful new research methods.

There seem to be at least two ways in which many psychotherapy researchers lose elegance by worshipping research methods that have almost uniformly been developed in and for fields outside psychotherapy, and by operating under an implicit principle that these research methods beget the research questions. One is that this common stance tends to truncate, restrict and sharply limit the range and scope of research questions asked by most psychotherapy researchers. A second is that this common stance has the same kind of deadening effect on the possibility of developing new and better psychotherapy research methods, methods that can be expressly useful and appropriate for answering the questions of psychotherapy researchers.

Elegance seems to be higher when the discovery-oriented researcher allows the research questions to beget the research methods, as compared with the common stance in which accepted research methods beget the research questions.

Do discovery-oriented research questions have little or no call for research methods such as 'experiments' or 'control groups'?

Starting with a rather careful framing of the discovery-oriented research questions, the job was how to develop a research strategy that was useful and also rigorous, careful, trustworthy, scientific. When the research methods were assembled and put into place, some almost universal research methods were seen to be missing. The discovery-oriented research strategy did not include research methods such as doing 'experiments' or using 'control groups'.

Could a research strategy be truly rigorous and scientific without including experiments and control groups? If the research methods are determined by the research questions, perhaps there really is no place for doing experiments and using control groups. If doing good research, doing research scientifically, means having experiments and using control groups, shouldn't the discovery-oriented research strategy include experiments and control groups? Yet there seemed to be no place in this research strategy for experiments and control groups. It seemed that, if research questions are allowed to beget research methods, an elegant research strategy can be put into place without using research methods such as experiments and control groups.

Does the more elegant principle replace 'the scientific method' with 'various scientific methods'?

In the field of psychotherapy research, it is common to think of the one and only grand scientific method, scientific research strategy, design, methodology. The idea is that the specific research methods are all to fall under one large scientific method.

Even at this higher level, the discovery-oriented research strategy holds to a principle that there can be various scientific methods, designs, strategies, and which one to use depends in large part on the particular research question(s), or the aim and intent of the research (Koch, 1959; Reichardt and Cook, 1979; Tharp and Gallimore, 1982; Williams, 1986; Geer and O'Donohue, 1989; Slife and Williams, 1995).

This way of looking at research declines the assumption of a single grand scientific method. 'The false assumption that there is a universal scientific method to which all forms of knowledge should conform plays a detrimental role in our society here and now, especially in the light of the fact that the version of the scientific method usually appealed to is some crude empiricist or inductivist one' (Chalmers, 1982, p. 141). When the work consists of answering the discovery-oriented research questions, elegance seems to lie more in thinking of the various scientific methods than in the common mind-set of 'the scientific method'.

Can the findings of discovery-oriented research provide especially fertile ground for elegant conceptualization?

Discovery-oriented research is always looking for new things, and the discovery of new things can and should be especially fertile ground for conceptual sense-making, elegant new conceptualization (compare Gelso, 1991). The findings almost proclaim that here is something new, something new that is specific, concrete, tangible, and these findings challenge the conceptualizer: 'How can these new findings lead you to arrive at new ways of conceptualizing these discovered new in-session impressive changes, these new sequences of impressive changes, these new ways of helping to bring about these impressive changes and these new ways of using these impressive changes once they occur?'

Some philosophers of science are skeptical about the ability of careful and rigorous methods, whether the methods of research or logic, to really shed much light on the discovery or creation of bold new ideas. 'There is no such thing as a logical method of having new ideas, or a logical reconstruction of this process. My view may be expressed by saying that every discovery contains "an irrational element", or "a creative intuition", in Bergson's sense' (Popper, 1980, p. 32; compare Gadamer, 1975).

I am inclined to disagree under particular conditions. I disagree when the conceptualizer allows him- or herself to concentrate on the fruits of discovery-oriented research. I disagree when the conceptualizer is ready and willing to allow the new findings to spark bold new conceptualizations. And I disagree when the conceptualizer knows how to go from the newly minted research findings to bold new conceptualizations, e.g. suppose that the conceptualizer starts with a finding that impressive change a seems to precede and be followed by impressive change b. Impressive change a is that the patient seems to have become an altogether new and different person, a wholesale change. Impressive change b is a substantially new perspective on things, new insights and ways of understanding things. The conceptualizer starts with this finding, is ready and willing to allow this finding to spark bold new conceptualizations, and knows how to let this finding grow and grow, become bigger and bigger, more and more expansive until it bumps into an established, commonly accepted, broad, basic principle of psychotherapy. The conceptualizer faces solving this problem: it is commonly presumed that insight and understanding help bring about substantial change; therefore, the therapist works at trying to promote heightened insight and understanding. But here is the opposite possibility: once the person undergoes qualitative change, becomes a whole new person, there is a whole new outlook, a whole new perspective, a whole new way of understanding things, insights. Therefore, perhaps therapists should work at finding how to have the person become a qualitatively new person, and insight and understanding are merely little indications that the person has indeed become a whole new person. The conceptualizer is on the threshold of creating some exciting bold conceptualization.

A relatively strong case can be made that the discovery-oriented research strategy is especially well suited for elegant conceptualization. Its findings are wonderfully fertile ground for the conceptualizer who is eager to do some elegant conceptualization and knows the skills of engaging in elegant conceptualization.

When does conceptualization occur in traditional research and in discovery-oriented research?

The traditional researcher usually does conceptual thinking before launching into the actual study. Arriving at some hypothesis to test almost always means starting with some conceptual system and reasoning down to a testable hypothesis. The researcher starts with some conceptual framework and does the theorizing in order to end up with a given study. Research on psychotherapeutic change generally starts by already holding, selecting or figuring out a theory of psychotherapeutic change (Kiesler, 1973; Marmar, 1990). Watch most traditional researchers, and the conceptualization is laid out, is done, well before the actual research is begun.

In discovery-oriented research, the situation is reversed. Once the findings are in, discovered, the discovery-oriented researcher can be ready to start conceptualizing, making conceptual sense of the findings. Where the traditional researcher may conclude by saying, 'I was right. My hypothesis was confirmed', the discovery-oriented researcher may say, 'Well! I wonder how I can make sense of this?'. Discovery-oriented findings are grist for the conceptual mill.

Some concluding concerns about and hopes for the discovery-oriented approach

Each of the previous chapters has concluded with a summary of the serious problems underlying that chapter's reason for doing research on psychotherapy. There probably are some serious problems associated with the discovery-oriented approach, but I believe that others are in a far better position than I am to identify and articulate these serious problems.

However, perhaps because I have helped to participate in the evolution of this reason for and way of doing research on psychotherapy, I do have some concluding concerns about and hopes for this particular approach:

1. I am concerned that so few researchers have a 'discovery-oriented' mind-set, and I hope that there can be more who think in terms of discovery. Somewhat more specifically, I have a few fond hopes:

(a) I hope that the small number of researchers whose way of thinking is somewhat cordial to the discovery-oriented approach can actually do some studies that are geared toward discovery. There are some studies. I picture that there can be more.

(b) I believe that one reason for the small number of discovery-oriented researchers is that the field of psychotherapy research does not seem to have a breadth and depth of appreciation and knowledge of the field of philosophy of science. It seems sensible to hope that future psychotherapy researchers can benefit from more emphasis on philosophy of science in their education and training.

(c) At present, with a rare exception here and there, virtually none of the psychotherapy researchers follows the discovery-oriented flag. I hope that these researchers can be kind enough to leave a non-threatening little bit of room for the discovery-oriented reason and approach, e.g. a brief mention of discovery-oriented research in authoritative reviews of psychotherapy research, a citation or so in the reading lists of courses on psychotherapy research, an occasional acceptance of a discovery-oriented article in a journal.

2. I sincerely hope that discovery-oriented researchers will make dedicated efforts to find tapes of sessions containing events that are special, unusual, magnificent, impressive, exciting. Such sessions can be available. It takes a few dedicated researchers to find them.

(a) I record each of my sessions, partly because my eyes are closed throughout the session, and writing down some notes about the session is helped by going over parts of the taped session, after the session. Once in a while, I keep the recording for later, more careful study, because I believe something happened in the session that was inexplicable, perhaps special and impressive.

My hope is that an increasingly larger proportion of psychotherapists will record most of their sessions, and will be willing to study, or to send to discovery-oriented researchers, those rare sessions where something magical and wondrous, something unusual and inexplicable, seemed to have happened.

(b) By all means, I value discovery-oriented study of tapes of distinguished exemplars of the various approaches, and of dedicated proponents of the dominant approaches. However, I hope that discovery-oriented researchers can also value locating and studying the work of gifted masters of the craft who are not especially well known; practitioners who are exploring new territory, pushing the outer limits of the field, are the creative innovators; and practitioners who are far outside the mainstream, on the periphery.

3. This chapter offered one way to do discovery-oriented research. There are, and there can be, other and perhaps better ways of doing this research. I hope that researchers make this way better and better, and find other and better ways of doing this kind of research.

   Partly because this way of doing research is relatively new, and only a small number of researchers use it, I had to turn to 'on-the-job' innovations and useful methods. I turned to trial and error to find useful methods. My impression is that the future can include sound and solid improvement and advancement in the working methods of carrying out discovery-oriented research.

   Doing research with the primary aim of discovering new things is relatively new, and it may therefore lead to the development of newer research methods on the presumption that research questions tend to beget research methods. Ask a new question, and you may well be inclined to lead to the development of new methods. The alternative presumption, unfortunately somewhat at home in the field of psychotherapy research, is that research methods beget research questions, so that the range of research questions is partly determined and restricted by the range of accepted research methods.

4. I have a naïve trust that the field of psychotherapy can move ahead when truly creative people study truly extraordinary events in actual sessions of psychotherapy. By truly creative people, I am picturing unusually creative psychotherapy researchers, practitioners and theorists, and other creative people who may be interested. My impression is that this does not happen much in the field of psychotherapy.

   My fond hope is that there can be much more room for such creative people to study these special sessions, and for the rest of us to appreciate what these truly creative people discover, to appreciate how much more these people can see, and how the field of psychotherapy can move ahead on the basis of what these truly creative people discover by studying these special sessions.

Conclusions and invitations

When I was reading about why researchers did research on psychotherapy, I had plenty of questions and plenty of curiosity. However, I had essentially no conclusions in mind when I was doing this reading. I had no preconceptions about the problems involved in doing this kind of research for whatever reasons researchers did this kind of research, or at least I was aware of no such preconceptions. I had essentially no idea about what the field of research might do differently on the basis of conclusions that were not even taking shape in a flimsy way. In other words, while I was doing most of the reading, especially in philosophy of science, I would not have been able to write even a rough draft of the non-existent conclusions and invitations.

Now it is time to spell out the conclusions and invitations. I hope that the following three points can help you to appreciate the spirit underlying the conclusions and invitations.

1. One is that these are presented as my conclusions and invitations, rather than as authoritative truths. I am trying to draw the conclusions that seem reasonable and sensible to me, rather than trying to approximate 'the truth' about why researchers do research on psychotherapy, and about the serious problems underlying each of these reasons. I can appreciate that others may well draw different conclusions.
2. Second, although the conclusions seem important to me, I regard the 'invitations' as even more important. In other words, much of the importance and worth of the conclusions lie in the actions that follow from the conclusions, in what researchers actually do if they accept the conclusions as reasonable and sensible. My excitement lies much more in the invitations that flow from the conclusions, rather than in the actual conclusions.
3. Third, I sincerely hope that these conclusions and invitations can help lead to further discussion, debate, serious consideration. Put differently, the intended contribution of this book is to stir up constructive

discussion and debate about these conclusions and invitations, to serve as a touchstone for interested others to study these conclusions and invitations, to go beyond these particular conclusions and invitations. It seems relatively easy to list the conclusions and invitations. It also seems relatively easy to pass them by, to dismiss them, to note and file them away. I sincerely hope that these conclusions and invitations are just the beginning of fruitful dialogue and discussion.

This is the spirit underlying the following conclusions and invitations.

The different reasons, aims and goals for doing research on psychotherapy

It seems possible to rise to a high enough level of almost meaningless abstraction at which all of the various reasons for doing research on psychotherapy blend together into a virtually meaningless mish-mash. However, at a more working level, a case can be made for a position that there seem to be a number of identifiably different reasons, aims and goals for doing psychotherapy research. It is, I believe, somewhat inaccurate to refer to 'psychotherapy research' as if it has a single, overriding, true purpose. It seems much more accurate and useful to hold a position that there are indeed quite different reasons, aims and goals for doing research on psychotherapy.

There are 10 proposed reasons for doing research on psychotherapy:

1. To show that this kind of psychotherapy thing goes with that kind of psychotherapy thing.
2. To show that psychotherapy is good, worthwhile, helpful, effective.
3. To show that this particular psychotherapy is good, worthwhile, helpful, effective.
4. To show that this psychotherapy is more helpful and effective than that psychotherapy for this particular problem/disorder.
5. To show that this particular in-session thing is connected with successful post-treatment outcome.
6. To show that these things are common across successful, effective therapies.
7. To show that this theory of psychotherapy is good.
8. To show that this theory of psychotherapy is better than that theory.
9. To contribute to the cumulative body of psychotherapeutic knowledge.
10. To discover more and more about what psychotherapy can achieve, and better and better ways of achieving what psychotherapy can achieve.

Keep improving the list of reasons for doing research on psychotherapy

The invitation is to keep improving this list. Make it better in all the ways that such a list can be made better. Help us to clearly appreciate that there are different reasons for doing research on psychotherapy, and here are the reasons.

Take your time and make a careful choice of your particular reason for doing research on psychotherapy before doing it

I have suggested 10 rather different reasons, aims and goals for doing research on psychotherapy. It seems all too easy just to plunge into a career of doing some kind of research, maybe even to get the grants and do the studies, and only much later, or never, come to realize that (1) the payoff or goal or reason for doing all that research is not what you had originally thought, or (2) it probably would have been better if you had started out doing research for some other reason, aim or goal.

The invitation is to take plenty of time to think about just why you are going to do research on psychotherapy, and whether or not it is the reason that you truly want. Study each of the reasons for doing this research. Which one truly excites you?

This invitation is extended to the student in training, to the psychotherapy researcher who is finishing one study and heading toward the next study, to the practitioner who stays clear of this alien thing called research and to the researcher in some related area of study. Simply check out the various reasons for doing research on psychotherapy and see if any of them seems sufficiently inviting at the present time.

Consider the possibility that there are deeper pools of ideas in you, a deeper framework inside, a kind of built-in mind-set. You may perhaps be surprised that you have a common factors kind of mind-set, or that your own deeper framework has genuine goodness of fit with a theory-checking or theory-enhancement kind of research, or that you have a discovery-oriented deeper framework. Accept the invitation to see if your own intrinsic framework or mind-set clicks with one or more of these 10 reasons for participating in research on psychotherapy.

There are different packages of serious problems associated with the different reasons for doing research on psychotherapy

For nine of the ten reasons, the case holds that (1) there are serious problems associated with each of the nine reasons and (2) these problems can be serious enough to sharply reduce the likelihood of success in doing research for these reasons, and also to effectively block, derail and defeat doing research for these reasons.

A few of these serious problems may be thought of as tied to several of the reasons for doing research on psychotherapy. However, to a large extent, most of these reasons are associated with their own relatively unique set of serious problems.

The nature and content of these serious problems are spelled out at the end of Chapters 1–9. When these are taken together, the main conclusion is that there are some exceedingly serious problems that may be understood as hampering and blocking most of the reasons for doing research on psychotherapy.

Will the conclusions include a list of the serious problems?

If the serious problems are so important, it may be appropriate for the conclusions to include a list of the serious problems. Here are a few reasons why I prefer not to try to assemble such a list:

1. At the ends of Chapters 1–9, the serious problems underlying each reason are identified. Although I can picture a simple list of all the serious problems, what seems more sensible to me is to identify the reason for doing research, and the small package of serious problems that go with that particular reason. That is already done. Just check the ends of Chapters 1–9.
2. The aim is to identify the serious problems that go with each reason for doing research on psychotherapy. If the aim were to provide a list of all the serious problems, I would face such issues as how to organize such a list, what topics or categories to use, how to deal with some serious problems being more basic than others. Trying to provide a concluding list of the serious problems runs into issues of how to organize such a list properly and well. I prefer to avoid these kinds of issues from trying to present a proper list.
3. One reason for avoiding issues of organizing and categorizing a list of serious problems is that I do not want to risk diffusing or diminishing the importance of these serious problems by deflecting attention to the poor way that I may have organized and categorized the list. What

seems important are the serious problems underlying each reason for doing research, rather than whether a concluding list is well or poorly done.

There are 42 serious problems that are identified. Each of the nine reasons for doing research is accompanied with its own package of about four to five serious problems, plus one serious problem that is common across all nine. Instead of a concluding list of the serious problems, please take a look at the conclusions to Chapters 1–9.

Researchers and others ready and willing to see these serious problems can see them

It may very well be that most researchers' ways of thinking have little or no room for being able to see these serious problems. These researchers can rather easily make a case that these serious problems do not exist, or dismiss them as not all that serious. On the other hand, there can be researchers with at least a tiny glow of readiness and willingness to see and appreciate that each of the nine reasons can be associated with its own package of serious underlying problems. I can appreciate the former group of researchers, although I would have a hard time talking with them. I can talk with the latter group of researchers and I have utmost appreciation that they are around.

Are the problems serious enough to raise serious questions about doing research for these reasons?

For those who are ready and willing to appreciate these serious problems, the message is that it can be essentially fruitless to set about doing research for these nine reasons. The serious problems can be too daunting, too much of an obstacle, too much of a road block. Instead of launching into these kinds of studies, perhaps some researchers can instead take some time out to take a more careful look into these serious problems. Perhaps it can be time to do something about these serious problems.

Solve the serious problems associated with most of the reasons for doing research on psychotherapy

The main invitation is for researchers and interested others to find solutions to these serious problems. If this volume has been able to put flags on many of the serious problems, hopefully it can be easier to arrive at effective solutions. This is the invitation. This is the hope.

This invitation is extended to interested researchers, both in and near the field of psychotherapy, and also to interested others, including theoreticians and practitioners, methodologists and philosophers of science. For interested psychotherapy researchers especially, the invitation is to take some time out to focus attention on solving these serious problems.

I have offered some amateur suggestions in the spirit of trying to solve some of the serious problems. The intent was merely to take a few swipes at solutions. What is needed is to go far beyond my provisional suggestions, and for interested researchers and others to engage in serious study and solutions to these serious problems.

Does solving these serious problems call for careful thinking rather than further research?

One of the apparent advantages of taking a close look at the serious problems is that it becomes rather clear that solution lies mainly in careful thinking, systematic reasoning and logical analysis. This avenue seems to be much more promising than trying to solve these serious problems by doing further research. Interested researchers are invited to take some time out from doing more research, and to join with interested others in doing some serious and careful thinking in an effort to solve these serious problems.

Does solving these serious problems help to remove some serious road blocks to doing research on psychotherapy?

For researchers dedicated to many of the reasons for doing research on psychotherapy, solving these serious problems can be a boon. It can effectively remove some of the serious road blocks that have hampered, constricted, derailed doing research for these reasons. In this important sense, solving these serious problems can be exceedingly friendly to researchers dedicated to these reasons for doing psychotherapy research.

Can solving these serious problems seriously weaken the case for many of the reasons for doing research on psychotherapy?

These problems are serious in part because they go to the very heart of the reasons for doing research. Serious problems can come from, and bear serious implications for, the reasons for the research. Accordingly, one of the risks in solving the serious problems is that the solution may dissolve much of the reason, the rationale, the justification for doing the research, or weaken the case for the reason tied to the serious problem, e.g. if the reason rests on the existence of some presumed entity, the risk is that the case for the reason can be seriously weakened if the solution includes the dissolution of the presumed entity. It can be hard to see which of several therapies is superior if the solution dissolves the current system for identifying therapies.

Can solving these serious problems help nudge the field of psychotherapy in the direction of revolutionary shift?

From a practical standpoint, many of the problems can be understood as serious because they pose serious difficulties for the researchers, and can interfere with and even block doing research for various reasons. There is also another way in which these problems can be serious. Many of these problems arise out of much deeper issues, foundational matters underlying psychotherapy theory, research and practice. Many of these serious problems are tied to the very core of the field of psychotherapy.

Accordingly, solving these serious problems can help nudge the field in the direction of a revolutionary shift. In this sense, solutions to these serious problems can have profound implications and consequences well beyond psychotherapy research, i.e. researchers can play a role in enabling a revolutionary shift in the field of psychotherapy, not so much by their research findings, but rather by helping to solve the serious problems underlying their reasons for doing psychotherapy research. If the flagging up of some of these serious problems can help pave the way toward such a revolutionary shift, clarification of the serious problems can be an exceedingly worthwhile enterprise.

Is doing research for nine of the ten reasons aimed at discovering more and more of what psychotherapy can accomplish and better and better ways of doing it?

It is unlikely that the nine reasons would lead to research that is designed to, or can tell us much about, discovering more and more of what psychotherapy can accomplish and how to accomplish these things better and better.

It is also unlikely that many researchers would readily admit this. They would more likely try to find some way of insisting that their reason for doing research does indeed provide findings that can show how to do psychotherapy better and better. I doubt if their case can be truly strong or genuinely convincing.

If researchers are interested in discovering more and more of what psychotherapy can accomplish, and better and better ways of accomplishing these things, the invitation is to consider doing discovery-oriented research.

What is an effective way of doing research to discover more and more of what psychotherapy can accomplish, and better and better ways of accomplishing this?

The discovery-oriented way of doing research is designed to uncover the secrets of psychotherapy, to find how to do psychotherapy better and better, to discover more and more of what psychotherapy can accomplish, and better and better ways of accomplishing this. None of the other nine reasons for doing research is, I believe, designed for these purposes.

The discovery-oriented way of doing research is not only designed for these purposes; I believe that it pays off. It is a useful and effective way of studying psychotherapy to discover more and more of what psychotherapy can accomplish, and better and better ways of accomplishing those things. And that holds three invitations. One is that researchers allow a little room for this additional reason for doing psychotherapy research. Second, researchers are invited to adopt and use the discovery-oriented way of doing research, if the researcher is interested in discovering more and more of what psychotherapy can accomplish, and better and better ways of accomplishing these things. Finally, researchers are invited to improve, extend and advance the discovery-oriented way of doing research on psychotherapy.

Become friends with the field of philosophy of science

Some of our researchers are knowledgeable about philosophy of science. Some are scholars of philosophy of science. But not many. My hope is that a continuously increasing proportion of psychotherapy researchers will become students and scholars in philosophy of science, especially as it relates to psychotherapy and psychotherapy research.

Studying philosophy of science can help us to know about the issues, problems, dilemmas, limitations and possibilities, the mind-sets and ways of thinking that relate to the field of psychotherapy and psychotherapy research. If we do not study philosophy of science, it is unlikely that we will have this knowledge.

Knowing what philosophy of science has to offer can help us see better the foundational problems and possibilities in the field of psychotherapy and psychotherapy research. Without this knowledge, it is unlikely that we can see these underlying problems and magnificent possibilities.

Being able to see these deep-seated problems and magnificent possibilities can help us to solve these serious problems and achieve these magnificent possibilities. If we do not see these deep-seated problems and magnificent possibilities, it is unlikely that we can enable the field of psychotherapy and psychotherapy research to become what it is magnificently capable of becoming.

The field of philosophy of science can have a great deal to offer us if we are ready and eager to appreciate our neighboring field, learn what it has to offer and put it to good use. The serious issues that are the subject matter of philosophy of science cut across most sciences. I believe it is time that the field of psychotherapy and psychotherapy research welcome and appreciate our neighboring field.

This invitation extends to the education and training of our students. At the very least, the invitation is for the education and training of psychotherapy researchers to include knowledge of philosophy of science. Hopefully, this invitation also extends to the education of psychotherapy practitioners and theoreticians, and even to undergraduates who study the field of psychotherapy and psychotherapy research.

This is what I wanted to say to you. Thank you for letting me talk with you. Now the conversation shifts over to you and it is your turn. If we can be in conversation, please write to me at School of Psychology, University of Ottawa, Ottawa, Canada K1N 6N5, or talk with me by e-mail at amahrer@uottawa.ca

References

Adams, D.K. (1937). Note on method. Psychological Review 44: 212–218.

Alexander, F. (1963). The dynamics of psychotherapy in light of learning theory. American Journal of Psychiatry 120: 440–448.

Allen, J.G., Gabbard, G.O., Newsom, G.E. and Coyne, L. (1990). Detecting patterns of change in patients' collaboration within individual psychotherapy sessions. Psychotherapy 27: 522–530.

Anderson, W.P. and Heppner, P.P. (1986). Counselor applications of research findings of practice: Learning to stay current. Journal of Counseling and Development 65: 152–155.

Andreozzi, L.L. (1985). Why outcome research fails the family therapist. In: Andreozzi, L.L. (ed.), Integrating research and clinical practice. Rockville, Md: Aspen, pp. 1–9.

Arachtingi, B.M. and Lichtenberg, G.W. (1999). Self-concept and self-esteem as moderators of client transference. Psychotherapy 36: 369–379.

Auerbach, A.H. and Luborsky, L. (1968). Accuracy of judgements of psychotherapy and the nature of the 'good hour'. In: Shlein, J.M., Hunt, H.F., Matarazzo, J.D. et al. (eds), Research in psychotherapy. Washington DC: American Psychological Association, pp. 155–168.

Barkham, M. and Shapiro, D.A. (1986). Counselor verbal response modes and experienced empathy. Journal of Counseling Psychology 33: 3–10.

Barlow, D.H. (1980). Behavior therapy: The next decade. Behavior Therapy 11: 315–328.

Barlow, D.H. (1994). Psychological intervention in the era of managed competition. Clinical Psychology: Science and Practice 1: 109–122.

Barlow, D.H. (1996). The effectiveness of psychotherapy: Science and policy. Clinical Psychology: Science and Practice 3: 236–240.

Beck, A.T. (1967). Depression: Causes and treatment. Philadelphia: University of Pennsylvania Press.

Beck, A.T. (1976). Cognitive Therapy and the Emotional Disorders. New York: New American Library.

Beck, A.T. (1987). Cognitive therapy. In: Zeig, J.K. (ed.), Evolution of Psychotherapy. New York: Brunner/Mazel, pp. 149–163.

Beck, A.T., Rush, A., Shaw, B. and Emery, G. (1979). Cognitive Therapy of Depression. New York: Guilford.

Bellack, A. and Hersen, M. (eds) (1985) Dictionary of Behavior Therapy Techniques. New York: Pergamon.

Benjamin, A. (1979). The Helping Interview. Boston: Houghton-Mifflin.

Bergin, A.E. (1971). The evaluation of therapeutic outcomes. In: Bergin, A.E. and Garfield, S.L. (eds), Handbook of Psychotherapy and Behavior Change. New York: Wiley, pp. 217–270.

Bergin, A.E. and Lambert, M.J. (1978). The evaluation of therapeutic outcomes. In: Bergin, A.E. and Garfield, S.L. (eds), Handbook of Psychotherapy and Behavior Change, 2nd edn. New York: Wiley, pp. 180–236.

Berrigan, L.P. and Garfield, S.L. (1981). Relationship of missed psychotherapy appointments to premature termination and social class. British Journal of Clinical Pychology 20: 239–242.

Beutler, L.E. (1986). Systematic eclectic psychotherapy. In: Norcross, J.C. (ed.), Handbook of Eclectic Psychotherapy. New York: Brunner/Mazel, pp. 94–131.

Beutler, L.E. (1991). Have all won and all must have prizes? Revisiting Luborsky et al.'s verdict. Journal of Consulting and Clinical Psychology 59: 226–232.

Beutler, L.E., Crago, M. and Arizmendi, T.G. (1986). Research on the therapist variables in psychotherapy. In: Bergin, A.E. and Garfield, S.L. (eds), Handbook of Psychotherapy and Behavior Change, 3rd edn. New York: Wiley, pp. 257–310.

Beutler, L.E., Machado, P.P., Engle, D. and Mohr, D. (1993). Different patient treatment maintenance among cognitive, experiential, and self-directed psychotherapies. Journal of Psychotherapy Integration 3: 15–31.

Blum, H.P. (1980). The curative and creative aspects of insight. In: Blum, H.P. (ed.), Psycho-analytic Explanations of Technique. New York: International Universities Press, pp. 41–69.

Bohart, A.C. (2002). A passionate critique of Empirically Supported Treatments and the provision of an alternative paradigm. In: Watson, J.C., Goldman, R. and Warner, M. (eds), Client-centered and Experiential Psychotherapy in the 21st Century. Langarron, UK: PCCS Books, pp. 258–277.

Bordin, E.S. (1948). Dimensions of the counseling process. Journal of Clinical Psychology 4: 240–244.

Bordin, E.S. (1979). The generalizability of the psychoanalytic concept of the working alliance. Psychotherapy: Theory, Research and Practice 16: 252–260.

Bordin, E.S. (1994). Theory and research on the therapeutic working alliance. In: Horvath, A.O. and Greenberg, L.S. (eds), The Working Alliance: Theory, research, and practice. New York: Wiley, pp. 13–37.

Borgen, F.H. (1992). Expanding scientific paradigms in counseling psychology. In: Brown, S.D. and Lent, R.W. (eds), Handbook on Counseling Psychology, 2nd edn. New York: Wiley, pp. 111–139.

Brogan, M.M., Prochaska, J.O. and Prochaska, J.M. (1999). Predicting termination and continuation status in psychotherapy using the transtheoretical model. Psychotherapy 36: 105–113.

Brooks, H. (1971). Can science survive in the modern age? Science 174: 21–30.

Bruner, J. (1990). Acts of Meaning. Cambridge, Mass: Harvard University Press.

Bunge, M. (1972). Toward a philosophy of technology. In: Mitcham, C. and Mackay, R. (eds), Philosophy and Technology. New York: Free Press, pp. 62–76.

Calhoun, K.S., Moras, K., Pilkonis, P. and Rehm, L.P. (1998). Empirically supported treatments: Implications for training. Journal of Consulting and Clinical
Psychology 66: 151–162.

Cape, J. (2000). Patient-rated therapeutic relationship and outcome in general
practitioner treatment of psychological problems. British Journal of Clinical
Psychology 39: 383–395.

Cashdan, S. (1973). Interactional psychotherapy: Stages and strategies in behavior change. New York: Grune & Stratton.

Caspar, F., Pessier, J., Stuart, J., Safran, J.D., Samstag, L.W. and Guirguis, M. (2000).
One step further in assessing how interpretations influence the process of psychotherapy. Psychotherapy Research 10: 309–320.

Chalmers, A.F. (1982). What is this Thing Called Science? Queensland, Australia:
University of Queensland Press.

Chambless, D.L. and Hollon, S.D. (1998). Defining empirically supported therapies. Journal of Consulting and Clinical Psychology 66: 7–18.

Chambless, D.L. and Ollendick, T.H. (2001). Empirically supported psychological
interventions: Controversies and evidence. Annual Review of Psychology 52:
685–716.

Chambless, D.L., Sanderson, W.C., Shoham, V. et al. (1996). An update on empirically validated therapies. Clinical Psychologist 49: 5–18.

Chambless, D.L., Baker, M.J., Baucom, D.H. et al. (1998). Update on empirically
validated therapies II. Clinical Psychologist 51: 3–16.

Chomsky, N. (1957). Review of verbal behavior, by B.F. Skinner, Language 35:
26–58.

Clarke, K.M. (1996). Change processes in a creation of meaning event. Journal of
Consulting and Clinical Psychology 64: 465–470.

Cohen, M.R. and Nagel, E. (1953). The nature of a logical or mathematical system.
In: Feigl, H. and Brodbeck, M. (eds), Readings in the Philosophy of Science.
New York: Appleton-Century-Crofts, pp. 129–147.

Conrad, C.F. (1978). A grounded theory of academic change. Sociology of
Education 51: 102–112.

Corsini, R.J. (ed.) (1981) Handbook of Innovative Psychotherapies. New York:
Wiley.

Council, J.R., Kirsch, I. and Hafner, L.P. (1986). Expectancy versus absorption in
the prediction of hypnotic responding. Journal of Personality and Social
Psychology 50: 182–189.

Cummings, A.L., Hallberg, E.T. and Slemon, A.G. (1994). Templates of client change
in short-term counseling. Journal of Counseling Psychology 41: 464–472.

Cummings, A.L., Martin, J., Hallberg, E.T. and Slemon, A.G. (1992). Memory for
therapeutic events, session effectiveness, and working alliance in short-term
counseling. Journal of Counseling Psychology 39: 306–312.

Curtis, J. and Silberschatz, G. (1986). Clinical implications of research on brief
dynamic psychotherapy: I. Formulating the patient's problems goals.
Psychoanalytic Psychology 3: 13–25.

Derisley, J. and Reynolds. S. (2000). The transtheoretical stages of change as a predictor of premature termination, attendance, and alliance in psychotherapy.
British Journal of Clinical Psychology 39: 371–382.

Dittes, J.E. (1959). Previous studies bearing on content analysis of psychotherapy. In: J. Dollard and F. Auld, Jr (eds), Scoring human motives: A manual, pp. 325–351). New Haven, Connecticut: Yale University Press.

Dowd, E.T. and Milne, C.R. (1986). Paradoxical interventions in counseling psychology. The Counseling Psychologist 14: 237–282.

Dubrin, J.R. and Zastowny, T.R. (1988). Predicting early attrition from psychotherapy: An analysis of a large private practice cohort. Psychotherapy 25: 393–408.

Duhem, P. (1953). Physical theory and experiment. In: Feigl, H.H. and Brodbeck, M. (eds), Readings in Philosophy of Science. New York: Appleton-Century-Crofts, pp. 235–252.

Duhem, P. (1962). The Aim and Structure of Physical Theory. New York: Atheneum.

Duhem, P. (1996). Essays in the History and Philosophy of Science. Indianapolis, Indiana: Hackett.

Duncan, S., Jr, Rice, L.N. and Butler, J.M. (1968). Therapists' paralanguage in peak and poor psychotherapy hours. Journal of Abnormal Psychology 22: 264–272.

Dunlap, K. (1928). A revision of the fundamental law of habit formation. Science 57: 360–362.

Eagle, M. (1984). Recent Developments in Psychoanalysis: A critical evaluation. New York: McGraw-Hill.

Eagle, M. (1993). The dynamics of theory change in psychoanalysis. In: Earman, J., Janis, A., Massey, G. and Rescher, N. (eds), Philosophical Problems of the Internal and External Worlds: Essays on the philosophy of Adolf Grunbaum. Pittsburgh: University of Pittsburgh Press, pp. 373–408.

Eckert, R., Luborsky, L., Barber, J. and Crits-Christoph, P. (1990). The narratives and CCRTs of patients with major depression. In: Luborsky, L. and Crits-Christoph, P. (eds), Understanding transference: The core conflictual relationship theme method. New York: Basic Books, pp. 222–234.

Edwards, D.J.A. (1998). Types of case study work: A conceptual framework for case-based research. Journal of Humanistic Psychology 38: 36–70.

Einstein, A. (1923). Sidelights of Relativity. New York: Dutton.

Elliott, R. (1983a). 'That in hour hands': A comprehensive process analysis of a significant event in psychotherapy. Psychiatry 46: 113–129.

Elliott, R. (1983b). Fitting process research to the practicing psychotherapist. Psychiatry: Theory, Research and Practice 20: 47–55.

Elliott, R. (1984). A discovery-oriented approach to significant change events in psychotherapy: Interpersonal process recall and comprehensive process analysis. In: L.N. Rice and L.S. Greenberg (eds), Patterns of change, pp. 249–286). New York: Guilford.

Elliott, R. (1985). Helpful and non-helpful events in brief counseling interviews: An empirical taxonomy. Journal of Counseling Psychology 32: 307–322.

Elliott, R. (1986). Interpersonal Process Recall (IPR) as a psychotherapy process research method. In: Greenberg, L.S. and Pinsoff, W.M. (eds), The Psychotherapeutic Process: A research handbook. New York: Guilford, pp. 503–528.

Elliott, R. and James, E. (1989). Varieties of client experience in psychotherapy: An analysis of the literature. Clinical Psychology Review 9: 443–467.

Elliott, R. and Shapiro, D.A. (1988). Brief Structured Recall: A more efficient method for identifying and describing significant therapy events. British Journal of Medical Psychology 61: 141–153.

Elliott, R. and Shapiro, D.A. (1992). Client and therapist as analysts of significant events. In: Toukmanian, S.S. and Rennie D.L. (eds), Psychotherapy Process Research. Newbury Park, Calif: Sage, pp. 163–186.

Elliott, R. and Wexler, D. (1994). Measuring the impact of sessions in process-experiential therapy of depression: The session impacts scale. Journal of Counseling Psychology 41: 166–174.

Elliott, R., Barker, C.B., Caskey, N. and Pistrang, N. (1982). Differential helpfulness of counselor verbal response modes. Journal of Counseling Psychology 29: 354–361.

Elliott, R., James, E., Reimschuessel, C., Cislo, D. and Sacks, N. (1985). Significant events and the analysis of immediate therapeutic impacts. Psychotherapy 22: 620–630.

Ertl, M.A. and McNamara, J.R. (2000). Predicting potential client treatment preferences. Psychotherapy 37: 219–227.

Erwin, E. (1978). Behavior Therapy: Scientific, philosophical and moral foundations. New York: Cambridge University Press.

Erwin, E. (1992). Current philosophical issues in the scientific evaluation of behavior therapy theory and outcome. Behavior Therapy 23: 151–171.

Erwin, E. (1997). Philosophy and Psychotherapy. London: Sage.

Erwin, E. and Siegel, E. (1989). Is confirmation differential? British Journal of Philosophy of Science 40: 105–119.

Eysenck, H. (1952). The effects of psychotherapy: An evaluation. Journal of Consulting Psychology 16: 319–324.

Eysenck, H. (1961). The effects of psychotherapy: In: Eysenck, H. (ed.), Handbook of Abnormal Psychology. New York: Basic Books, pp. 137–156.

Eysenck, H. (1966). The Effects of Psychotherapy. New York: International Science Press.

Feigl, H. (1959). Philosophical embarrassments of psychology. American Psychologist 14: 115–128.

Feyerabend, P.K. (1962). Explanation, reduction, and empiricism. In: Feigl, H. and Maxwell, G. (eds), Minnesota studies in the philosophy of science. Minneapolis: University of Minnesota Press, pp. 27–97.

Feyerabend, P.K. (1971). Problems of empiricism. In: Colodny, R.G. (ed.), The Nature and Function of Scientific Theories. Pittsburgh: University of Pittsburgh Press, pp. 45–260.

Feyerabend, P.K. (1972). Against Method: Outline of an anarchistic theory of knowledge. London: New Left Books.

Feyerabend, P.K. (1977). Changing patterns of reconstruction. British Journal of Philosophy of Science 28: 351–382.

Feyerabend, P.K. (1978). Science in a Free Society. London: New Left Books.

Fine, A. and Forbes, M. (1986). Grunbaum on Freud: Three grounds for dissent. Behavioral and Brain Sciences 9: 237–238.

Fisher, L., Anderson, A. and Jones, J.E. (1981). Types of paradoxical interventions and indications/counterindications for use in clinical practice. Family Process 20: 25–35.

Fiske, D.W. (1977). Methodological issues in research on the psychotherapist. In: Gurman, A.S. and Razin, A.M. (eds), Effective Psychotherapy: A handbook of research. Oxford: Pergamon, pp. 23–43.

Foreman, S. and Marmar, C.R. (1985). Therapist actions that address initially poor therapeutic alliances in psychotherapy. American Journal of Psychiatry 142: 922–966.

Frank, J.D. (1971). Therapeutic factors in psychotherapy. American Journal of Psychiatry 25: 350–361.

Frank, J.D. (1973). Persuasion and Healing. Baltimore, Md: Johns Hopkins University Press.

Frank, J.D. (1982). Therapeutic components shared by all psychotherapies. In: Harvey, J.H. and Parks, M.M. (eds), Psychotherapy Research and Behavior Change. Washington DC: American Psychological Association, pp. 5–37.

Frankl, V.E. (1960). Paradoxical intention: A logotherapeutic technique. American Journal of Psychotherapy 14: 520–535.

Friedlander, M.L. and Phillips, J.P. (1984). Stochastic process analysis of interactive discourse in early counseling interviews. Journal of Counseling Psychology 31: 139–148.

Friedlander, M.L., Thibodeau, J.R. and Ward, L.G. (1985). Discriminating the 'good' from the 'bad' therapy hour: A study of dyadic interaction. Psychotherapy 22: 631–642.

Frieswyk, S.H., Colson, D.B. and Allen, J.G. (1984). Conceptualizing the therapeutic alliance from a psychoanalytic perspective. Psychotherapy 21: 460–464.

Fuller, S. (1996). Social epistemology and psychology. In: O'Donohue, W. and Kitchener, R.F. (eds), The Philosophy of Psychology. London: Sage, pp. 33–49.

Gabbard, G.O., Horowitz, L.M., Frieswyk, S.H. et al. (1988). The effect of therapist interventions on the therapeutic alliance with borderline patients. Journal of the American Psychoanalytic Association 36: 697–727.

Gadamer, H.G. (1975). Truth and Method. New York: Seabury.

Garduk, E. and Haggard, E. (1972). Immediate effects on patients of psychoanalytic interpretations. Psychological Issues 7: whole issue no. 28.

Garfield, S.L. (1980). Psychotherapy: An eclectic approach. New York: Wiley.

Garfield, S.L. (1981). Evaluating the psychotherapies. Behavior Therapy 12: 295–307.

Garfield, S.L. (1994). Research on client variables in psychotherapy. In: Bergin, A.E. and Garfield, S.L. (eds), Handbook of Psychotherapy and Behavior Change, 4th edn. New York: Wiley, pp. 190–228.

Garfield, S.L. and Kurtz, R. (1977). A study of eclectic views. Journal of Consulting and Clinical Psychology 45: 78–83.

Garrett, R. (1996). Skinner's case for radical behaviorism. In: O'Donohue, W. and Kitchener, R.F. (eds), The Philosophy of Psychology. London: Sage, pp. 141–148.

Geer, J.H. and O'Donohue, W.T. (1989). Introduction and overview. In: Geer, J.H. and O'Donohue, W.T. (eds), Theories of Human Sexuality. New York: Plenum, pp. 1–19.

Gelso, C.J. (1979). Research in counseling: Methodological and professional issues. Counseling Psychologist 8: 7–35.

Gelso, C.J. (1991). Galileo, Aristotle, and science in counseling psychology: To theorize or not to theorize. Journal of Consulting Psychology 38: 211–213.

Gergen, K.J. (1985). The social constructionist movement in modern psychology. American Psychologist 40: 266–275.

Gergen, K.J. (1994). Exploring the postmodern: Perils or potentials? American Psychologist 49: 414–416.

Giorgi, A. (1975). An application of phenomenological method in psychology. In: Giorgi, A., Fisher, C. and Murray M.E. (eds), Duquesne Studies in Phenomenological Psychology. Pittsburgh: Duquesne University Press, pp. 82–103.

Giorgi, A. (1985). Sketch of a psychological phenomenological method. In: Giorgi, A. (ed.), Phenomenological and Psychological Research. Pittsburgh: Duquesne University Press, pp. 8–22.

Giorgi, A. (1986). Theoretical justification for the use of description in psychological research. In: Ashworth, P.D., Giorgi, A. and de Koninck, A.J. (eds), Qualitative Research in Psychology. Pittsburgh: Duquesne University Press, pp. 3–32.

Giorgi, A. (1997) The theory, practice, and evaluation of the phenomenological method as a qualitative research procedure. Journal of Phenomenological Psychology 28: 235–260.

Gladis, M.M., Gosch, E.A., Dishuk, N.M. and Crits-Christoph, P. (1999). Quality of life: Expanding the scope of clinical significance. Journal of Consulting and Clinical Psychology 67: 320–331.

Glass, G.V., Wilson, V.L. and Gottman, J.M. (1975). Design and Analysis of Time-series Experiments. Boulder, Colo: University of Colorado Press.

Glazer, B.G. (1978). Theoretical Sensitivity: Advances in the method of grounded theory. Mill Valley, Calif: Sociology Press.

Glazer, B.G. and Strauss, A.L. (1967). The Discovery of Grounded Theory: Strategies for qualitative research. Chicago: Aldine/Atherton.

Goldfried, M.R. (1980). Toward the delineation of therapeutic change principles. American Psychologist 35: 991–999.

Goldfried, M.R. and Padawer, W. (1982). Current status and future directions in psychotherapy. In: Goldfried, M.R. (ed.), Converging Themes in Psychotherapy. New York: Springer, pp. 3–49.

Goldfried, M.R., Raus, P.J. and Castonguay, L.G. (1998). A therapeutic focus in significant sessions of master therapists: A Comparison of cognitive–behavioral and psychodynamic-interpersonal interventions. Journal of Consulting and Clinical Psychology 66: 803–810.

Goldman, L. (1977). Toward more meaningful research. Personnel and Guidance Journal 55: 363–368.

Goldman, L. (1979). Research is more than just technology. Counseling Psychologist 8: 41–44.

Goldman, L. (1989). Moving counseling research into the 21st century. Counseling Psychologist 17: 81–85.

Goldman, L. (1996). Psychology of science. In: O'Donohue, W. and Kitchener, R.F. (eds), The Philosophy of Psychology. London: Sage, pp. 50–65.

Gottman, J.M. (1979). Time-series analysis of continuous data in dyads. In: Lamb, M.E., Suomi, S.J. and Stephenson, G.R. (eds), Social Interaction Analysis. Madison: University of Wisconsin Press, pp. 87–112.

Grafinaki, S. and McLeod, J. (1999). Narrative processes in the construction of helpful and hindering events in experiential psychotherapy. Psychotherapy Research 9: 289–303.

Gray, C. (1993). A way to end Parkinson's law in therapeutic process-sequential psychotherapy. Psychotherapy in Private Practice 12: 43–56.

Greenberg, L.S. (1980). The intensive analysis of recurring events from the practice of Gestalt therapy. Psychotherapy: Theory, Research and Practice 17: 143–152.

Greenberg, L.S. (1984). A task analysis of intrapersonal conflict resolution. In: Rice, L.N. and Greenberg, L.S. (eds), Patterns of Change. New York: Guilford, pp. 67–123.

Greenberg, L.S. and Clarke, K. (1979). The differential effects of the two-chair experiment and empathic reflections at a conflict marker. Journal of Counseling Psychology 26: 1–8.

Greenberg, L.S. and Dompierre, L.M. (1981). Specific effects of Gestalt two-chair dialogue on intrapsychic conflict in counseling. Journal of Counseling Psychology 28: 4: 288–294.

Greenberg, L.S. and Higgins, H. (1980). The effects of two-chair dialogue and focusing on conflict resolution. Journal of Counseling Psychology 27: 221–224.

Greenberg, L.S. and Pinsoff, W. (eds) (1986). The Psychotherapeutic Process: A research handbook. New York: Guilford.

Greenberg, L.S. and Webster, M.C. (1982). Resolving decisional conflict by Gestalt two-chair dialogue: Relating process to outcome. Journal of Counseling Psychology 29: 468–477.

Grunbaum, A. (1984). The Foundations of Psychoanalysis: A philosophical critique. Berkeley, Calif: University of California Press.

Haley, J. (1986). The Power Tactics of Jesus Christ and Other Essays, 2nd edn. Rockville, Md: Triangle.

Hansen, N.R. (1958). Patterns of Discovery. Cambridge: Cambridge University Press.

Hardy, G.E., Barkman, M., Field, S.D., Elliott, R. and Shapiro, D.A. (1998). Whingeling versus working: Comprehensive process analysis of a 'vague awareness' event in psychodynamic-interpersonal therapy. Psychotherapy Research 8: 334–353.

Harper, R.A. (1975). The New Psychotherapies. Englewood Cliffs, NJ: Prentice-Hall.

Hatcher, R.L. (1999). Therapists' views of treatment alliance and collaboration in therapy. Psychotherapy Research 9: 405–423.

Hattie, J.A., Sharpley, C.F. and Rogers, H.F. (1984). Comparative effectiveness of professional and paraprofessional helpers. Psychological Bulletin 95: 534–541.

Hayes, J.A. and Erkis, A.J. (2000). Therapist homophobia, client sexual orientation, and source of client HIV infection as predictors of therapist reactions to clients with HIV. Journal of Counseling Psychology 47: 71–78.

Hayes, S.C., Follette, V.M., Dawes, R.M. and Grady, K.E. (1995) (eds), Scientific standards of psychological practice: Issues and recommendations. Reno, Nev: Context.

Heaton, J.M. (1976). Theoretical practice: The place of theory in psychotherapy. Journal of the British Society for Phenomenology 7: 73–85.

Held, B.S. (1995). Back to Reality: A critique of postmodern theory in psychotherapy. New York: Norton.

Hempel, C. (1953). On the nature of mathematical truth. In: Feigl, H. and Brodbeck, M. (eds), Readings in the Philosophy of Science. New York: Appleton-Century-Crofts, pp. 148–162.

Hempel, C. and Oppenheim, P. (1953). The logic of explanation. In: Feigl, H. and Brodbeck, M. (eds), Readings in the Philosophy of Science. New York: Appleton-Century-Crofts, pp. 319–352.

Heppner, P.P., Rosenberg, J.I. and Hedgespeth, J. (1992). Three methods in measuring the therapeutic process versus actual therapeutic events. Journal of Counseling Psychology 39: 20–31.

Herbert, J.D., Lilienfeld, S.O., Lohr, J.M. et al. (2000). Science and pseudoscience in the development of eye movement desensitization and reprocessing: Implications for clinical psychology. Clinical Psychology Review 20: 945–971.

Hertel, R.K. (1972). Application of stochastic process analysis to the study of psychotherapeutic processes. Psychological Bulletin 77: 421–430.

Hill, C.E. (1990). Exploratory in-session process research in individual therapy: A review. Journal of Consulting and Clinical Psychology 58: 288–294.

Hill, C.E. (1992). Research on therapist techniques in brief individual therapy: Implications for practitioners. The Counseling Psychologist 20: 689–711.

Hill, C.E. (1996). Working with dreams in psychotherapy. New York: Guilford.

Hill, C.E., Carter, J.A. and O'Farrell, M.K. (1983). A case study of the process and outcome of a time-limited counseling. Journal of Counseling Psychology 30: 3–18.

Hill, C.E., Helms, J.E., Tichenor, V., Spiegel, S.B., O'Grady, K.E. and Perry, E.S. (1988). Effects of therapist response modes in brief psychotherapy. Journal of Counseling Psychology 25: 222–233.

Hill, C.E., Zack, J.S., Wonnell, T.L. et al. (2000). Structured brief therapy with a focus on dreams or loss for clients with troubling dreams and recent loss.. Journal of Counseling Psychology 47: 90–101.

Hill, K.A. (1987). Meta-analysis of paradoxical interventions. Psychotherapy 24: 266–270.

Hitchcock, R.A. (1986). An epistemology of counseling: Implications for counselor education and research. Counselor Education and Supervision 26: 95–102.

Hobbs, N. (1962). Sources of gain in psychotherapy. American Psychologist 17: 18–34.

Hollon, S.D. and Flick, S.N. (1988). On the meaning and significance of clinical significance. Behavioral Assessment 10: 197–206.

Holsti, L.R. (1969). Content analysis for the Social Sciences and Humanities. Reading, Mass: Addison-Wesley.

Horowitz, H., Siegelman, E., Wolfson, A. and Weiss, J. (1975). On the identification of warded-off mental contents: An empirical and methodological contribution. Journal of Abnormal Psychology 84: 545–558.

Horowitz, H., Rosenberg, S.E., Ureno, G., Kalehzan, B.M. and O'Halloran, P. (1989). Psychodynamic formulation, consensual response method, and interpersonal problems. Journal of Consulting and Clinical Psychology 57: 599–606.

Horvath, A.O. and Symonds, B.D. (1991). Relations between working alliance and outcome in psychotherapy: A meta-analysis. Journal of Counseling Psychology 38: 139–149.

Hoshmand, L.T. (1989). Alternative research paradigms: A review and teaching proposal. The Counseling Psychologist 17: 3–79.

Howard, G.S. (1985). The role of values in the science of psychology. American Psychologist 40: 255–265.

Howard, G.S. (1986). The scientist-practitioner in counseling psychology: Toward a deeper integration of theory, research and practice. Counseling Psychologist 14: 61–105.

Howard, K.I., Moras, K., Brill, P.L., Martinovich, Z. and Lutz, W. (1996). Evaluation of psychotherapy. American Psychologist 51: 1059–1064.

Hoyt, M.F. (1980). Therapist and patient actions in 'good' psychotherapy sessions. Archives of General Psychiatry 37: 159–161.

Hunter, J. (1786). A Treatise on the Venereal Disease. London: J. Hunter.

Hycner, R.H. (1985). Some guidelines for the phenomenological analysis of interview data. Human Studies 8: 279–303.

Imber, S.D. (1992). Then and now: Forty years in psychotherapy research. Clinical Psychology Review 12: 199–204.

Jacobs, M.K., Christensen, A., Snibbe, J.R., Dolezal-Woods, S., Huber, A. and Polterok, A. (2001). A comparison of computer-based versus traditional individual psychotherapy. Professional Psychology: Research and Practice 32: 92–96.

Jacobson, N.S. and Revenstorf, D. (1988). Statistics for assessing the clinical significance of psychotherapy techniques: Issues, problems, and new developments. Behavior Assessment 10: 88–101.

Jacobson, N.S. and Truax, P. (1991). Clinical significance: A statistical approach to defining meaningful change in psychotherapy research. Journal of Consulting and Clinical Psychology 59: 12–19.

Jacobson, N.S., Follette, W.C. and Revenstorf, D. (1984). Psychotherapy outcome research: Methods for reporting variability and evaluating clinical significance. Behavior Therapy 15: 336–352.

Johnson, E.L. and Sandage, S.J. (1999). A postmodern reconstruction of psychotherapy: Orienteering, religion, and the healing of the soul. Psychotherapy 36: 1–15.

Kagan, N., Krathwohl, D.R. and Miller, R.L. (1963). Stimulated recall in therapy using videotape: A case study. Journal of Counseling Psychology 10: 237–243.

Kantor, J.R. (1945). Psychology and Logic, Vol. 1. Bloomington, Ind: Principia.

Kantor, J.R. (1950). Psychology and Logic, Vol. 2. Bloomington, Ind: Principia.

Karasu, T.B. (1986). The specificity versus nonspecificity dilemma: Toward identifying therapeutic agents. American Journal of Psychiatry 143: 687–695.

Kazdin, A.E. (1979). Nonspecific treatment factors in psychotherapy outcome research. Journal of Consulting and Clinical Psychology 47: 846–851.

Kazdin, A.E. (1986). Comparative outcome studies of psychotherapy: Methodological issues and strategies. Journal of Consulting and Clinical Psychology 54: 95–105.

Kazdin, A.E. and Wilson, G.T. (1978). Evaluation of behavior therapy: Issues, evidence, and research strategies. Cambridge: Ballinger.

Keen, E. (1975). A Primer in Phenomenological Psychology. New York: Holt, Rinehart, & Winston.

Kelman, H. (1969). Kairos: The auspicious moment. American Journal of Psychoanalysis 29: 59–82.

Kendall, P.C. (1998). Empirically supported psychological therapies. Journal of Consulting and Clinical Psychology 66: 3–6.

Kendall, P.C. and Grove, W. (1988). Normative comparisons in therapy outcome. Behavioral Assessment 10: 147–158.

Kernberg, F. and Clarkin, J.F. (1994). Training and the integration of research and clinical practice. In: Talley, P.F., Strupp, H.H. and Butler, S.F. (eds), Psychotherapy Research and Practice. New York: Basic Books, pp. 39–59.

Kiesler, D.J. (1973). The process of psychotherapy: Empirical foundations and systems of analysis. Chicago: Aldine.

Kiesler, D.J. (1994). Standardization of intervention: The tie that binds psychotherapy research and practice. In: Talley, P.F., Strupp, H.H. and Butler, S.F. (eds), Psychotherapy Research and Practice. New York: Basic Books, pp. 142–153.

Kiesler, D.J. and Watkins, L.M. (1989). Interpersonal complementarity and the therapeutic alliance: A study of relationship. Psychotherapy 26: 183–194.

Kitchener, R.F. (1996). Skinner's theory of theories. In: O'Donohue, W. and Kitchener, R.F. (eds), The Philosophy of Psychology. London: Sage, pp. 108–125.

Kivlighan, D.M., Jr and Angelone, E.O. (1991). Helpee introversion, novice counselor intention use, and helpee-rated session impact. Journal of Counseling Psychology 38: 25–29.

Kivlighan, D.M., Jr and Arthur, E.G. (2000). Convergence in counselor recall of important session events. Journal of Counseling Psychology 47: 79–84.

Kivlighan, D.M., Jr and Schmitz, P.J. (1992). Counselor technical activity in cases with improving working alliances and continuing-poor working alliances. Journal of Counseling Psychology 39: 32–38.

Kivlighan, D.M., Jr and Shaunessy, P. (2000). Patterns of working alliance development: A typology of clients' working alliance ratings. Journal of Counseling Psychology 47: 362–371.

Kivlighan, D.M., Jr, Multon, K.D. and Patton, M.J. (2000). Insight and symptom reduction in time-limited psychoanalytic counseling. Journal of Counseling Psychology 47: 50–58.

Klein, G. (1970). Perception, Motives, and Personality. New York: Knopf.

Klonsky, E.D. (2000). The DSM classification of personality disorders: Clinical wisdom or empirical truth? A response to Alvin R. Mahrer's problem 11. Journal of Clinical Psychology 56: 1615–1621.

Kneale, W. (1953) Induction, explanation, and transcendent hypotheses. In: Feigl, H. and Brodbeck, M. (eds), Readings in the Philosophy of Science. New York: Appleton-Century-Crofts, pp. 353–367.

Knox, S., Hess, S.A., Petersen, D.A. and Hill, C.E. (1991). A qualitative analysis of client perceptions of the effects of helpful therapist self-disclosure in long-term therapy. Journal of Counseling Psychology 44: 274–283.

Koch, S. (1959). Psychology: A study of a science. New York: McGraw-Hill.

Kolden, G.G. (1996). Change in early sessions of dynamic therapy: Universal processes and the generic model of psychotherapy. Journal of Consulting and Clinical Psychology 64: 489–496.

Kuhn, T.S. (1959). The Copernican Revolution. New York: Random House.

Kuhn, T.S. (1970). The Structure of Scientific Revolutions. Chicago: University of Chicago Press.

Kuhn, T.S. (1973). Second thoughts on paradigms. In: Suppe, F. (ed.), The structure of scientific theories. Urbana, Ill: University of Illinois Press, pp. 459–482.

Kuhn, T.S. (1977). The Essential Tension. Chicago: University of Chicago Press.

Kutash, S.B. (1976). Modified psychoanalytic therapies. In: Wolman, B.B. (ed.), The Therapist's Handbook: Treatment methods of mental disorders. New York: Van Nostrand Reinhold, pp. 87–116.

Labov and Fanshel, D. (1977). Therapeutic Discourse. New York: Atheneum.

Lakatos, I. (1963). Proofs and refutations. British Journal for the Philosophy of Science 14: 1–25.

Lakatos, I. (1970). Falsification and the methodology of scientific research programs. In: Lakatos, I. and Musgrave, A. (eds), Criticism and the Growth of Knowledge. Cambridge: Cambridge University Press, pp. 91–196.

Lakatos, I. (1974). Popper on demarcation and induction. In: Schilpp, P.A. (ed.), The Philosophy of Karl Popper. LaSalle, Ind: Open Court, pp. 241–273.

Lambert, M.J., Shapiro, D.A. and Bergin, A.E. (1986). The effectiveness of psychotherapy. In: Garfield, S. and Bergin, A.E. (eds), Handbook of Psychotherapy and Behavior Change, 3rd edn. New York: Wiley, pp. 157–211.

Lazarus, A.A. (1967). In support of technical eclecticism. Psychological Reports 21: 415–416.

Lazarus, A.A. (1971). Behavior Therapy and Beyond. New York: McGraw-Hill.

Lebow, J. (1982). Consumer satisfaction with mental health treatment. Psychological Bulletin 91: 244–259.

Lewis, T., Amini, F. and Lannon, R. (2000). A General Theory of Love. New York: Random House.

Lichtenberg, J.W. and Barké, K.H. (1981). Investigation of transactional communication relationship patterns in counseling. Journal of Counseling Psychology 28: 471–480.

Lichtenberg, J.W. and Heck, E.J. (1979). Interactional structure of interviews conducted by counselors of differing levels of cognitive complexity. Journal of Counseling Psychology 26: 15–22.

Lichtenberg, J.W. and Hummel, T.J. (1976). Counseling as a stochastic process: Fitting a Markov chain to initial counseling interviews. Journal of Counseling Psychology 23: 310–315.

Lietaer, G. (1992). Helping and hindering processes in client-centered/experiential psychotherapy. In: Toukmanian, S.G. and Rennie, D.L. (eds), Psychotherapy Process Research. Newbury Park, Calif: Sage, pp. 134–162

Llewelyn, S.P., Elliott, R., Shapiro, D.A., Firth-Cozens, J. and Hardy, G. (1988). Client perceptions of significant events in prescriptive and exploratory periods of individual therapy. British Journal of Clinical Psychology 27: 105–114.

Luborsky, L, and Auerbach, A.H. (1969). The symptom context method: Quantitative studies of symptom formation in psychotherapy. Journal of the American Psychoanalytic Association 17: 68–99.

Luborsky, L, and Crits-Christoph, P. (1998). Understanidng Transference: The core conflictual relationship theme method, 2nd edn. New York: Basic Books.

Luborsky, L., Barber, J.P. and Crits-Christoph, P. (1990). Theory-based research for understanding the process of dynamic psychotherapy. Journal of Consulting and Clinical Psychology 58: 281–287.

Luborsky, L, Singer, B., Hartke, J., Crits-Christoph, P. and Cohen, M. (1984). Shifts in depressive state during psychotherapy: Which concepts of depression fit the context of Mr. Q's shifts? In: Rice, L.N. and Greenberg, L.S. (eds), Patterns of Change. New York: Guilford, pp. 157–193.

Maccia, G. S. (1973). Pedagogical epistemology. In: Brownson, W.E. and Carter, J.E. (eds), Proceedings of the Ohio Valley Philosophy of Education Society. Terre Haute, Ind: Indiana State University Press, pp. 57–76.

MacCorquodale, K. and Meehl, P.E. (1948). On a distinction between hypothetical constructs and intervening variables. Psychological Review 55: 95–107.

McCullough, J.P. (1984). Single-case investigative research and its relevance for the nonoperant clinician. Psychotherapy 21: 382–388.

McGuire, W.J. (1989). A perspectivist approach to the strategic planning of programmatic scientific research. In: Ghoulson, B., Houts, A., Neimeyer, R. and Shadish, W.R. (eds), Psychology of Science: contributions to metascience. New York: Cambridge University Press, pp. 214–245.

McGuire, W.J. (1997). Creative hypothesis generating in psychology: Some useful heuristics. Annual Review of Psychology 48: 1–30.

Machado, P.P., Beutler, L.E. and Greenberg, L.S. (1999). Emotion recognition in psychotherapy: Impact of therapist level of experience and emotional awareness. Journal of Clinical Psychology 55: 39–57.

McLeod, J. (1990). The client's experience of counselling and psychotherapy: A review of the research literature. In: Means, D. and Dryden, W. (eds), Experiences of Counselling in Action. London: Sage, pp. 1–19.

McMullin, E. (1983). Values in science. In: Asquith, P.D. and Nickles, T. (eds), Proceedings of the 1982 Philosophy of Science Association, vol. 2. East Lansing, Michigan: Philosophy of Science Association, pp. 3–23.

Madanes, C. (1984). Behind the One-way Mirror. San Francisco, Calif: Jossey-Bass.

Mahrer, A.R. (1985). Psychotherapeutic Change: An alternative approach to meaning and measurement. New York: Norton.

Mahrer, A.R. (1988a). Discovery-oriented psychotherapy research: Rationale, aims, and methods. American Psychologist 43: 694–702.

Mahrer, A.R. (1988b). Research and clinical applications of 'good moments' in psychotherapy. Journal of Integrative and Eclectic Psychotherapy 7: 81–93.

Mahrer, A.R. (1989a). Experiencing: A humanistic theory of psychology and psychiatry. Ottawa, Canada: University of Ottawa Press.

Mahrer, A.R. (1989b). The Integration of Psychotherapies: A guide for practicing therapists. New York: Human Sciences Press.

Mahrer, A.R. (1995). An introduction to some disposable myths, how to detect them, and a short list. Psychotherapy 32: 484–488.

Mahrer, A.R. (1996a). Discovery-oriented research on how to do psychotherapy. In: Dryden, W. (ed.), Research in Counselling and Psychotherapy: Practical applications. London: Sage, pp. 232–258.

Mahrer, A.R. (1996b). Studying distinguished practitioners: A humanistic approach to discovering how to do psychotherapy. Journal of Humanistic Psychology 36: 31–48.

Mahrer, A.R. (1996/2004). The Complete Guide to Experiential Psychotherapy. Boulder, CO: Bull.

Mahrer, A.R. (2000a). Philosophy of science and the foundations of psychotherapy. American Psychologist 55: 1117–1125.

Mahrer, A.R. (2000b). So many researchers are sincerely scientific about factitious fictions: Some comments on the DSM classification of personality disorders. Journal of Clinical Psychology 56: 1623–1627.

Mahrer, A.R. (2002). Becoming the Person You Can Become: The complete guide to self-transformation. Boulder, Colo: Bull.

Mahrer, A.R. (2003). What are the foundational beliefs in the field of psychotherapy? Psychology: Journal of the Hellenic Psychological Society 10: 1–19.

Mahrer, A.R. (2004). Theories of Truth and Models of Usefulness: Toward a revolution in the field of psychotherapy. London: Whurr.

Mahrer, A.R. and Boulet, D.B. (1999). How to do discovery-oriented psychotherapy research. Journal of Clinical Psychology 55: 1481–1493.

Mahrer, A.R. and Fairweather, D.R. (1993). What is 'experiencing'? A critical review of meanings and applications in psychotherapy. The Humanistic Psychologist 21: 2–25.

Mahrer, A.R. and Gagnon, R. (1991). The care and feeding of a psychotherapy research team. Journal of Psychiatry and Neuroscience 16: 188–192.

Mahrer, A.R. and Nadler, W.P. (1986). Good moments in psychotherapy: A preliminary review, a list, and some promising research avenues. Journal of Consulting and Clinical Psychology 54: 10–15.

Mahrer, A.R., Nordin, S. and Miller, L.S. (1995). If a client has this kind of problem, prescribe that kind of post-session behavior. Psychotherapy 32: 194–203.

Mahrer, A.R., Paterson, W.E., Theriault, A.T., Roessler, C. and Quenneville, A. (1986a). How and why to use a large number of clinically sophisticated judges in psychotherapy research. Voices: The Art and Science of Psychotherapy 22: 57–66.

Mahrer, A.R., Nadler, W.P., Gervaize, P.A. and Markow, R. (1986b). Discovering how one therapist obtains some very good moments in psychotherapy. Voices: The Art and Science of Psychotherapy 22: 72–83.

Mahrer, A.R., Nadler, W.P., Dessaulles, A., Gervaize, P.A. and Sterner, I. (1987). Good and very good moments in psychotherapy: content, distribution, and facilitation. Psychotherapy 24: 7–14.

Mahrer, A.R., White, M.V., Howard, M.T. and Lee, A.C. (1991a). Practitioner methods for heightening feeling expression and confrontational strength. Psychotherapy in Private Practice 9: 11–25.

Mahrer, A.R., White, M.V., Souliere, M.D., MacPhee, D.C. and Boulet, D.B. (1991b). Intensive process analysis of significant in-session client change events and antecedent therapist methods. Journal of Integrative and Eclectic Psychotherapy 10: 38–55.

Mahrer, A.R., Gagnon, R., Fairweather, D.R. and Cote, P. (1992a). How to determine if a session is a very good one. Journal of Integrative and Eclectic Psychotherapy 11: 8–23.

Mahrer, A.R., White, M.V., Howard, M.T., Gagnon, R. and MacPhee, D.C. (1992b). How to bring about some very good moments in psychotherapy sessions. Psychotherapy Research 2: 252–265.

Mahrer, A.R., Gagnon, R., Fairweather, D.R., Boulet, D.B. and Herring, C.B. (1994). Client commitment to carry out post-session behaviors. Journal of Counseling Psychology 41: 407–414.

Mahrer, A.R., Fairweather, D.R., Passey, S., Gingras, N. and Boulet, D.B. (1999). The promotion and use of strong feelings in psychotherapy. Journal of Humanistic Psychotherapy 39: 35–53.

Maione, P.V. and Chenail, R.J. (1999). Qualitative inquiry in psychotherapy: Research on common factors. In: Hubble, M.A., Duncan, B.L. and Miller, S.D. (eds), The Heart and Soul of Change: What works in therapy? Washington DC: American Psychological Association, pp. 57–88.

Maling, M.S. and Howard, K.I. (1994). From research to practice to research to . . . . In: Talley, P.F., Strupp, H.H. and Butler, P.F. (eds), Psychotherapy Research and Practice: Bridging the gap. New York: Basic Books, pp. 246–253.

Marmar, C.R. (1990). Psychotherapy process research: Progress, dilemmas, and future directions. Journal of Consulting and Clinical Psychology 58: 265–272.

Marmar, C.R., Wilner, N. and Horowitz, M.J. (1984). Recurrent client states in psychotherapy: Segmentation and quantification. In: Rice, L.N. and Greenberg, L.S. (eds), Patterns of Change. New York: Guilford, pp. 194–212.

Marmar, J. (1969). Neurosis and the psychotherapeutic process: Similarities and differences in the behavioral and psychodynamic conceptions. International Journal of Psychiatry 7: 514–519.

Marmar, J. (1976). Common operational factors in diverse approaches to behavior change. In: A. Burton (ed.), What Makes Behavior Change Possible? New York: Brunner/Mazel, pp. 47–71.

Martin, J. (1992). Cognitive-mediational research in counseling and psychotherapy. In: Toukmanian, S.G. and Rennie, D.L. (eds), Psychotherapy Process Research. Newbury Park, Calif: Sage, pp. 108–133.

Martin, J., Martin, W. and Slemon, Ag.G. (1987). Cognitive mediation in person-centered and rational-emotive therapy. Journal of Counseling Psychology 34: 251–260.

Martin, J. and Stelmaczonek, K. (1988). Participants' identification and recall of important events in counseling. Journal of Counseling Psychology 35: 385–390.

Mathieu-Coughlan, P. and Klein, M.N. (1984). Experiential psychotherapy: Key events in client-centered interaction. In: Rice, L.N. and Greenberg, L.S. (eds), Patterns of Change. New York: Guilford, pp. 194–211.

Mays, W. (1977). Whitehead's Philosophy of Science and Metaphysics. The Hague, Netherlands: Martinus Nijhoff.

Mazzoni, G.A., Lombardo, P., Malragia, S. and Loftus, E.F. (1999). Dream interpretation and false beliefs. Professional Psychology: Research and Practice 30:
45–50.

Medawar, P. (1969). Induction and Intuition in Scientific Thought. London:
Methuen.

Meehl, P.E. (1978). Theoretical risks and tabular asterisks: Sir Karl, Sir Ronald, and
the slow progress of soft psychology. Journal of Consulting and Clinical
Psychology 46: 806–834.

Meier, A. and Boivin, M. (2000). The achievement of greater selfhood: The application of theme-analysis to a case study. Psychotherapy Research 10: 57–77.

Meltzoff, J. and Kornreich, M. (1970). Research in Psychotherapy. New York:
Atherton.

Mercier, M.A. and Johnson, M. (1984). Representational system predicate use and
convergence in counseling: Gloria revised. Journal of Counseling Psychology
31: 161–169.

Messer, S.B., Tishby, O. and Spillman, A. (1992). Taking context seriously in psychotherapy research: Relating therapist interventions to patient progress in
brief psychodynamic therapy. Journal of Consulting and Clinical Psychology
60: 678–688.

Mickelson, D.J. and Stevic, R.R. (1971). Differential effects of facilitative behavioral counselors. Journal of Counseling Psychology 18: 314–319.

Milbrath, C., Bauknight, R., Horowitz, M.J., Amoro, R. and Sugahara, C. (1995).
Sequential analysis of topics in psychotherapy discourse: A single-case study.
Psychotherapy Research 5: 199–217.

Monsen, J.T. and Monsen, K. (1999). Affects and affect consciousness – a psychotherapy model integrating Silvan Tomkins' affect and script theory within
the framework of self-psychology. Progress in Self-Psychology 15: 287–306.

Monsen, K. and Monsen, J. T. (2000). Chronic pain and psychodynamic body therapy: A controlled outcome study. Psychotherapy 37: 257–269.

Morgenstern, K.P. (1988). Behavioral interviewing. In: Bellack, A.S. and Hersen,
M. (eds), Behavioral Assessment: A practical handbook. New York: Pergamon,
pp. 86–118.

Moras, K. (1994). Spence and Havens: Examples of practitioner contributions to
bridging the chasm. In: Talley, P.F., Strupp, H.H. and Butler, S.F. (eds),
Psychotherapy Research and Practice: Bridging the gap. New York: Basic
Books, pp. 181–195.

Mueller, M. and Pekavik, G. (2000). Treatment duration prediction: Client accuracy and its relationship to dropout, outcome, and satisfaction. Psychotherapy
37: 117–123.

Muran, J.C., Gorman, B.S., Safran, J.D., Twining, L., Samstag, L.W. and Winston, A.
(1995). Linking in-session change to overall outcome in short-term cognitive
therapy. Journal of Consulting and Clinical Psychology 63: 651–657.

Murray, M.E. (1976). A dynamic synthesis of analytic and behavioral approaches
to symptoms. American Journal of Psychotherapy 30: 561–569.

Nathan, P.E. (1998). Practice guidelines: Not yet ideal. American Psychologist 53:
290–299.

Newman, F.J. and Tejeda, M.J. (1996). The need for research that is designed to support decisions in the delivery of mental health services. American Psychologist 51: 1040–1049.

Nichols, M.P. (1984). Family Therapy: Concepts and methods. New York: Gardner.

Norcross, J.C. (ed.) (2001) Empirically supported therapy relationships: Summary report of the Division 29 Task Force. Psychotherapy 39(4).

Norcross, J.C. (2002) (ed.), Psychotherapy Relationships that Work: Therapist contributions and responsiveness to patient needs. New York: Oxford University Press.

O'Connor, L.E., Edelstein, S., Burry, J.W. and Weiss, J. (1992). Change in the patient's level of insight in brief psychotherapy: Two pilot studies. Psychotherapy 29: 554–559.

O'Donohue, W. (1989). The (even) bolder model: The clinical psychologist as metaphysician–scientist–practitioner. American Psychologist 44: 1460–1468.

O'Donohue, W. and Kitchener, R.F. (eds) (1996). The Philosophy of Psychology. London: Sage.

O'Donohue, W. and Vass, J. (1996). What is an irrational belief? Rational-emotive therapy and accounts of rationality. In: O'Donohue, W. and Kitchener, R.F. (eds), The Philosophy of Psychology. London: Sage, pp. 371–380.

Orlinsky, D.E. (1994). Research-based knowledge as the emergent foundation for clinical practice in psychotherapy. In: Talley, P.I., Strupp, H.H. and Butler, S.F. (eds), Psychotherapy Research and Practice: Bridging the gap. New York: Basic Books, pp. 99–123.

Orlinsky, D.E. and Howard, K.I. (1967). The good therapy hour: Experiential correlates and therapists' evaluations of therapy sessions. Archives of General Psychiatry 16: 621–632.

Orlinsky, D.E. and Howard, K.I. (1986). Process and outcome in psychotherapy. In: Garfield, S.L. and Bergin, A.E. (eds), Handbook of Psychotherapy and Behavior Change. New York: Wiley, pp. 311–381.

Orlinsky, D.E. and Ronnestad, M.H. (2000). Ironies in the history of psychotherapy research: Rogers, Bordin, and the shape of things that came. Journal of Clinical Psychology 56: 841–851.

Pairio, S.C. and Patterson, L.A. (1999). Alliance development in therapy for resolving child abuse issues. Psychotherapy 36: 343–354.

Parloff, M. (1976). Shopping for the right therapy. Saturday Review, 14–16 February.

Parloff, M. (1979). Can psychotherapy research guide the policymaker? A little knowledge may be a dangerous thing. American Psychologist 34: 296–306.

Patterson, C.H. and Hidore, S. (1997). Successful Psychotherapy: A caring, loving relationship. Northvale, NJ: Jason Aronson.

Patton, M. (1986). Utilization-focused Evaluation, 2nd edn. Newbury Park, Calif: Sage.

Patton, M., Kivlighan, D.M. and Milton, K.M. (1997). The Missouri psychoanalytic counseling research project: Relation of changes in counseling process to client outcomes. Journal of Counseling Psychology 44: 189–208.

Paul, G.L. (1967). Strategy of outcome research in psychotherapy. Journal of Consulting Psychology 31: 109–118.

Peebles, J. (2000). The future of psychotherapy outcome research: Science or political rhetoric? Journal of Psychology 134: 659–669.

Persons, J.B. and Silberschatz, G. (1998). Are results of randomized controlled trials useful to psychotherapists? Journal of Consulting and Clinical Psychology 66: 126–135.

Peterson, D.R. (1968). The Clinical Study of Social Behavior. New York: Appleton-Century-Crofts.

Piper, W.E., Ogrodniczuk, J.S., Joyce, A.S., McCallum, M., Rosie, J.S. and O'Kelly, J.G. (1999). Prediction of dropping out in time-limited interpretive individual psychotherapy. Psychotherapy 36: 114–122.

Pittenger, R.E., Hockett, C.F. and Danehy, J.J. (1960). The First Five Minutes. Ithaca, NY: Paul Martineau.

Polanyi, M. (1962). Personal Knowledge. Chicago: University of Chicago Press.

Polkinghorne, D.E. (1988). Narrative Knowing and the Human Sciences. New York: State University of New York Press.

Popper, K.R. (1972a). Conjectures and Refutations: The growth of scientific knowledge. New York: Harper & Row.

Popper, K.R. (1972b). Objective Knowledge. Oxford: Oxford University Press.

Popper, K.R. (1974). Replies to my critics. In: Schilpp, P.S. (ed.), The Philosophy of Karl Popper. LaSalle: Open Court, pp. 984–985.

Popper, K.R. (1980). The Logic of Scientific Discovery. New York: Harper & Row.

Prochaska, J.O. and DiClemente, C.C. (1984). The Transtheoretical Approach: Crossing the traditional boundaries of therapy. Homewood, Ill: Dow Jones-Irwin.

Prochaska, J.O. and DiClemente, C.C. (1992). Stages of changes in the modification of problem behaviors. In: Hersen, M.M., Eisler, R.M. and Miller, P.M. (eds), Progress in Behavior Modification. Sycamore, Ill: Sycamore Press, pp. 184–214.

Quine, W.V. (1961). Two dogmas of empiricism. In: Quine, W.V. (ed.), From a Logical Point of View. New York: Harper & Row, pp. 20–46.

Rector, N.A., Zuroff, D.C. and Segal, Z.V. (1999). Cognitive change and the therapeutic alliance: The role of technical and nontechnical factors in cognitive therapy. Psychotherapy 36: 317–338.

Reichardt, C.S. and Cook, T.D. (1979). Beyond qualitative versus quantitative research. In: Cook ,T.D. and Reichardt, C.S. (eds), Qualitative and Quantitative Methods in Evaluation Research. Beverly Hills, Calif: Sage, pp. 7–32.

Reichenbach, H. (1938). Experience and Prediction. Chicago: University of Chicago Press.

Renk, K., Dinger, T.M. and Bjugstad, K. (2000). Predicting therapy duration from therapist experience and client psychopathology. Journal of Clinical Psychology 56: 1604–1614.

Reynolds, S., Stiles, W.B., Barkham, M., Shapiro, D.A., Hardy, G.E. and Rees, A. (1996). Acceleration of changes in session impact during contrasting time-limited psychotherapies. Journal of Consulting and Clinical Psychology 64: 577–586.

Rice, L.N. and Greenberg, L.S. (eds) (1984). Patterns of Change. New York: Guilford.

Richards, G. (1996). On the necessary survival of folk psychology. In: O'Donohue, W. and Kitchener, R.F. (eds), The Philosophy of Psychology. London: Sage, pp. 270–275.

Rimm, D.C. and Masters, J.C. (1979). Behavior Therapy: Techniques and empirical findings. New York: Academic Press.

Rogers, C.R. (1957). The necessary and sufficient conditions of therapeutic personality change. Journal of Consulting Psychology 21: 95–103.

Roos, J.P. (1979). From oddball research to the study of real life: The use of qualitative methods in social sciences. Acta Sociologica 22: 63–74.

Rose, E.M., Westefeld, J.S. and Ansley, T.N. (2001). Spiritual issues in counseling: Clients' beliefs and preferences. Journal of Counseling Psychology 48: 61–71.

Rotgers, F. (1988). Social learning theory, philosophy of science, and the identity of behavior therapy. In: Fishman, D., Rotgers, F. and Franks, C. (eds), Paradigms in Behavior Therapy: Present and promise. New York: Springer, pp. 206–228.

Rubenstein, E.A. and Parloff, M.B. (eds) (1959). Research in Psychotherapy. Washington DC: American Psychological Association.

Russell, R.L. and Trull, T.J. (1986). Sequential analysis of language variables in psychotherapy process research. Psychotherapy 54: 16–21.

Rychlak, J.E. (1981). Introduction to Personality and Psychotherapy: A theory – construction approach, 2nd edn. Boston: Houghton-Mifflin.

Safran, J.D., Greenberg, L.S. and Rice, L.N. (1988). Integrating psychotherapy research and practice: Modeling the change process. Psychotherapy 25: 1–17.

Sarbin, T.R. (1986). The narrative as a root metaphor for psychology. In: Sarbin T.R. (ed.), Narrative Psychology: The storied nature of human conduct. New York: Praeger, pp. 1–27.

Saunders, S.M. (1999). Clients' assessments of the affective environment of the psychotherapy session: Relationship to session quality and treatment effectiveness. Journal of Clinical Psychology 55: 597–605.

Schofer, G., Black, F. and Koch, U. (1979). Possible applications of the Gottschalk–Gleser content analysis of speech in psychotherapy research. In: Gottschalk, L.A. (ed.), The Content Analysis of Verbal Behavior. New York: SP Medical and Scientific Books, pp. 857–870.

Schon, D.A. (1982). The Reflective Practitioner: How professionals think in action. New York: Basic Books.

Schutz, A. (1964). Collected Papers: II. Studies in social theory. The Hague: Martinus-Nijhoff.

Seligman, M.E.P. (1995). The effectiveness of psychotherapy: The Consumer Reports Study. American Psychologist 50: 965–974.

Seltzer, L.F. (1986). Paradoxical Strategies in Psychotherapy. Toronto, Canada: Wiley.

Sexton, H. (1993). Exploring a psychotherapeutic change sequence: Relating process to intersessional and posttreatment outcome. Journal of Consulting and Clinical Psychology 61: 128–136.

Sexton, H. (1996). Process, life events, and symptomatic change in brief eclectic psychotherapy. Journal of Consulting and Clinical Psychology 64: 358–365.

Sexton, H., Hembre, K. and Kvarme, G. (1996). The interaction of the alliance and therapy microprocess: A sequential analysis. Journal of Consulting and Clinical Psychology 64: 471–480.

Sexton, T.L. and Whiston, S.C. (1996). Counseling: An interpersonal influence process. Journal of Counseling Psychology 15: 215–224.

Shaffer, L.F. and Shoben, E.J., Jr (1967). Common aspects of psychotherapy. In: Berenson, B.G. and Carkhuff, R.R. (eds), Sources of Gain in Counseling and Psychotherapy. New York: Holt, Rinehart, & Winston, pp. 63–70.

Shapiro, M.B. (1951). An experimental approach to diagnostic psychological testing. Journal of Mental Science 97: 748–764.

Shapiro, M.B. (1957). Experimental method in psychological description of the individual psychiatric patient. International Journal of Social Psychiatry 3: 89–102.

Shapiro, M.B. (1964). The measurement of clinically relevant variables. Journal of Psychosomatic Research 8: 245–254.

Shapiro, M.B. (1969). A clinically oriented strategy in individual-centred research. British Journal of Social Clinical Psychology 8: 290–291.

Shlien, J.M., Hunt, H.F., Matarazzo, J.D. and Savage, C. (eds) (1968). Research in Psychotherapy, Vol. 3. Washington DC: American Psychological Association.

Shoham-Salomon, V. (1990). Interrelating research processes of process research. Journal of Consulting and Clinical Psychology 58: 295–303.

Siegel, H. (1996). Naturalism and the abandonment of normativity. In: O'Donohue, W. and Kitchener, R.F. (eds), The Philosophy of Psychology. London: Sage , pp. 4–18.

Silberschatz, G. and Curtis, G.T. (1986). Clinical implications of research on brief dynamic psychotherapy: II. How the therapist helps or hinders therapeutic progress. Psychoanalytic Psychology 3: 27–37.

Silberschatz, G. and Curtis, G.T. (1993). Measuring the therapist's impact on the patient's therapeutic progress. Journal of Consulting and Clinical Psychology 61: 403–411.

Silberschatz, G., Curtis, G.T. and Nathans, S. (1989). Using the patient's plan to assess progress in psychotherapy. Psychotherapy 26: 40–46.

Skinner, B.F. (1938). The Behavior of Organisms. New York: Appleton-Century-Crofts.

Skinner, B.F. (1957). Verbal Behavior. New York: Appleton-Century-Crofts.

Slife, B.D. and Williams, R.N. (1995). What's Behind the Research? Discovering hidden assumptions in the behavioral sciences. London: Sage.

Smith, M.L. and Glass, G.V. (1977). Meta-analysis of psychotherapy outcome studies. American Psychologist 32: 752–760.

Snyder, W.U. (1945). An investigation of the nature of nondirective psychotherapy. Journal of General Psychology 33: 193–223.

Spence, D.P. (1994). The failure to ask the hard questions. In: Talley, P.F., Strupp, H.H. and Butler, S.F. (eds), Psychotherapy Research and Practice: Bridging the gap. New York: Basic Books, pp. 19–38.

Spence, K.W. (1953). The postulates and methods of 'behaviorism'. In: Feigl, H. and Brodbeck, M. (eds), Readings in the Philosophy of Science. New York: Appleton-Century-Crofts, pp. 571–584.

Spiegelberg, H. (1972). Phenomenology in Psychology and Psychiatry: A historical introduction. Evanston, Ill: Northwestern University Press.

Spitzer, R., Endicott, J. and Gibson, M. (1979). Crossing the border into borderline personality and borderline schizophrenia. Archives of General Psychiatry 36: 17–24.

Standahl, S.W. and Corsini, R.J. (eds) (1959). Critical Incidents in Psychotherapy. New York: Prentice-Hall.

Steering Committee (2001). Empirically supported therapy relationships: Conclusions and recommendations of the Division 29 Task Force. Psychotherapy 39: 4: 495–497.

Stiles, W.B. (1980). Measurement of the impact of psychotherapy sessions. Journal of Consulting and Clinical Psychology 48: 176–185.

Stiles, W.B. (1982). Psychotherapeutic process: Is there a common core? In: Abt, L.E. and Stuart, I.R. (eds), The Newer Therapies: A sourcebook. New York: Van Nostrand Reinhold, pp. 4–17.

Stiles, W.B. (1988). Psychotherapy process-outcome correlations may be misleading: Psychotherapy 25: 27–37.

Stiles, W.B. and Snow, J.S. (1984). Dimensions of psychotherapy session impact across sessions and across clients. British Journal of Clinical Psychology 23: 59–63.

Stiles, W.B., Shapiro, D.A. and Elliott, R. (1986). Are all psychotherapies equivalent? American Psychologist 41: 120–130.

Stiles, W.B., Elliott, R., Llewelyn, S.P. et al. (1990). Assimilation of problematic experiences by clients in psychotherapy. Psychotherapy 27: 411–420.

Stone, M.H. (1982). Turning points in psychotherapy. In: Slipp, S. (ed.), Curative Factors in Dynamic Psychotherapy. New York: McGraw-Hill, pp. 259–279.

Strauss, E.W. (1966). Phenomenological Psychology. New York: Basic Books.

Strauss, E.W. (1980). A naturalistic experiment investigating the effects of hypnotic induction upon creative imagination scale performance in a clinical setting. International Journal of Clinical and Experimental Hypnosis 28: 218–224.

Strupp, H.H. (1971). Psychotherapy and Modification of Abnormal Behavior. New York: McGraw-Hill.

Strupp, H.H. (1973). On the basic ingredients of psychotherapy. Journal of Consulting and Clinical Psychology 41: 1–8.

Strupp, H.H. (1974). On the basic ingredients of psychotherapy. Psychotherapy and Psychosomatics 24: 249–260.

Strupp, H.H. (1977). A reformulation of the dynamics of the therapist's contribution. In: Gurman, A.S. and Razin, A.M. (eds), Effective Psychotherapy: A handbook of research. Oxford: Pergamon, pp. 3–22.

Strupp, H.H. (1986a). Psychotherapy: Research, practice, and public policy (How to avoid dead ends). American Psychologist 41: 120–130.

Strupp, H.H. (1986b). The nonspecific hypothesis of therapeutic effectiveness: A current assessment. American Journal of Orthopsychiatry 56: 513–520.

Strupp, H.H. (1989). Can the practitioner learn from the researcher? American Psychologist 44: 717–724.

Strupp, H.H. (1994). Psychotherapists and (or versus) researchers. Voices 30: 55–62.

Strupp, H.H. (1996). The tripartile model and the Consumer Reports Study. American Psychologist 51: 1017–1024.

Strupp, H.H. and Hadley, S.W. (1977). A tripartile model of mental health and therapeutic outcomes. American Psychologist 32: 187–196.

Strupp, H.H. and Luborsky, L. (eds) (1962), Research in Psychotherapy, Vol. 2. Washington DC: American Psychological Association.

Strupp, H.H., Fox, R.E. and Lessler, K. (1969). Patients view their psychotherapy. Baltimore, Md: Johns Hopkins University Press.

Sue, S., McKinney, H.L. and Allen, D.B. (1996). Predictors of the duration of therapy for clients in the community mental health system. Community Mental Health Journal 12: 365–373.

Szasz, T.S. (1961). The Myth of Mental Illness. New York: Hoeber-Harper.

Talley, P.F., Strupp, H.H. and Butler, S.F. (1994). Conclusion. In: Talley, P.F., Strupp, H.H. and Butler, S.F. (eds), Psychotherapy Research and Practice: Bridging the gap. New York: Basic Books, pp. 254–261.

Task Force on Promotion and Dissemination of Psychological Procedures (1995). Training in and dissemination of empirically validated psychological treatments: Report and recommendations. The Clinical Psychologist 48: 3–23.

Taylor, C. (1973). Peaceful coexistance in psychology. Social Research 40: 55–82.

Taylor, J. and Bogdan, R. (1984). Introduction to Qualitative Analysis: A research tool for scientists-practitioners. New York: Wiley.

Telch, M.J., Schmid, N.B., Jaimez, L., Jacquin, K.M. and Harrington, P.J. (1995). Impact of cognitive-behavioral treatment on quality of life in panic disorder patients. Journal of Consulting and Clinical Psychology 63: 823–830.

Tharp, R.G. and Gallimore, R.L. (1982). Inquiry process in program development. Journal of Community Development 10: 103–118.

Tracey, T.J. (1985). Dominance and outcome: A sequential examination. Journal of Counseling Psychology 32: 119–122.

Tracey, T.J. (1987). Stage differences in the dependencies of topic initiation and topic following behavior. Journal of Counseling Psychology 34: 123–131.

Tracey, T.J. and Ray, P.B. (1984). Stages of successful time-limited counseling: An interactional examination. Journal of Counseling Psychology 31: 13–27.

Valle, R.S. and King, M. (1978). Existential–Phenomenological Alternatives for Psychology. New York: Oxford University Press.

van Zuuren, F.J., Wertz, F. and Mook, B. (eds) (1987) Advances in Qualitative Psychology: Themes and variations. Berwyn, PA: Swets North America.

Vickery, A.R, Kirsch, I., Council, J.R. and Sirkin, M.I. (1985). Cognitive skill and traditional trance hypnotic inductions: A within-subjects comparison. Journal of Consulting and Clinical Psychology 53: 131–133.

Viney, L.L. (1983). The assessment of psychological states through content analysis of psychological communications. Psychological bulletin 84: 542–563.

von Eckartsberg, R. (1971). On experiential methodology. In: Giorgi, A., Fischer, W.F. and von Eckartsberg, R. (eds), Duquesne Studies in Phenomenological Psychology, Vol. 1. Pittsburgh: Duquesne University Press, pp. 70–76.

von Knorring-Giorgi, B. (1998). A phenomenological analysis of the experiencing of pivotal moments in therapy as defined by clients. Unpublished doctoral dissertation. University of Québec at Montréal.

Vonk, M.E. and Thyer, B.A. (1999). Evaluating the effectiveness of short-term treatment of a university counseling center. Journal of Clinical Psychology 55: 1095–1106.

Walsh, R., Perrucci, A. and Severns, J. (1999). What's in a good moment?: A hermeneutic study of psychotherapeutic values across levels of psychotherapy training. Psychotherapy Research 9: 304–326.

Wampold, B.E. and Kim, K.H. (1989). Sequential analysis applied to counseling process and outcome: A case study revisited. Journal of Counseling Psychology 36: 357–364.

Watson, J.B. (1913). Psychology as the behaviorist views it. Psychological Review 20: 158–177.

Watson, J.C. and Greenberg, L.S. (1996). Pathways to change in the psychotherapy of depression: Relating process to session change and outcome. Psychotherapy 33: 262–274.

Weeks, G.R. and L'Abate, L. (1982). Paradoxical Psychotherapy: Theory and practice with individuals, couple, and families. New York: Brunner/Mazel.

Weiss, J. (1986). Theory and clinical observations. In: Weiss, J., Sampson, H. and The Mount Zion Psychotherapy Research Group (eds), The Psychoanalytic Process: Theory, clinical observation, and empirical research. New York: Guilford, pp. 3–138.

Weiss, J., Sampson, H. and The Mount Zion Psychotherapy Research Group (eds) (1986), The Psychoanalytic Process: Theory, clinical observation, and empirical research. New York: Guilford.

Wertz, F. and van Zuuren, F.J. (1987). Qualitative research: Educational considerations. In: van Zuuren, F.J., Wertz, F., and Mook, B. (eds), Advances in Qualitative psychology: Themes and variations. Berwyn, PA: Swets North America, pp. 3–23.

Westen, D. and Morrison, K. (2001). A multidimensional meta-analysis of treatment for depression, panic, and generalized anxiety disorder: An empirical examination of the status of empirically supported therapies. Journal of Consulting and Clinical Psychology 69: 875–889.

White, M. and Epston, D. (1990). Narrative means to therapeutic ends. New York: Norton.

Whitehead, A.N. (1929). Process and Reality: An essay in cosmology. Cambridge: Cambridge University Press.

Williams, D.D. (1986). When is naturalistic evaluation appropriate? In: Williams, D.D. (ed.), Naturalistic Evaluation. San Francisco, Calif: Jossey-Bass, pp. 85–92.

Wilson, G.T. and Evans, I.M. (1977). Adult behavior therapy and the therapist-client relationship. In: Franks, C.M. and Wilson, G.T. (eds), Annual Review of Behavior Therapy: Theory and practice. New York: Brunner/Mazel, pp. 156–179.

Wiseman, H. and Rice, L.N. (1989). Sequential analysis of therapist-client interaction during change events: A task-focused approach. Journal of Consulting and Clinical Psychology 57: 281–286.

Wolberg, L. (1954). The Technique of Psychotherapy. New York: Grune & Stratton.

Wonnell, T.L. and Hill, C.E. (2000). Effects of including the action stage in dream interpretation. Journal of Counseling Psychology 47: 372–374.

Index